Urban
Odyssey

Urban Odyssey

A Multicultural History of Washington, D.C.

Edited by
Francine Curro Cary

Smithsonian Institution Press
Washington and London

Editor: Jenelle Walthour
Designer: Linda McKnight

Library of Congress Cataloging-in-Publication Data
Cary, Francine.
Urban odyssey : a multicultural history of Washington, D.C. /
   edited by Francine Curro Cary.
      p.   cm.
   Includes bibliographical references and index.
   ISBN 1-56098-545-3 (cloth : alk. paper).
   1. Washington (D.C.)—Emigration and immigration—
History.   2. Migrant labor—Washington (D.C.)—History.
3. Alien labor—Washington (D.C.)—History.   4. Immigrants—
Washington (D.C.)—History.   5. Washington (D.C.)—Ethnic
relations.   6. Pluralism (Social sciences)—Washington
(D.C.)—History.   I. Cary, Francine.
JV6940.U73   1995
304.8'09753—dc20   94-44018

British Library Cataloguing-in-Publication Data is available

Manufactured in the United States of America
01 00 99 98 97 96 95   5 4 3 2 1

⊗ The paper used in this publication meets the minimum
requirements of the American National Standard for Permanence
of Paper for Printed Library Materials Z39.48-1984.

For permission to reproduce illustrations appearing in this book,
please correspond directly with the owners of the works, as listed
in the individual captions. The Smithsonian Institution Press
does not retain reproduction rights for these illustrations individu-
ally, or maintain a file of addresses for photo sources.

For my daughters, Elissa and Michelle,
and my grandchildren,
Julia, Tony, and Allison Rachel

Contents

Part Three. Multicultural Washington

Preface and
Acknowledgments

Urban Odyssey: A Multicultural History of Washington, D.C. has entailed its own journey. It originated in curiosity that has not abated with its completion. Who peopled Washington, D.C., and built its communities? How did migrants and immigrants across cultures and time change the city, and how did the city change them? What factors have influenced their community building in a new environment? Who are the diverse newcomers arriving today in unprecedented numbers and changing the social landscape yet again? *Urban Odyssey* begins to address these questions and to tell the story of the migrant and immigrant experience in the nation's capital.

This collection of essays, intended for the general reader, is presented in the hope of encouraging further research into a subject whose field of inquiry proved more vast than any one volume could contain. The book moved from concept to manuscript to publication on a path of discovery that raised more questions than it answered. As our migrant and immigrant forebears learned, a destination is only a new beginning. So too is *Urban Odyssey*. The highways and byways of Washington's migrant and immigrant heritage have yet to be fully explored, and they promise a rewarding journey to those who undertake it.

This book grew out of a series of public programs on Washington's cultural diversity sponsored by the Humanities Council of Washington D.C., the non-profit affiliate of the National Endowment for the Humanities in the District of Columbia. The project included a television series, which was based on dramatizations of the lives of seven migrants and immigrants, and produced by Howard University's WHMM-TV32 and filmmaker Michelle Parkerson, and a conference at the Charles Sumner School Museum and Archives, which featured presentations by the authors in this collection. The project received its principal funding from the National Endowment for the Humanities through an Exemplary Award from the Division of State Programs, and additional funding from the D.C. Commission on the Arts and Humanities, the Morris and Gwendolyn D. Cafritz Foundation, the Eugene and Agnes E. Meyer Foundation, Adams National Bank, and numerous individuals. This volume does not, however, necessarily reflect the opinions or views of the project's funders or those of the Humanities Council of Washington, D.C.

Many people contributed to *Urban Odyssey*. I thank Doug Foard, Kathryn Gibson, and Carole Watson for moral support as the project unfolded; Joseph Jordan, Lee Ellen Friedland, and Carren Kaston for their work in the early stages; the Historical Society of Washington, D.C., the George Washington University's Gelman Library, the Jewish Historical Society, and the D.C. Public Library's Washingtoniana Division for resources on local history; James Early, Dorn McGrath, Jerome Paige, Robert Manning, Brett Williams, Desmond Dinan, and Suzanne Meyer for thoughtful discussions about ideas; Renee DeGross for assistance with photo research; the *Washington Post* for contributing photographs; Daniel Goodwin and Mark Hirsch at the Smithsonian Institution Press for their wisdom and patience during an extended publishing journey; and Jenelle Walthour for her masterful copyediting. I am grateful to consulting editors Lee Halper and Jane Freundel Levey, who combined their talents with bursts of enthusiasm at just the right moments during the final stretch. My greatest debt is to the council's board members and staff, whose extraordinary support of their executive director is gratefully acknowledged. The council's commitment, and that of all those involved in the project, does not extend to any shortcomings of this volume, which I accept as my own. My parents, Frank and Roselynn Curro, my sister, Andrea, and my brother, Loren, have always been my greatest source of strength. My children, Elissa and Michelle, and my grandchildren, Julia, Tony, and Allison Rachel, have shown me new ways of seeing the journey. I dedicate this book to them.

Introduction

Washington, D.C., is considered a city of transients. Home of the nation's capital, it is a government town where elected officials and bureaucrats come to represent the interests of people in other places, stay a short time, and then leave. It has also been called a "sojourner city," a temporary way station for migrants and immigrants from around the nation and the world, who hope to return eventually to their real homes elsewhere. Many have, indeed, come and gone. Yet, from the beginning, some residents have stayed—perhaps longer than they had intended—put down roots, and built communities on the wide avenues and the open spaces of the capital city designed by French architect Pierre Charles L'Enfant. Many a transient and a sojourner have "slid over the invisible line to become Washingtonians."[1]

Interspersed among the national monuments and federal buildings that dot the urban landscape of Washington are other institutions—both religious and secular—that stand as silent sentinels in a city whose role as the nation's capital has eclipsed its own social history. If these structures of myriad purpose, lineage, and architecture could speak, they would tell the untold stories of the community-building efforts of thousands of migrants and immigrants who came to Washington in search of opportunity, and stayed to shape the social fabric of an evolving city and changing region. They would illuminate the ways in which people from diverse birthplaces contributed to the mosaic of cultures that make up Washington. They would also remind us that the culture and identity of the city, as well as that of its individual communities, are "in a continual state of construction."[2]

Urban Odyssey begins to explore the migrant and immigrant experience in Washington, D.C. This collection of essays focuses on the community-building efforts and social relations of diverse groups of native-born and foreign-born newcomers in a city bypassed by the industrial revolution and overshadowed by the federal presence. The common thread that emerges from the essays is the quest for community, a quest embodied in efforts to transplant cultural traditions and rebuild familiar social networks, rituals, and support institutions on unfamiliar terrain. For migrants throughout the city's history, building community—recreating a sense of home, affinity, and identity—has both fashioned and cushioned the adjustment to changing circumstances and to a new environment.

The essays show that the process of adaptation and resettlement encompassed in community building is a multifaceted phenomenon influenced by a variety of factors. These factors include the race, ethnicity, gender, and social class of newcomers; the resources, skills, and connections they have carried with them; the reasons for and circumstances that led to migration (the "context of exit"); and the shifting economic and social conditions—including public policies and prevailing climates of opinion—that newcomers encounter upon their arrival (the "context of reception").[3]

The interplay of these factors has affected the odyssey experience across time—from the earliest migrations of Native Americans spurred by contact with Europeans in the seventeenth century, to those of native-born blacks and whites, who predominated in the District, to the migrations of foreign-born groups in the nineteenth century, and up to the contemporary global movement of people from Africa, Asia, Central and South America, and the Caribbean. These factors, in a range of permutations, have aided, inhibited, or facilitated the quest for community and the patterns and processes of adaptation in Washington, D.C., as elsewhere.

Much of the research needed to reconstruct the migrant and immigrant experience in Washington has yet to be undertaken. Until recently, few scholars writing on U.S. migration and immigration have discussed the nation's capital. Lacking the magnet of industry, which drew millions of unskilled immigrants to other cities, and situated geographically between the North and the South, Washington does seem peculiar enough to have warranted its scholarly neglect. Fortunately, a resurgence of interest in the city's past—which is reflected in the publication of *Urban Odyssey*—is beginning to address the gaps in scholarship.[4]

The essays in this collection gather together for the first time scattered and unexamined materials that illuminate the odysseys of specific groups. As several authors have noted, reconstructing this story is like putting together pieces of a puzzle. The pieces include published and unpublished primary sources; local and federal government records—including census materials, naturalization and court records, and building permits; oral histories and ethnographic studies; city directories and newspapers; and the primary material generated by neighborhood and local history projects, such as exhibits and documentary films. The raw data for social histories often resides in the memories and memorabilia of current residents. Unarchived and unpreserved, such material may be "discovered" in the basements or attics of residences, religious institutions, businesses, and other community organizations. The essayists included in *Urban Odyssey*, like detectives searching for clues to a mystery, have relied on a combination of these sources; many have also drawn from their own experiences as members of a particular community.

The essays, coming from a wide spectrum of disciplines, interests, and views, have been written by historians, anthropologists, sociologists, and folklorists, independent scholars, graduate students, and members of new communities in the process of formation. Above all, each essay reflects its author's own point of view and, in this sense, is thought of—like the volume itself—as a springboard to further inquiry, rather than as a definitive or comprehensive work. Indeed, the authors and I are sensitive to the many migrants and immigrants not represented in this volume—from the enduring Irish community, to native-born white migrants who came to work for the federal government (including the ubiquitous "government girls"), and the more recent immigrants from the Middle East, the Pacific Islands, and many other parts of the world.[5] These groups are important subjects for research.

Part One of *Urban Odyssey* presents the three major ethnic groups that dominated the area that in 1791 would become Washington, D.C.: Native Americans, Africans, and Europeans. In Chapter 1, William M. Gardner describes the intricate cultures of the Washington area's indigenous populations, the Piscataway and other Native American cultural groups—some of whom still live in the area today. Gardner contends that Native Americans were among the first groups of people to exist on the margins of an emerging hegemonic Anglo-American culture. Their survival strategies and the mutability of indigenous cultures and identities over time resonate with those of successive waves of newcomers to Washington. The issues that arose with Native Americans' contact with early Europeans are present in the ongoing national conversation about American pluralism. These issues are also raised throughout *Urban Odyssey*.

In Chapter 2, James Oliver Horton, studying the consequences of a forced migration experience and the aspirations of people seeking freedom, traces the genesis of Washington's African American community. According to Horton, by the 1790s the area's blacks, both slave and free, had created "a family-centered community life" that sustained an increasing number of newcomers over several generations and throughout the Civil War. The steady growth of the District of Columbia's free black community, with its own social institutions and kinship networks, had far-reaching effects on the odyssey from slavery to freedom.

Margaret H. McAleer's discussion in Chapter 3 of the earliest Irish immigrants, who were among the federal city's fluid heterogeneous labor force, provides a close look at the process of early nineteenth-century city building. The experiences of Irish artisans, laborers, grocers, and tavern keepers, builders, architects, and a host of other tradespeople echo in the stories of successive immigrants.

Part Two traces the city's development through the nineteenth century and into the twentieth century, emphasizing the various factors that influenced the origins and evolution of several migrant and immigrant communities. Common to the experiences of newcomers was adjusting to a city that lacked industry and local control over its political affairs. As Kathryn Smith contends in *Washington at Home*, it was the expansion of the federal government from a few hundred workers in the early 1800s to more than 276,000 employees after World War II—not the rise of factory smokestacks, manufacturing plants, or skyscrapers—that served as the main barometer of the rate of the city's growth.[6]

Without industry the capital drew a larger percentage of skilled and entrepreneurial immigrants than other U.S. cities, and its foreign-born populations were smaller. At the same time, it attracted large numbers of African American migrants from the rural South well into the twentieth century. Thus, the common threads of Washington's urban experience in the century between 1860 and 1960 did not include the major labor struggles or ethnic political coalitions that characterized the histories of such cities as Chicago, New York, and Philadelphia. Instead, the locus of community life lay within religious institutions, charitable organizations, businesses and entrepreneurial activities, schools, neighborhood coalitions, and, occasionally, craft traditions transplanted from native countries. Family, kinship, and birthplace networks—both in spatially concentrated communities and, over time, in loosely anchored, scattered communities—also played an important role in sustaining migrants and immigrants. The quest for community, as the essays in Part Two demonstrate, varied according to race, ethnicity, and social class. These factors shaped the daily lives of newcomers and the nature and role of the communities they built.

The essays on African American migration and community building elucidate the longest continuous narrative thread in the city's history. In Chapter 4, Lois E. Horton examines the profound changes in Washington's African American community resulting from the Civil War and Reconstruction, when former slaves flooded the capital in search of a new life in freedom. In Chapter 6, Elizabeth Clark-Lewis views the migration experience through the voices of African American women, whose only means for self-support was domestic work—often in the homes of wealthy white migrants who came to the city at the same time. These women's insistence on maintaining ties with their southern birthplaces helped them to adjust to an urban environment and, ultimately, to force concessions from their employers. Spencer R. Crew, in Chapter 12, traces the development and increasing complexity and diversity of the segregated city's black communities, as well as the impact of shifting patterns of migration from the border states to the deep South. He also examines the pioneering protest movements that eventually cut across social divisions. Many native Washingtonians today trace their heritage to the city's earliest free black community, while others have roots in the migrations that began during the Civil War and continued throughout the next century.

In Chapter 5, Kathryn Allamong Jacob's history of the wealthy migrants who came to participate in the city's increasingly dominant federal society highlights the polarities of the migration experience. The majority of native-born white migrants were ordinary citizens seeking jobs with an ever-expanding government. Washington had its elites, too: elected officials, judges, military personnel, a small circle of descendants of New England literary families, and a substantial proportion of southerners. On the heels of the destruction of slavery, however, came not only newly freed people—many with barely the clothes on their backs—but also millionaires from the American heartland, which represented an unusual but forceful migration. Their transitory presence left its mark on the city's built environment. It not only created the District's first fashionable neighborhood, in what is now Dupont Circle, but it also forced the movement of black and immigrant residents who had long lived in that area to other parts of the city. This shift created further overcrowding in the poorest neighborhoods, a condition that eventually spurred both migration out of the District and civil reform movements for the Washingtonians who stayed.

While wealthy white migrants pulled the city's political and economic identification northward, African American migrants helped maintain the city's social and cultural ties to the Old South. The changing regional dimensions of the nation's capital— fueled by an expanding federal bureaucracy, the diversification of the economy, and the emergence of a metropolitan region after World War II—continues to reflect these poles.[7]

The essays in Part Two on European immigrants in Washington trace the evolution of ethnic enclaves from their inception to their relocation or dispersion throughout the city and then into the suburbs. The role of spatial concentration of immigrant communities in affording labor and markets for the entrepreneurial efforts of the first generation of newcomers, as well as emotional and social support, is a common thread. In Chapter 11, Esther Ngan-ling Chow concentrates on the transformation of Chinatown and highlights similarities and differences with other ethnic groups. She shows how a beleaguered Chinese community struggled to achieve stability for its members in a volatile racial environment. Chow's essay also explores the relationship between public policies and the nature of community formation, which remains an important issue today.

Some ethnic communities, such as those of the Christian and Jewish Germans, had their roots in early Washington, D.C. In Chapter 7, Mona E. Dingle traces the development of the Christian component of the German community, showing that its identity construction and ethnic institution-building peaked at the end of the nineteenth century. In Chapter 8, Hasia R. Diner and Steven J. Diner extend the discussion of German community building in their study of the Jewish community, whose early German and central European immigrants were joined later by eastern European Jews, and then by American-born Jews.

Other ethnic communities emerged primarily in the 1880s and 1890s, and in the early decades of the twentieth century, a period of unprecedented immigration to America. Howard Gillette Jr. and Alan M. Kraut's essay on the Italian immigrant community describes the "plural opportunity structure" offered by nonindustrial Washington. This environment, they contend, attracted Italians with craft or entrepreneurial skills, afforded "intraethnic" opportunities for mobility, and reinforced ethnic identities. Gillette and Kraut observe that many Italians who had tried industrial wage labor elsewhere engaged in Washington in a range of service trades or small business enterprises, supported by family networks and social institutions—especially the local Catholic church, built in 1913 by and for the Italian community.

These patterns of community building, including the universal endeavor to establish religious institutions that anchored new communities, are also evident among the Greek and the Jewish immigrants who arrived in the city during the same period. In Chapter 10, Christine M. Warnke examines how the Greeks' "disdain" for wage labor, coupled with quick-rooting kinship and village networks, translated into their eventual dominance of certain retail and wholesale industries. The essay also uncovers the little-known social relations among the Greeks, Italians, Jews, and African Americans who lived and worked side-by-side in the downtown commercial districts and around the bustling markets that serviced the city's residents. In Chapter 8, the Diners document the community building efforts of Jewish migrants who, much like their Greek and Italian counterparts, often moved up the social and economic ladder by establishing free-loan societies and pooling resources to become shop-keepers and business owners.

The emergence of entrepreneurial enclaves in Washington is an important theme in the essays. The activities of Italians, Greeks, Jews, and Chinese reverberate in those of Koreans, Ethiopians, Vietnamese, Salvadorans, and other immigrant groups today. The efforts of African American migrants to carve out autonomous spheres of economic and social endeavors are also a part of this experience.

But the path of incorporation into the mainstream culture and the middle class varied in pace and degree for Europeans, Chinese, and African Americans. The Chinese, for example, entered the laundry and later the restaurant business because no other jobs were available to them besides low-wage, menial labor. Even with that alternative, racial discrimination combined with public policy to limit their options even further. The situation was similar for African Americans. The rise of small businesses in the African American community emerged from a strong tradition of self-help. However, the increase in black economic enterprise—particularly from 1890 to 1920—also represented a response to severely restricted opportunities in a racially hostile environment, which was only exacerbated by the Woodrow Wilson administration's elimination of federal jobs for African Americans.[8] Thus, on the one hand, many Chinese and African Americans, like their European counterparts, embraced self-employment as preferable to other options. On the other hand, the choice of self-employment or entrepreneurship was often as much a means of economic survival as a strategy for economic mobility. The persistence of these issues as factors in the experiences of new communities is evident in the essays on the contemporary odyssey.

Not all migrants and immigrants in Washington were entrepreneurs or business owners, of course. The same economic and social restrictions that propelled some African Americans into entrepreneurial ventures forced the majority of them into low-wage work. African American women from the rural

South were barred from the increasing numbers of clerical and retail jobs that drew native-born white women to the city at the turn of the century. The meager earnings of African American domestic workers nonetheless contributed to household incomes, enhancing their value within their own communities.

Many European newcomers also worked for wages in, for example, businesses or shops owned by co-ethnics, construction, the building trades, retail, clerical work, domestic labor, and teaching. Sometimes immigrants combined wage work with service to their compatriots, perhaps running stores and restaurants from their homes. During the New Deal and World War II, the enormous expansion of white-collar jobs in the federal government not only attracted new migrants and immigrants, but also opened opportunities for the wives and children of those already living in the city. The contributions of wage workers to household economies, as well as the pooling of wages among family and kinship groups, offered an alternative avenue to economic advancement. Such efforts remain conspicuous today among immigrant newcomers.

Cooperative self-help strategies took place initially within the supportive communities of compatriots. The responses of ethnic minorities to nativist or antiforeign sentiment, however, reflected both the fragility of their communities and the pressures to assimilate. While the Chinese turned inward to pursue their own way of life in an insulated enclave, Germans and Greeks responded by lowering their visibility, particularly during and after World War I when their loyalty came under virulent attack. For both Germans and Greeks in this period, and for Italians a few decades later, such attacks lent what Warnke describes as "a sense of urgency" to their efforts to enter the American mainstream. On the other hand, antiforeign sentiment also heightened ethnic sensibilities, creating identifications that did not necessarily break down with the communities' dispersion.

The question of whether a sense of ethnicity persisted, however, remains another subject for ongoing inquiry. Some authors argue that upward mobility and dispersion dissolved the initial sense of community and the identity associated with it. Other authors indicate that ethnicity persisted in the personal, if not the public, lives of immigrants. They argue that a new sense of community—one bound not by place but by shared values, traditions, and social life— was extended across the permeable boundaries of the District. Although ethnic Washingtonians became part of larger social, occupational, and regional networks, they retained patterns of community and identity forged in the early years of settlement and adjustment. There may be some evidence of persistence across generations as well, but in new forms, since ethnicity "at will" is only one among many identities that the descendants of immigrants can choose.[9] Still, the religious and other institutions that marked the first generation's earlier concentration continue to draw participants back into the city even today.

These issues of ethnicity and acculturation are explored further in Part Three, which focuses on the contemporary immigration to Washington and its metropolitan area. During the 1950s and 1960s, when the struggle for civil rights and home rule dominated local politics, the movement of people into and out of the District again altered the residential city's cultural dynamics and initiated a transformation that continues to the present. The nation's capital attained a black majority in 1957. While the African American population increased, white Washingtonians—encouraged by government policies that subsidized the construction of new housing, highways, and transportation systems—increasingly moved to the suburbs. Since then the District has become a part of a rapidly expanding metropolitan region whose changing economy, demographics, and communities are often intertwined, thus reconfiguring social relationships and networks across jurisdictional boundaries.

During the 1970s and 1980s Washington and the metropolitan region attracted an inflow of immigrants that was unprecedented in terms of its numbers and diversity. The Washington area is now home to the nation's third-largest concentration of Central American immigrants, the fourth-largest group of Korean immigrants, the sixth-largest group of Indochinese immigrants, and the largest group of Ethiopian immigrants. The diversity of this contemporary urban odyssey is reflected in the origins of the newcomers, who, in contrast to the earlier immigration to the city, are predominantly non-European and non-white. This diversity is also evident in the regional distinctiveness within national groups and the circumstances that motivated migration.

Washington's growing ethnic diversity, and that of other urban centers, resulted from the U.S. Immigration Act of 1965. That legislation eliminated the forty-year-old national origins quota system, which had given preference to European immigrants, and replaced it with a system that emphasized family reunification and skills needed in the American job market. It thus eased entry for Latin American and Asian nationals. Additionally, the Refugee Act of 1980 offered asylum to increasing numbers of political refugees, specifically those fleeing communist regimes and other governments the United States did not support. The impact of these policies is reflected dramatically in the 1990 U.S. census. In the Washington metropolitan area, the foreign-born population grew from 253,000 in 1980 (8 percent of the total population) to 484,000 in 1990 (12 percent of the total population). While the region's African American population increased at about the same rate as total population growth, the numbers of Asians and Hispanics more than doubled.[10]

Within the District, total population declined to 606,900, a loss of some 31,000 people between 1980 and 1990 (although the census figures are in dispute). In contrast to the 1950s pattern, this decline was due almost entirely to the out-migration of African Americans to the suburbs.[11] Meanwhile, the percentage of foreign-born residents almost doubled to 10 percent of the population, and unofficial counts are much higher for every emerging ethnic community. The District's Hispanic population, estimated at 40,000 to 52,000 depending on who is counting, is the largest ethnic group within the city.

William Alonso, a Harvard University population scholar, argues that while the District's African American population is declining, an increasing number of blacks now living in the city are

> immigrants from countries with cultures and traditions starkly different from that of the rural South where most African Americans have their roots. . . . Many of these new immigrants who have been pouring in may not even consider themselves black in the American sense.[12]

The essays on African and Caribbean newcomers show that the new African diasporan presence, which also includes Spanish-speaking blacks from Latin America and the Caribbean ("Afro-Latinos"), and creole-speaking blacks from Haiti, and French-speaking Africans from such nations as Senegal, offers new perspectives on black identity.

The essays in Part Three only begin to suggest the variety of national, social, and ethnic origins of Washington's newcomers and the ways they are adjusting to their new environment, redefining their identities, and reconstructing Washington's urban landscape and the relations of its people to one another. The racial and ethnic composition of the District's contemporary immigrants, combined with the continuing presence and increasing visibility in the Washington area of Native Americans (some tracing their ancestry to the Piscataway, others to tribal cultures from across the nation) brings the odyssey narrative full circle. The emerging multicultural communities are indeed addressing insistent questions about the nature of the American "melting pot" and the very meaning of race, ethnicity, and acculturation—areas that are now undergoing considerable scholarly revision and public debate.

In Chapter 13, Olivia Cadaval's analysis of the evolution of Washington's Latino community raises some key issues arising from the contemporary encounter of cultures. Her discussion of the adjacent Adams Morgan and Mount

Pleasant neighborhoods in northwest Washington describes the city's principal commercial and cultural hub for emergent communities of African, Asian, Caribbean, and South and Central American immigrants. Cadaval traces the intricate process of community formation among different Spanish-speaking national groups, as well as the impetus for their immigration and the changes within the community since the 1960s. Despite the fact that Washington's Latinos come from a wide range of backgrounds and circumstances, argues Cadaval, they are forging a new identity and sense of community based on a common language and the shared hardship of migration and adaptation—"without losing their individual national identities." The Latino community in the Adams Morgan–Mount Pleasant barrio remains central to this emerging pan-Hispanic identity as a time-tested means of increasing political clout and supporting economic mobility. At the same time, the increasing number of Latinos now living in the suburbs, where they are finding affordable housing and service jobs, is creating a more decentralized community with networks that crisscross the region. The forging of a Latino political consciousness and agenda, still in a formative stage, thus suggests new possibilities for the city's and the region's multicultural future.

The diversity of the immigration and the rapidity with which new communities are formed and transformed have become a hallmark of the late twentieth-century immigrant experience in America. As each of the authors discusses, what plays a major role in shaping communities is the legal status of newcomers—whether they are immigrants intending to become citizens, political refugees eligible for U.S. assistance, or sojourners struggling with decisions about staying or returning to homelands. The fact that numerous émigrés are here illegally compounds the difficulties of survival. For example, many Salvadorans, who are now the dominant group among Latinos, were denied asylum and have thus become, along with other nationals without refugee status, a part of the growing but undocumented subculture that has developed within the contemporary urban odyssey.

Also critical to community formation and adaptation among today's immigrants are the conditions in countries of origin that lead to migration and determine whether or not sojourners return, and the opportunities and support networks that draw them to Washington. The availability of entry-level jobs in the region's multifaceted services sector is a major attraction to immigrants. Securing such jobs is a first step into the labor market for the majority of newcomers, although it might initially be a step backward for more educated immigrants and refugees. However, for those with limited English language skills and contacts—and even for those with professional skills—service work is often the only option available. Such limited options are also an impetus for many immigrants to engage in entrepreneurial activities, which they are doing at an astonishing rate and in a variety of ways. The proliferation of ethnic-owned businesses, restaurants, and shops, as well as ethnic street vendors, attests to a modern-day revival of Washington's entrepreneurial tradition.

In Chapter 14, Keith Q. Warner examines the evolution of the English-speaking Caribbean community. The old support networks were established in the 1960s by Caribbean students at Howard University and by embassy domestic staffs and others who remained. In the last two decades these networks have drawn successive waves of immigrants and have grown tremendously. Warner discusses Caribbeans' involvement in local politics as an example of their "becoming Americanized"; but he also emphasizes that a receding sojourner mentality has not diminished the maintenance of a Caribbean identity, which is manifested in the exuberant adherence to cultural traditions. These Washingtonians, many now U.S. citizens, are developing new ethnic identities linked to the distinct histories of their homelands. In the process, they are reconstructing the categories of race and ethnicity that have developed out of the North American experience.

In Chapter 15, Bereket H. Selassie discusses the experiences and adaptation strategies of the new Africans in Washington. Ethiopians, Eritreans, and Nigerians, the focus of Selassie's essay, are only a few of the many diverse African national groups now living and working in the city. The Africans, like many Caribbeans, were drawn to the District first by Howard University and the capital's international community, and then, as political crises and civil wars pushed them out of their homelands, by the networks established by earlier arrivals. Unlike the Latinos and the Caribbeans, however, the Africans' cultural presence has not yet developed into a political presence. Still, many of the African-born refugees are making new homes in Washington, supported by ethnic organizations, businesses, and birthplace networks that are as characteristic to today's emerging communities as they were to those of the past. At the same time, the maintenance of African identities remains paramount. Like their Caribbean contemporaries, Africans are developing ethnic identities tied closely to the cultures of their countries of origin.

In Chapter 16, Beatrice Nied Hackett examines the traumatic odyssey of Vietnamese, Cambodian, and Laotian refugees who came to America in the aftermath of the Vietnam War. These refugee groups largely maintain their distinctive traditions and cultures, but sometimes coalesce as "Indochinese" for reasons of expediency. Hackett discusses their adjustment to American life through their reliance on family networks, religious and ethnic institutions, traditional rituals, businesses, and the exchanges between them and the American culture that are facilitating new multiethnic relations.

Unyong Kim and Meeja Yu's portrait of Korean immigrants in Chapter 17 brings a particular insight into a story that haunts us in newspaper headlines and civic meetings: the conflict that has strained relations between Korean merchants and some residents of central-city neighborhoods in which they do business. Yu and Kim describe Korean history, traditions, and values in order to address what may be some sources of culture clashes that have led to violence and tragically, in some instances, to death. They also highlight the diversity of Asian cultures. The fact that even fifth-generation Chinese Americans and Japanese Americans are often mistaken for foreigners in their own land compounds the dilemma for Korean immigrants. The majority of Koreans have come as permanent settlers, and many are now American citizens. Today, Koreans are one of the fastest growing ethnic minorities in the country. Yu and Kim affirm a common thread of the urban odyssey over time in discussing how Koreans' reliance on the labor of family and co-ethnics, and their traditional methods of financial support, underlie their efforts to achieve economic self-sufficiency and security. The Koreans' dreams thus reflect those of all migrants and immigrants in every era.

As each of the recent immigrant groups copes with the new American culture, another common thread emerges: the changing relationships between immigrants and their children. As Hackett observes among Vietnamese, Cambodian, and Laotian immigrants, parents want their children to be "American enough to carry on business and be good citizens," but not so American that they will forget their cultures or their languages. Kim and Yu underscore this observation in their essay, noting that Korean parents find that "their relations with their children embody the tensions of their new life," a point which Warner and Selassie also make for Caribbean and African immigrant parents. For some groups the process of adaptation suggests new roles for women, while for others it means forging ties based not on kinship but on other commonalities. As immigrants struggle to understand their changing environment and their changing familial lives, they find themselves, as Hackett writes, "redefining the meaning of family and community for all of us."

The contemporary immigrant experience raises a host of questions that confront Washingtonians as the urban odyssey continues into a new century. The formation of new communities and the ongoing reconstruction of identities, which began with the migrations of Native Americans, African Americans, European Americans, and Chinese Americans more than a century ago, continues to transform the social terrain of the District of Columbia and the

Washington metropolitan area. This odyssey informs our present and is shaping our future.

NOTES

1. Constance McLaughlin Green, *Washington: A History of the Capital, 1800–1950* (Princeton: Princeton University Press, 1962), 1:123.

2. Alice Kessler Harris, "Multiculturalism Can Strengthen, Not Undermine, a Common Culture," *Chronicle of Higher Education* 39, no. 9 (21 October 1992): B3, B7.

3. "Context of exit" and "context of reception" refer to, respectively, the conditions in countries of origin that impel emigration and those in the host society that receives them. See Alejandro Portes and Rubén G. Rumbaut, *Immigrant America: A Portrait* (Berkeley: University of California Press, 1990).

4. See, for example, Kathryn Schneider Smith, ed., *Washington at Home: An Illustrated History of Neighborhoods in the Nation's Capital* (Northridge, Calif.: Windsor Publications, 1988); Kathryn Schneider Smith, *Port Town to Urban Neighborhood: The Georgetown Waterfront of Washington, D.C., 1880–1920* (Washington, D.C.: Center for Washington Area Studies of The George Washington University, 1989); David Brinkley, *Washington Goes to War* (New York: Harper and Row, 1988); and Brett Williams, *Upscaling Downtown: Stalled Gentrification in Washington, D.C.* (Ithaca, N.Y.: Cornell University Press, 1988).

5. The variety of ethnic Americans living in the Washington area is suggested in Margaret S. Boone, ed., "Metropolitan Ethnography in the Nation's Capital," *Anthropological Quarterly* 54, no. 2 (April 1981). This volume contains ethnographic research reports on the following post–World War II immigrant groups: Sephardic Jews, Palestinians, Armenians, Serbians, Hungarians, Vietnamese, and Cubans. See also Al Kamen, "The Changing Face of America," *Washington Post,* 12 August 1991, A1, A8; D'Vera Cohn and Barbara Vobejda, "English Is Foreign in More Homes," *Washington Post,* 22 April 1992, A1; Barbara Vobejda, "A Nation in Transition," *Washington Post,* 29 May 1992, A1, A18–19; and Robert D. Manning, "Multicultural Change in Washington, D.C.," *Occasional Report Series,* no. 91 (3), Smithsonian Institution, 1991.

6. Kathryn Schneider Smith, *Washington At Home,* 10.

7. For a thoughtful exploration of the changing nature of Washington's regional orientation, see Carl Abbott, "Dimensions of Regional Change in Washington, D.C.," *American Historical Review* 95 (August 1990): 1367–93. Abbott concludes that:

> Regional change in Washington has not operated in parallel in the public spheres of business and politics and the private realms of personal behavior and allegiance. Washington at the end of the twentieth century has experienced substantial and almost certainly permanent accommodation to the public values of the North and has been integrated into the communication networks of the northeastern core. At the same time, improvements in transportation and communication have enhanced its role as a metropolitan focus for southern culture.

8. On African American entrepreneurship between 1890 and 1920, see Michael Andrew Fitzpatrick, "'A Great Agitation for Business': Black Economic Development in Shaw," *Washington History* 2, no. 2 (Fall/Winter 1990–91): 49–73.

9. A new body of scholarship is emerging on these issues, and several books and articles are cited in the essays. See also Alan Jabbour, "Ethnicity and Identity in America," *Library of Congress Folklife Center News* (Spring 1993): 6–10. Jabbour argues that the salient features of ethnicity in America include selectivity, tenacity, "the recombinant development of symbolic forms," and versatility. According to Jabbour, "once ethnicity is severed from the identification with turf . . . then it must compete with crosscutting groups such as region, religion, or occupation in the cultural marketplace where Americans select the elements of their interlocking identity." In short, Jabbour suggests that the American cultural process "generates a multitude of interlocking, overlapping, and constantly changing categories of human organization."

10. Robert E. Griffiths, "A Decade of Change in Metropolitan Washington: A COG Special Report on the 1990 Census," in *1990 COG Census Products* (Washington, D.C.: Metropolitan Washington Council of Governments, 1992), 1–16.

11. See Charlotte Allen, "The Incredible Shrinking District," *Washington City Paper*, 12 June 1992, 14–31, and Griffiths, "Decade of Change in Metropolitan Washington," 1–16.

12. William Alonso is quoted in Allen, "Incredible Shrinking District," 24.

PART ONE

Foundations of a Shared Past

1.

Native Americans
Early Encounters

William M. Gardner

In 1608 a barge, moved by wind against billowing sails, approached the area that would become Washington, D.C. The boat, on an exploratory expedition from the Jamestown, Virginia, settlement down the coast, carried fifteen English colonists, including Capt. John Smith. Along the shores, watching with wary but not unwelcoming eyes, were the region's native inhabitants. Whether these Europeans were the first they had seen is unknown; it is known, however, that they had heard of the Europeans and had gained access to some of their goods.

This encounter was the beginning of the end for the watchers on the shore. Most, if not all, of their descendants would die or move away, virtually disappearing from the historical record. In the century that followed, both good and bad times marked the inter-relations between the Europeans and the Native Americans—people of markedly diverse heritage and perspective. In the long run, however, the bad times prevailed for the Native Americans. In the early eighteenth century, less than one hundred years following their initial contact with the American Indians, the newcomers had virtually replaced the indigenous people. The Washington area was then in the process of becoming one of England's colonial outposts, complete with a plantation economy. The remaining vestiges of American Indian heritage included a few place names, lost arrowheads, scattered pieces of broken pottery, and burial grounds.[1]

Ethnohistorians categorize the American Indians who resided in what is now the greater Washington area as the Piscataway. Most of the tribes classified as such probably spoke a coastal Algonquian language, although some may have spoken a language that was Iroquoian in origin. A variety of names, many of which were derived from villages, districts, or individuals, designated the

American Indians of the region. A partial listing of native groups inhabiting the area in 1608 from Indianhead, Maryland, northward included the Pamacocack, the Pamunkey, the Cinquaoteck, the Moyaons, the Tessamatuck, the Nacotchtank, and the Anacostank. In Virginia, there were additional Pamacocack, as well as the Namaraughquend, the Assaomeck, the Namassingakent, the Tauxenent, the Matchipongo, the Quiyough, and the Patawomeke. On later maps and lists, other American Indian culture groups appear, such as the Doeg (perhaps synonymous with Tauxenent), the Mattawoman, and the Necostin.

Usage of the inclusive term "Piscataway," however, has become common. This is so primarily because at some point during the tumultuous history of the seventeenth century, just before the arrival of the Europeans, almost all culture groups living on the Maryland and District shores—and probably on the Virginia shore as well—became allied in a powerful confederacy dominated by the Piscataway (also called the Conoy in the Iroquoian language).

When the English settled Jamestown they encountered Native Americans whose predecessors had hunted in the region as far back as the end of the Pleistocene period, or the last ice age, some 11,000 years ago. Over the next several millennia, seasonally migrant populations visited the Washington area with greater frequency. By 3000 to 2000 B.C. the post-Pleistocene warming had reached its peak. Seasonal runs of anadromous fish—shad, herring, rockfish, and sturgeon—became available for harvesting. These fish were important to the American Indians and, later, to the Europeans as well. Because the migrating fish could not get over Great Falls, the rivers and streams of Washington, D.C., served as a natural funnel, and hundreds of prehistoric Indian communities lined the banks to harvest the natural bounty. In addition to the fish, archaeological evidence suggests that the cobble beds in what is now Rock Creek Park constituted one of the region's major attractions for "early Washingtonians." There, the Indians quarried raw material and fashioned tools for procuring and processing fish.

From 1800 B.C. onward, prehistoric populations inhabited the District more or less continuously. A break in cultural continuity occurred around A.D. 200, when a different style of pottery and projectile points appeared. This suggests the intrusion into the area of the southernmost ancestors of the coastal Algonquian tribes—the residents of the coastal plain extending from North Carolina to Maine. By A.D. 900 the primarily fishing and foraging society underwent another significant change with the adoption of agriculture and the bow and arrow. Evidence of these changes consists of pottery artifacts that have been traced to the resident Nanticoke and Powhatan culture groups, and others

Map of the Chesapeake region by Emanuel Bowen, 1752. (Courtesy Geography and Maps Division, Library of Congress)

of the Delmarva Peninsula (Maryland's eastern shore), Tidewater Virginia, and the North Carolina Algonquian groups.

Fundamental shifts in patterns of settlement resulted when foraging and subsistence ways of life were supplemented by agriculture, particularly the cultivation of cultigens such as corn, beans, and squash, as well as sunflower and amaranth. Fishing grounds became secondary, while cultivating arable land became primary. Settlement in permanent communities in turn required a new social order. The stable and predictable food base resulting from agricultural society also provided a storable surplus, which shortly thereafter caused major demographic changes that included internal population growth and subsequent migrations into new areas.

Like a stone dropped into a pool of water, the migrations that occurred throughout the Mid-Atlantic produced a ripple effect with varied results from place to place. In some regions, assimilation followed the contact of different tribal cultures. In the Potomac Piedmont, the original homeland of the ancestral Piscataway, the resident Piscataway population chose to abandon the region and to move downriver to below the Fall Line rather than to assimilate into a new culture. This migration subsequently forced the existing indigenous groups of the Washington area (probably Coastal Algonquian speakers, such as the Nanticoke) to retreat across the Chesapeake Bay. The ancestral Piscataway located in southern Maryland, the area from St. Mary's City to the Patuxent River, west across the District to the Fall Line, then south along the Virginia shore to just below Potomac Creek.

To the west, a later migration occurred during the Little Ice Age (approximately A.D. 1400 to 1700), when a sustained period of cool weather adversely affected agricultural productivity. The migration of expanding populations into western Pennsylvania and West Virginia culminated in the arrival of new groups into the northern Shenandoah Valley and the Potomac Piedmont as far east as the mouth of the Monocacy River. It was also during this interval that palisaded villages and towns sprang up to replace a more dispersed hamlet or farmstead pattern of housing.

The emergence of the palisaded villages provides the first indication of ongoing, endemic intergroup hostilities. It has yet to be determined whether the defensive posture of the region's American Indian communities was prehistoric—engendered by changes in tribal organization and geography that preceded European contact—or historic—precipitated primarily by the changes wrought directly and indirectly by the arrival of Europeans.

The historic period for the Native Americans of the Washington area began in 1608 with their first recorded contact with Europeans. Throughout the sixteenth century, however, European explorers had moved up and down the Atlantic coast, west along the Saint Lawrence River to the Great Lakes, and, in the case of the Spanish, as far north as the mouth of the Potomac River.[2] While it may never be known what impact these early explorations had on the Indians of the Washington area, we can assume that they had heard of the Europeans long before they saw them. What they had heard may not have been uniformly ominous. Although virtually all early contacts between Europeans and Indians quickly degenerated into hostilities, many Indians—despite repeated perfidy—continued to regard the Europeans as friends.

Some forms of betrayal were unintentional, though no less harmful. The separation of Europe and the Americas for millions of years before Columbus's voyage resulted in great immunological differences between the peoples of the two land masses. The arrival of Europeans among the Indians was thus tantamount to unintentional germ warfare. The Europeans carried diseases that were often transmitted far into the American interior in advance of their actual face-to-face contact with indigenous peoples. Thus, in many cases the Indians did not even realize that the Europeans were the source of the infections. Both direct and indirect evidence indicates great loss of life among Native Americans along the Atlantic coast from measles, small pox, chicken pox, and whooping cough. In addition, even before the Native American communities died out, the failure of time-honored herbal and ritual practices to stop the escalating mortality rate probably caused many Indians to doubt the efficacy and the value of their social and cultural norms.

Trade goods also exerted an influence on the Native Americans in the interior well before any actual encounter with the Europeans and, over time, undermined traditional culture. Although no archaeological evidence exists, Capt. John Smith and Henry Spelman, an English adventurer who was captured by the Patawomeke in 1609, suggested that the Washington area's Indians had contact with other native groups who were trading with one or more European groups to the north and west. Europeans had initiated the fur trade in the Northeast as early as the first quarter of the sixteenth century. By 1550 to 1580 the industry had reached such significant economic proportions that it affected virtually everyone from as far as the northern Chesapeake Bay region up the coast. The profit-driven competition and the greed engendered—particularly by the beaver pelt trade—altered the relationships of the Native American culture groups not only to the Europeans but also to each other and to the environment.

In 1608, when the English first appeared in the area, Indian villages hugged the shorelines near the mouths of streams. In such locations they had access to the resources in the tidal bays formed by the streams—fish, mussels, turtles, and eels, as well as the lush vegetation that grew along the wetlands. Further up the shoreline, the streams formed natural funnels for the spring runs of anadromous fish. The lower terraces of the stream valleys broadened, providing arable land for the corn, bean, squash, sunflower, tobacco, and other plants that comprised the Indian diet. From springs flowing from the bases of the bluffs, Native Americans obtained fresh water for drinking. They used the uplands and the interiors primarily for general foraging and seasonal movements to hunting grounds.

The Indians were technologically in the Stone Age when the Europeans arrived. They made tools and weapons from stone obtained from the local cobbles, and the bow and arrow was their primary weapon. Corn was ground with wooden mortars and pestles, and shells and stones were used as hoes and digging sticks to cultivate fields. Additionally, pottery and basketry were important aspects of Indian culture. Clothing was made from bark and skins. Shell beads and copper were used as currency and to symbolize rank and wealth. However, only males—and not all of them—could trade in or wear copper. Native American housing, consisting of pole frameworks covered by brush or mats, was a variation of the longhouse, in which entire kin groups may have lived under one roof.

American Indians' basic method of planting was to dig hillocks three feet apart, on which they planted corn. Once the cornstalks began to grow, the Indians planted beans, and the stalks served as bean poles. With their nitrogen-fixing capacity, the beans acted as a fertilizer. Squash was also planted on the hillocks and spread across the space between them. Because tobacco was considered sacred, the Indians planted it in separate fields. Other than the nitrogen-fixing crops, no other form of soil regeneration was used. Periodic migration of villages was thus the norm.

Each village probably consisted of independent, kin-related groups—although more than one kin group may have been present in the larger villages. Villagers were also allied by fictive kinship ties; and judging from the Powhatan chiefdom, the personalities of the leaders influenced the social dynamic of the villages. Individual villages or tribes were headed by a chief, or *werowance*. The chief's position was hereditary, but authority passed to his older brother or his sister's oldest male child—not to his own. Those in line for succession had to have some demonstrated abilities. The Powhatan model suggests that power politics and manipulation may also have played a role in who became chief.

The Indians of the upper Potomac were matrilineal and matrilocal in residence—at least until the end of the seventeenth century. At the time of the

"The Town of Secota," by John White, 1590. This drawing, depicting a Native American village at the time of European contact, shows a ceremonial feast (C and D); a tobacco field (E); a corn field with a watchtower "for guarding against marauding beasts and birds"; and a pumpkin and squash garden (I). (Courtesy City of Washington Collection, Prints and Photographs Division, Library of Congress)

Europeans' initial contact with the Patawomeke, or the Potomac, the paramount ruler of the confederacy, the *tayac,* was a male child who was advised and guided by an elder male, probably a maternal uncle. Ranked below the *tayac* (whom the Europeans called "emperor" after models familiar to them from their own history) were a series of lesser chiefs who often represented the paramount leader in other villages within the larger polity. They may have been kin of the *tayac,* rather than simply town or tribe chiefs. Other categories of rank included priests and war captains. These positions were probably both hereditary and achieved through a combination of ability and tutelage.

When the English first entered the area, they encountered two especially powerful culture groups: the Susquehannock and the Powhatan. Both of these groups had an impact on other Indians and Europeans alike. The Susquehannock—who spoke an Iroquoian language and lived to the north in what is now Lancaster County, Pennsylvania—dominated a large area to the south and west as far as Romney, West Virginia, on the southern branch of the Potomac River. The Susquehannock were a well-organized and militarized political entity. They emphasized egalitarianism and achievement more than hereditary authority. In contrast, an all-powerful hereditary chief ruled the highly centralized and rank-conscious Powhatans. In fact, the "confederacy" of Powhatan, the paramount chief (also the father of Pocahontas), was coercive and advanced through conquest. The Powhatan Confederacy, however, was strongest at its core and weakest at its extremities. Smaller polities that were similar to the Powhatan and Susquehannock Confederacies also existed throughout the Chesapeake Bay and the Potomac region. The Piscataway Confederacy, for example, seems to have been as much a pragmatic alliance as a firmly developed "empire," again, perhaps, with the core group showing greatest allegiance. The loyalty of tribes in the confederacy seems to have been contingent on whomever they saw as the most beneficial to their needs.

The total population of Indians at time of contact with the Europeans can only be estimated. Capt. John Smith noted approximately 1,000 people for the Piscataway in 1608, with up to 3,600 in the confederacy. Recent demographic work, however, suggests that the total population of Native Americans in the Washington area during early contact was at least 12,000. In 1632 the journal of Henry Fleet, a British fur trader, recorded the figure at 5,000.[3] If such estimates are correct, the population had declined by more than 50 percent in just twenty-four years. Despite the vagaries of the data, such population loss is highly probable considering the introduction of diseases and the endemic warfare among Native Americans that contact with Europeans only exacerbated.

During the early years of white settlement the Indians of the upper Potomac coastal plain, unlike the Powhatan and other culture groups near the Virginia Colony, were well removed from the English. When Captain Smith sailed into the Washington area, the Indians received him with friendliness, a stark contrast to his reception downriver, where other Patawomeke closer to the Powhatan Confederacy had met the English with hostility. Indeed, Smith indicated that some Patawomeke were allied with Powhatan's group against the English. Also, at that time, the Patawomeke were not on friendly terms with their upriver kin. The Piscataway were not mentioned by name in Smith's first visit. Instead, he specified that he had friendly visits with the Moyaons, probably then at or just below the mouth of Piscataway Creek; the Nacotchtank, on the east bank of the Potomac just below the mouth of the Anacostia River; and the Tauxenent, at or near the mouth of Hunting Creek near Mount Vernon.

Relations between the Jamestown colonists and the Washington area culture groups fluctuated with outbreaks of intertribal warfare. Following the first Powhatan War in 1609, the English, regarding nearby Native American groups as enemies, recognized the need to ally themselves with Indians farther from their immediate settlements. The Jamestown group cultivated amiable relations with the Patawomekes up the coast, although some of the Potomac tribes joined the Powhatan in launching a coordinated attack against the Virginia colonists in 1622. In 1623, following the outbreak of this second Powhatan War, in which the Powhatan suffered greatly, the English and the Patawomeke, who apparently had been waiting for just such an opportunity to avenge themselves against their traditional enemies, attacked the Piscataway, the Moyaons, and the Necostins. Culture groups from the interior—presumably one or more Iroquoian-speaking groups, including the Susquehannock—also attacked the Moyaons at about this time.

In 1623 at Nacotchtank (Necostin), near the mouth of what came to be called the Anacostia River, Henry Fleet, in attempting to corner the fur trade of the upper Potomac coastal plain, encountered a number of Native American groups speaking different languages, notably the Massomacks (the Erie) and other "Cannyda" Indians. The Nacotchtank were, and had been since the beginning of the fur trade, middlemen in that industry, hence, the iron tools that had worked their way into the upper Potomac coastal plain. The area now called Washington, D.C., appears to have been an entrepôt between the tidewater and the interior. According to Fleet, the Nacotchtank, protected by the powerful Indian groups to the north, relished their role as middlemen, much to the consternation of the Piscataway, who viewed them as overly independent. Ultimately, the fur trade hurt rather than helped Indian groups engaged in it, because it resulted in their growing dependence on European rather than traditional technologies.

A major change in Piscataway history, which was initially a change for the better, occurred when the English arrived in Maryland in 1634. Prior to this time the Indians had dealt directly and indirectly with colonial fur traders and the English in Virginia, who were primarily Protestant. The English who established the Maryland Colony, however, were Catholics. At first, Maryland's Jesuit settlers were more interested in the religious conversion of Native Americans than in trading with or removing them.

The first encounter between the Marylanders and the Piscataway produced a notable response from the *tayac*. Addressing a Jesuit leader's announcement that the settlers had come to "bring the Indians enlightenment in the form of Christianity and civilization," the chief reportedly said "he would not bid him goe, neither would hee bid him stay, but that he might use his own discretion."[4] In retrospect, it is puzzling why, after so many years of dismal encounters with the English, the *tayac* did not refuse the newcomers permission to stay. At the time, however, the Piscataway were under great stress—some of it internal, much of it external—and they probably hoped to gain technological and strategic advantage from any relationship that developed with the Maryland colonists.

The Marylanders settled in St. Mary's City, considerably removed from the Piscataway. The Marylanders categorized the Piscataway of the western shore into four groups. They called those on the western shore of the bay the Patuxent and the Matapanian, and those who resided on the Potomac River the Piscataway and the Portobacke (near present-day Port Tobacco). The Nacotchtank are not mentioned in the records.

The Marylanders assigned Father John White to minister to the Piscataway, and in June 1639 he went to live with them in the *tayac's* "palace." By 1640 he had baptized the chief. In 1642 White visited the Patawomeke, who were now reduced to a small village and an insignificant power. Although attacks by the Susquehannock had forced the mission at Piscataway to be moved south that year, more than 130 Indians had been baptized into the Catholic faith. Ultimately, the conversions complicated Piscataway relations with the Europeans because of the intolerance that had developed between Protestants and Catholics in the Maryland Colony.

As the population of Maryland increased, the English expanded northward up the southern Maryland peninsula and created new counties. An English population of approximately 200 in 1634 had approached 5,000 by 1657, which by that time was probably five times greater than that of the native population. The balance of power had shifted. The Marylanders, increasingly involved in Indian affairs, enacted laws designed to make the Indians dependents. For example, in 1641, when the Piscataway *tayac*, Kittamaquundi, died, he had given the English governor the right to choose his successor. In concert with a council of the Piscataway, the colony continued to exercise this right. Seven years later the colony passed an act making it legal to give "friendly" Indians arms for the defense of the Colony's frontiers, but forbidding the provision of guns or ammunition to any other native groups for any other purpose.

Acts to regulate American Indians grew out of the colonists' own needs. Since the Marylanders had declared war on the Susquehannock, they needed the Piscataway to provide a buffer between them and their powerful enemy. By 1666, however, the balance of power among the Indians to the north shifted, and the English made a treaty with the Susquehannock so that they would provide a buffer between them and the ascendant League of the Iroquois. The treaty formalized the right of the colony's governor to appoint a new *tayac*, levied the death penalty against Indians who killed English colonists, and stipulated that Indians must lay down their arms to indicate their friendly intentions when encountering an English colonist. Among the groups from the Washington area included in the treaty were the Anacostank and the Doeg (formerly, apparently, the Tauxenent). The 1666 treaty also provided reservation land for the Indian signatories; in turn, the Marylanders were to provide protection for them against the Iroquois tribes invading from the north. However, the reservation, which was approximately 10,000 acres, spanning from the Piscataway to the Mattawoman creeks, became subject to continued encroachment by the colonizing Marylanders.

As an indication of their changed status, the Piscataway, at a renewal of the treaty in 1670, noted that their population had dwindled considerably, and poignantly suggested that "when their Nation may be reduced to nothing perhaps they may not be Scorned and Chased out of our [the colony's] protection."[5] Subsequent events, however, further threatened the tribe's survival. By 1674 the Susquehannock, who had also suffered various kinds of population decimation, moved into the Washington area at the invitation of the Maryland colonists and settled on Piscataway Creek in the heartland of the Piscataway. The Susquehannock became involved in raids and counter-raids between the Doeg, who had settled across the river, and the English settlers. The Piscataway entered the fray apparently siding with the Virginians, since the Susquehannock had begun a series of fierce and destructive raids against the Piscataway. To their further detriment, the Piscataway, battered and weakened, also became involved in the animosities between Catholic and Protestant colonists. Infighting, as well as alcoholism, among the Piscataway added to the continuing internal strife and the breakdown of authority within the culture group. The Maryland colonists, who had expanded up to and beyond the Piscataway settlement, forced the Piscataway to relocate near Fort Washington and Prince Georges County. Piscataway relations with the advance guard of the Maryland colonists continued to degenerate, with hostilities and mistrust persisting between them and the Virginia colonists.

The Piscataway attempted to resolve their problems, as would many other Indian culture groups in the centuries succeeding them, by migrating away from their ancestral homeland to other parts of the country. Increasingly, they shifted toward the west at the foothills of the Blue Ridge Mountains probably in Rappahannock County, Virginia. By 1697 most had left Maryland. Reports indicated that they settled with the Seneca, with whom they had become friendly and had merged with to become "one people." Virginia, however, refused to accept the Piscataway. The Marylanders then offered to let them move to Piscataway Creek, or the mouth of Rock Creek. In 1699 the Piscataway, along with some Nacotchtank, were living on Conoy Island in the Potomac. Pennsylvania offered the Indians safe haven, and in 1702 the movement to that colony began. Thus was initiated a protracted northern and westward drift and a merging with the Iroquois. By 1718 the Piscataway had relocated to Conoy Town on the western branch of the Susquehanna. In 1743, again in response to continued pressure by expanding European settlements, they moved to the Juniata River. By 1758 they had merged with the remaining Nanticoke in western New York.

The experience of Washington's Indians was repeatedly replicated in different regions, as successive waves of white Americans expanded settlements into the west. Approximately fifty years after the Piscataway had been removed from the immediate environs of the District of Columbia, the French and Indian War erupted, pushing the native populations even further west. By 1791, the year that the District of Columbia became the nation's capital, similar encounters recurred across the Appalachian Mountains into the Ohio territory. On the shores of the Potomac and Anacostia rivers, whose names are among the few tangible reminders of an ancient heritage, a new series of cultural encounters would take place.

Over the past few decades scholars have argued that perhaps not all the Piscataway actually left the Washington area. While no indisputable evidence exists to demonstrate their continuous presence, it seems likely that the Piscataway, who under the pressure of continued encroachment had become factionalized and split apart, did not leave the area en masse.[6] Moreover, several

Piscataway descendants Turkey Tayac, Mark Tayac, and Jenice Bigbee during Indian Awareness Week at the University of Maryland in 1974. (Courtesy National Anthropological Archives, Smithsonian Institution)

people from southern Maryland claim to be Piscataway descendants. Today they are petitioning the state to recognize them as a designated Native American culture group. The Piscataway do not necessarily need such official recognition for their own self-identity, but they are aware that it does confer certain legal rights.[7] The petition also reflects ongoing efforts, part of a growing American Indian pride movement, to reclaim a heritage that has sustained Native Americans through a bitter history of religious and racial intolerance.

Like other "outsiders," or nonwhite Americans, many Native Americans reside on the periphery of society. Today, the race-oriented perspective of the dominant culture, which not only questions the Piscataway's identity as "pure" American Indians but also views them as less than white, has exacerbated their entry into the American "melting pot." Members of Native American culture groups have often been viewed as "black" by the U.S. Census and by society at large, further submerging their Indian identity and complicating their social relations with other ethnic Americans.

*District native Rose Powhatan,
a member of the Pamunkey tribe
of the Powhatan Confederacy
and a descendant of Pocahontas's uncle, at the opening of her
art exhibit, "Jubilation, Tribula-
tion, Positive Vibration," at the
Fondo del Sol Gallery in Washington in 1990. Powhatan's art
is infused with American Indian
culture. (Photograph by Cyrena
Chang, © Washington Post)*

It is estimated that more than 7,000 people of probable Piscataway descent now live in scattered but definite concentrations in Prince Georges,
Prince Charles, and St. Mary's counties in Maryland. They live on the ancestral land of their forebears, some as small farmers, some as laborers and blue-
collar workers, and a few, having overcome enormous barriers, as white-collar
clerical workers and professionals. Increasing numbers have followed the contemporary trend and migrated to Washington and the metropolitan area. Most
have remained Catholics; however, many consciously endeavor to preserve the
stories, sacred images, and customs of their native culture groups. In their ongoing struggle for survival, local Native Americans are making Washington's
Indian past visible again.

NOTES

1. A thorough discussion of the Washington area's prehistory has yet to be written, but there exist numerous studies covering the past and present of the Piscataway
Indians. In addition, there are documents, including dissertations, in such places as
the Mullen Library at Catholic University in Washington, D.C. The most informa-
tive recent summary of the ethnohistory of the Piscataway, which should be supplemented with other published studies, is Paul B. Cissna, "The Piscataway Indians of
Southern Maryland: An Ethnohistory from Pre-European Contact to the Present"
(Ph.D. diss., American University, 1986). For information on the historical back-

ground of the Piscataway, see Wayne E. Clark, "The Origins of the Piscataway and Related Indian Cultures," *Maryland Historical Magazine* 75, no. 1 (1980): 8–22; Christian F. Feest, "Nanticoke and Neighboring Tribes" and "Virginia Algonquians" in *Northeast*, ed. Bruce G. Trigger, *Handbook of North American Indians*, ed. William Sturtevant (Washington, D.C.: Smithsonian Institution, 1978), 15:240–52, 253–70; William M. Gardner, "The Prehistory of the Greater Washington, D.C., Area" (paper presented at the American Anthropological Association annual meeting, Washington, D.C., 1986 [on file Department of Anthropology, Catholic University, Washington, D.C.]); Robert L. Humphrey and Mary E. Chambers, *Ancient Washington: American Indian Cultures of the Potomac Valley*, Center for Washington Area Studies at George Washington University, 6th ser. (Washington, D.C.: Center for Washington Area Studies at George Washington University, 1977); Francis Jennings, "Susquehannock," in *Northeast*, ed. Trigger, 362–67; and James H. Merrell, "Cultural Continuity among the Piscataway Indians of Colonial Maryland," *William and Mary Quarterly* 37 (1979): 548–70.

2. In 1570–71 a small band of Spanish Jesuits led by Juan Bautista de Ségura attempted unsuccessfully to establish a Spanish mission on the York River. Ségura was accompanied, and subsequently thwarted, in his missionary effort by Don Luis. (Luis was the son of an Indian chief whom the Spanish had captured in 1561 off the coast of Virginia near the York River. He was renamed, converted, and raised as a Catholic in Spain, then brought back with them to the place of his birth.) There had thus been direct European contact with Native American culture groups in the area at least 50 years before the founding of the Jamestown settlement. See Clifford M. Lewis and Albert J. Loomie, *The Spanish Jesuit Mission in Virginia, 1570–1572* (Chapel Hill: University of North Carolina Press, 1953).

3. For a discussion of demographics, see Feest, "Nanticoke and Neighboring Tribes," 242. Scholars use different estimates, but the actual population figures remain a mystery.

4. Anonymous, "A Relation of Maryland, together with a Map of the Countrey, the Conditions of the Plantation, with his majesties Charter to the Lord Baltemore, translated into English," in *Narratives of Early Maryland, 1633–1684*, ed. Clayton C. Hall (New York: Charles Scribner and Sons, 1910; New York: Barnes and Noble, 1967): 70–112.

5. As quoted in William H. Browne, ed. *Proceedings of the Council, 1667–1678/9*, vol. 5 (Baltimore: Maryland Historical Society).

6. A number of other Indian groups have also survived in the surrounding area. For example, the Pamunkey and the Mattaponi have lived continuously on reservations that the state of Virginia granted to them in the eighteenth century. Both culture groups have established museums that document their prehistoric and historic experiences. Other tribes that once lived in Virginia apparently sold their reservation land and disappeared into the general population. Many Assateague, for example, ended up living with the Nanticokes. Another segment of the Nanticokes continues to live near their old reservation in southern Delaware. In a similar fashion, there are groups of people living in Virginia who have been linked with the Rappahannock, the Powhatan, and the Nansemond.

7. I had a long friendship with the late Philip Sheridan Proctor, also known as

Chief Turkey Tayac, the twenty-seventh chief of the Piscataway. We first met at the head of the Chesapeake Bay during a hurricane in the fall of 1967. Over the following years, we traveled together throughout much of the countryside and attended local archaeological society meetings. Adept at social and cultural adaptation, Tayac lived in several worlds. He was a sought-after herbalist, even treating prominent anthropologists in the early 1970s. Ethnohistorians, anthropologists, and journalists often interviewed him. In his medicine bundle, he kept a Library of Congress card listing a published interview he had given to the noted ethnographer Frank Speck in the 1930s. He was a veteran of World War I and had been gassed during that "war to end all wars." He lacked formal education, lived modestly, was a conservative Catholic, a southern Marylander, and, above all, a Piscataway Indian in mind and heart, as well as in physical characteristics. The maintenance of his "Indianness" was no mean feat after nearly four hundred years of forced submergence of that identity. He was my friend and teacher. I dedicate this article to his memory.

ADDITIONAL READING

Axtell, James. *After Columbus: Essays in the Ethnohistory of Colonial North America.* New York: Oxford University Press, 1988.

———. *The European and the Indian: Essays in the Ethnohistory of Colonial North America.* New York: Oxford University Press, 1981.

———. *The Invasion Within: The Contest of Cultures in Colonial North America.* New York: Oxford University Press, 1985.

Barbour, Philip L., ed. *The Complete Works of Captain John Smith.* 3 vols. Chapel Hill: University of North Carolina Press, 1986.

Fausz, Frederick. "Patterns of Anglo-Indian Aggression and Accommodations along the Mid-Atlantic Coast, 1584–1634." In *Cultures in Contact: The Impact of European Contacts on Native American Cultural Institutions, 1000–1800,* edited by William W. Fitzhugh. Washington, D.C.: Smithsonian Institution Press, 1985.

Fitzhugh, William W., ed. *Cultures in Contact: The Impact of European Contacts on Native American Cultural Institutions, 1000–1800.* Washington: Smithsonian Institution Press, 1985.

Kupperman, Karen Ordahl, ed. *Captain John Smith: A Select Edition of His Writings.* Chapel Hill: University of North Carolina Press, 1988.

Nash, Carole L. "A Little Town Called the Nacostin: Archeological Collecting and Model Building along the Anacostia," n.d. Department of Anthropology. Catholic University, Washington, D.C.

———. "When There Are No Sites Left," n.d. Department of Anthropology. Catholic University, Washington, D.C.

Rountree, Helen C. *The Powhatan Indians of Virginia: Their Traditional Culture.* Norman: University of Oklahoma Press, 1989.

Stephenson, Robert L., and Alice L. L. Ferguson, "The Accokeek Creek Site: A Middle Atlantic Seaboard Culture Sequence," *Anthropological Papers.* Ann Arbor: University of Michigan Press, 1963.

Turner, Randolph E. "Socio-Political Organization within the Powhatan Chiefdom and the Effects of European Contact, A.D. 1602–1646." In *Cultures in Contact: The Impact of European Contacts on Native American Cultural Institutions, 1000–1800,* edited by William W. Fitzhugh. Washington, D.C.: Smithsonian Institution Press, 1985.

Wood, Peter, et al., eds. *Powhatan's Mantle: Indians in the Colonial Southeast.* Lincoln: University of Nebraska Press, 1989.

2.

The Genesis of Washington's African American Community

James Oliver Horton

The migration of black people to the District of Columbia began long before the creation of the national capital on the banks of the Potomac River. This migration constituted an integral part of the first British settlement in North America. Twenty Africans, who landed in Jamestown, Virginia, in 1619 aboard a Dutch trading ship, marked the beginning of a forced migration that brought tens of thousands of blacks to the Chesapeake region. Those twenty Africans, and others who came after them, became unwilling participants in one of American history's most important and savage chapters—the Atlantic slave trade.

The first Africans imported into Virginia were treated not as slaves but as indentured servants, bound for a term of service, then allowed their freedom. A few—like Anthony Johnson, who became a prominent landholder on Virginia's eastern shore—prospered after their indenture had ended. The seventeenth century, however, saw the evolution of the American slave system, which severely limited the chances of many Africans to follow Johnson's example. By 1700 colonial statutes in Virginia and Maryland gave legal sanction to the emerging institution that would become the region's dominant labor system during the next century. This system defined class status and social relations, significantly influencing the political structure of the Chesapeake area and ultimately of the capital city carved from it.

The region's black people represented a variety of mainly West African national and cultural groups. They came primarily from the Bight of Biafra along the Nigerian coast, from Angola, from the Gold Coast, and from Senegambia in Guinea, West Africa. Some passed through the sugar islands of the West Indies; as the eighteenth century progressed, however, increasing numbers came directly from Africa. Enslaved Africans arrived in the Chesa-peake region on slave ships, or slavers, and spent weeks, sometimes months, being transported to regional ports, where they were auctioned. A slaver might visit Yorktown, Virginia, then move up river to settlements along the Rappa-hannock, selling its human cargo to area planters who traveled to port trading centers to replenish their slaveholdings.[1]

Africans adjusted to their new slave status in a variety of ways. Most were forced to labor in the tobacco fields, a task generally familiar to those who came from African agricultural societies in which tobacco was grown. Although they were given new names, for generations many continued to use their African names when not under the direct supervision of whites. Most were confined to plantations, away from colonial settlements. If they were on a large plantation with extensive slaveholdings, Africans had enhanced prospects for the estab-lishment of a supportive slave community. Plantation size was thus particularly important to slaves because it often determined their quality of life.

Common bondage created special difficulties for the captives, who came from many diverse culture groups and areas of Africa. Those who might have been tribal enemies in Africa now found themselves bound together as part of the same community and dependent upon one another for survival. Because Africa was more linguistically diverse than Europe, the slaves needed to over-come language differences. The large number of Angolans and the substantial representation of Ibos ensured a basis for a common language. For those unable to converse with their fellow slaves, however, it was important that they break language barriers quickly, because linguistic isolation could be unbearable. One who experienced such alienation firsthand reported, "I had no person to speak to that I could understand. In this state I was constantly grieving and pining, and wishing for death."[2]

Some Africans became multilingual, gaining facility with a number of Eu-ropean languages (French, English, Portuguese, Spanish, and Dutch) and mas-tering many African tongues. This allowed for their communication within and without the slave communities that were emerging by the early decades of the eighteenth century. Others employed the African trading language, WAPE (West African Pidgin English), to speak with their fellows. WAPE could also be understood by many British settlers, thus providing an additional vehicle for limited communication between slave and master.

By the 1720s slaves had established a comparatively stable community life. The African family in America was becoming what it had been in Africa: central to black life. As more African women arrived, the gender imbalance that had inhibited formation of family life began to disappear. Yet, on the scattered farms where slaveholdings were small, or even on the larger plantations with a sizable black population, maintenance of family life was difficult. Slaves' marriages were not legally recognized, and masters had absolute power to split families through sale or forced migration of some family members to another region. Slaves could also be gambled away, given as gifts, or used as collateral for planters' debts. Family separation was invoked as a powerful threat to control slave behavior.

Nevertheless, slave families were established—and in several forms. In the mid-eighteenth century some black males, generally African-born or first-generation American-born, continued the practice of polygyny, which was common to several cultures in West Africa. However, too few African women had been brought to the Chesapeake region—even late in the century—for the practice to be widespread or practical. Instead, two-parent families, sometimes within households sheltering extended kin, became the norm, especially among American-born blacks. By the end of the century, slaves, almost all of whom were American-born, lived in these family arrangements at a rate comparable to that of whites. By the time the new federal government began to bargain for the land on which the capital city would stand, area blacks, who were predominantly slaves, had already established a family-centered community life.

In 1800, when the First Congress convened and Washington became the federal government's official seat, 3,244 slaves and 783 free blacks accounted for 29 percent of the District of Columbia's 14,000 inhabitants. In addition, by the 1800s almost all blacks in Virginia and Maryland were native-born—some second- or third-generation Americans. Many worked in tobacco fields or as domestics. A significant number were skilled workers. Two-thirds of black skilled laborers worked and resided in either the port city of Georgetown at the headwaters of the Potomac River, or the more sophisticated and prosperous Alexandria, five miles downstream on the Virginia side. Slaves served the affluent merchant families of those communities as domestic servants, or manned the docks that served the commercial economies. Dick, an Alexandria slave, was a wagoner for the Harrison family. He transported barrels of flour from the port to merchants in the city. Services like those Dick provided were rendered by hundreds of other slaves as well, and helped to fuel the Washington area's economic expansion and, in turn, its rapid population growth.[3]

Many slaves and free blacks were involved in building the federal city. Some members of the city's small European immigrant community advocated measures to limit competition from black labor, which they believed undercut wages and devalued white labor. As a result of employment restrictions, the work available for blacks declined by the Civil War. However, in Washington's earlier years, when much of the initial construction of public buildings was under way, the need for workers was so great that Congress refused to restrict the use of slave labor in that enterprise. Both slaves and free blacks worked alongside Irish and German laborers. Together they constructed the nation's capital.[4]

The rise of the federal city shaped the character of slavery in the area, as well as its significance to the nation. The emergence of the capital and its attendant officialdom brought black people from other regions of the country. Congressional delegations and their staff members—many of whom were attended to by slaves—came from Georgia and the Carolinas, as well as Delaware and several other northern states, such as Pennsylvania, New Jersey, and New York—all of which in 1800 still tolerated slavery. Black migrants and those from the Chesapeake region swelled the ranks of the District's slave population. Before 1800 slavery in the Chesapeake area had been confined to rural or small-town locales that were relatively removed from outsiders' view. In Washington, slavery—now on public display not only to the country at large but also to a world eager to evaluate America's bold experiment in liberty—stood out more vividly than elsewhere as the grossest contradiction of the new nation's professed democratic values.

For the slave, however, urbanization generally afforded greater personal freedom than on the plantation, where isolation enhanced the planter's power as dictator in his private fiefdom. In the city, local political authority, the pressure of public opinion, and the moral authority of the church diluted such absolute power. Although slaveholders in the District of Columbia could elicit broad support for their exercise of power, the lack of isolation tended to limit their dominance. Additionally, the presence of a free black community—small at the turn of the nineteenth century but growing through succeeding generations—provided support for those in bondage and assistance for fugitive slaves. Despite their efforts, masters never fully succeeded in precluding contact between their slaves and free blacks, who were seen as a threat to the slave system.

The city also offered slaves the opportunity to be "hired out," a practice entitling a master to collect a fee for work done by his slave for a third party. In a city constantly under construction, slaveowners often found it financially lucrative to hire out their slaves to building contractors short of laborers. Jane Ashley hired out her slave, Harrison Cary, an accomplished bricklayer, for the then considerable sum of $22 per month. William Rowe contracted his slave, Thomas, to the National Hotel for $30 per month.[5]

Hired-out slaves sometimes lived with their short-term employers, away

"A Slave-Coffle Passing the Capitol," engraving in Popular History of the U.S. *(William Cullen Bryant and Sydney Howard Gay, 1880). (Photo courtesy Prints and Photographs Division, Library of Congress)*

from the master's residence. A more desirable arrangement, from a slave's viewpoint, was independent housing. Although District regulations required a slave to live either with a master or a designated employer, authorities often turned a blind eye if slaves made independent living arrangements with their owner's consent. These possibilities of substantial profit for masters and independent housing for slaves made Washington attractive to both parties and encouraged the migration of hired bondsmen.

During the 1790s and the early 1800s a few slaves employed in construction and living independently found housing in shanties on F Street, behind St. Patrick's Church near Blodgett's Hotel, or in scattered shacks north of F

Street. Accommodations were not comfortable, but slaves seeking to live with family members and unconstrained by their masters favored such arrangements.[6]

If hiring-out brought an immediate cash return on human capital, it also tended to erode slavery's omnipotence. In their associations with one another and with the growing free black community, slaves became more independent—sometimes too much so—for a system that demanded absolute obedience. John, "a well-made yellow man," expressed his independence and his anger when his master, George Coleman of Fairfax, Virginia, hired him out to "very hard white people." Having been hired out before, John knew he could command at least $150 a year and refused to tolerate what he considered unfair treatment from his temporary employers. He decided to attempt an escape to the North, in his words, "to be free or die, to kill or be killed, in trying to reach free land somewhere." Supporters of slavery viewed John's attitude as a direct result of his having spent so much time independent of his master's control.[7]

In the urban environment slaves were sometimes allowed liberties even beyond those of selecting their own employers and living in their own quarters. John probably knew slaves who sold their own produce in area markets and retained the profits for themselves. Sophia Bell, an Alexandria slave, sold vegetables from her garden in a marketplace near her home. Allowed to keep her earnings, she saved $400—enough to buy freedom for her husband George, an Anacostia slave. Shortly after his emancipation, George purchased Sophia's freedom. The couple then settled in southeast Washington, where both lived into their eighties.[8]

The growing difficulty of controlling urban slaves and the profitability of allowing them greater mobility help to explain the deterioration of slavery in Washington throughout the first half of the nineteenth century. After increasing until 1830—though decreasing as a percentage of the black population—the slave population began a steady decline. On the eve of the Civil War there were fewer slaves in Washington than there had been at the beginning of the century. The 1800 and 1860 censuses for the District indicate that although almost all Washington blacks were slaves in 1800, when Abraham Lincoln took office in 1860 only one in five blacks was so designated.

Although the ratio of slaves to free blacks in the city dropped steadily after the early nineteenth century, Washington and its surrounding areas witnessed the growth of a vigorous slave-trade market. The trading of slaves into and out of the city provided hefty returns for slave traders but painfully disrupted black family and community life. As the soil in the Chesapeake region deteriorated after generations of depleting tobacco agriculture, the center of southern economic and political power shifted. The Deep South now provided new opportunities for planter investment, and cotton became the choice crop. Eli Whitney's cotton gin increased the productivity of slave labor by 500 percent, making cotton extremely profitable to grow and inflating the value of slaves in the territory acquired by the United States through the Louisiana Purchase. This region became known as the Black Belt and the Cotton Kingdom, where by 1815 plantations were producing the nation's most profitable export. By the Civil War the Deep South had absorbed the nation's largest concentration of blacks, as the demand for slave labor increased and slave prices spiraled upward.

The District of Columbia was directly implicated in the growth of slavery in the Black Belt. Slaves purchased in Virginia and Maryland and sold at auction in Washington or Alexandria at moderate prices could be resold in the lower South at tremendous profits. A prime field hand who sold for a few hundred dollars in the District might bring several thousand dollars in Natchez, Mississippi, or in New Orleans. Slave traders thus did a brisk business in the District, despite the steady pressure from black and white abolitionists, who petitioned the federal government throughout the nineteenth century with demands that the slave trade be outlawed in the capital. One Washingtonian, sickened by the presence of the trade in his city, speculated that "in no part of the earth . . . was there so great, so infamous, a slave market as in the metropolis in the seat of government of this nation which prides itself on freedom."[9]

Slave-holding cells (often called "Georgia pens") and auction blocks were scattered around the city—for example, in what became Potomac Park, in Robey's Tavern at Seventh Street and Maryland Avenue, in southwest Washington on B Street, in Georgetown at McCandless's Tavern, and on F Street near Thirteenth Street, NW, and elsewhere. One of the most notorious was located near Lafayette Square in sight of the White House. The Alexandria offices of slave traders Franklin and Armfield were among the largest in the country and through branch offices in the Deep South the firm supplied the massive cotton plantations of Mississippi and Louisiana.

Although slaves in Washington faced fewer restrictions than did those in Virginia and Maryland, the significant presence of slave traders and the frequent slave auctions were constant reminders of their vulnerability. Any slave could be literally sold down the river at any time. The immense profit to be made in the trade also endangered the well-being of free blacks, who were sometimes kidnapped into bondage and sold south. In an autobiographical narrative, *Twelve Years a Slave*, Solomon Northrup, a free black from New York, described how he was kidnapped while visiting Washington and taken by boat to New Orleans, where he was held in slavery for twelve years. Finally, in 1852

Old slave pen on north side of G Street, NW, between 4th and 6th Streets. (Photo courtesy Prints and Photographs Division, Library of Congress)

Northrup was able to get word to his wife about his plight and his whereabouts. Only through her efforts and the influence of the governor of New York was he restored to liberty.[10]

While Washington's slave population declined in the pre–Civil War decades, the free black population increased by 12 percent, more than twice the rate for the District's total population. The steady rise in the number of free blacks constituted one of the most significant trends in early Washington history. Free blacks thus figured prominently at every stage of the city's development. Like the slaves, most free blacks came to the District from adjoining states. For example, Benjamin Banneker, an astronomer, mathematician, and almanac author from Maryland, was part of the survey team that laid plans for the federal city in 1791. Banneker worked closely with Maj. Andrew Ellicott in setting out the District's boundaries. Together they produced the first printed

Mariah Sharp, a free woman born in Virginia, was included in the 1810 U.S. census. Some of Mariah's descendants—including her great-great grandson, Johnarthur Lightfoot—still live in Washington. (Photograph reproduced by Robert Sherbow and reprinted with permission of Johnarthur Lightfoot)

version of the federal city plan as conceived by French architect Pierre Charles L'Enfant.

Banneker's role in the earliest days of the District's planning foreshadowed the continuing significance of free blacks, as Washington grew from a settlement of "straggling, confused . . . crazy wooden sheds, and filthy pigsties"[11] in the early nineteenth century to the city it was to become. The evolving capital city attracted free blacks hoping to find a measure of truth in the new government's idealistic slogans. In the afterglow of the American Revolution, when talk of freedom and liberty punctuated the national discourse, state legislatures in Virginia and Maryland instituted regulations that made it easier for masters to manumit their slaves. A faltering upper-South tobacco economy, suffering from soil depletion that reduced crop yields and depressed the value of slaves, also encouraged such relatively progressive laws. In this more tolerant atmosphere numerous slaves gained their freedom.

Many of the newly freed blacks moved to Washington in search of work and found jobs in the building trades or in the service sector as cooks, waiters, and hotel workers, as well as in private homes as domestics. Though low-paying and unstable, such work was far preferable to slavery and offered the possibility of economic independence.

Although the need for labor encouraged tolerance of free black migration to Washington, uneasiness remained about the growth of a large free black community. Local authorities therefore established special structures of racial control for free African Americans. Starting in 1808, the same year the Atlantic slave trade was constitutionally prohibited, the first of several "black codes" was passed, restricting the movements of free blacks and imposing on them a 10 P.M. curfew, which could be adjusted whenever local whites felt particularly threatened. The codes also forbade free blacks from operating or frequenting gambling or drinking establishments, swearing in public, keeping dogs, racing horses through the streets, carrying firearms, bathing in the river, or attending "disorderly" meetings. By the 1820s the law required free blacks to post a bond guaranteeing their solvency and good conduct and to secure white guarantors who would attest to their character. As elsewhere in the South, black persons in the District were assumed to be slaves unless they could prove otherwise; after 1812 all free blacks were required to register with local authorities and to carry "freedom papers" to prove their status.[12]

Such restrictive codes reflected common anxieties among whites, many of whom feared a flood of African American migrants from the slave states. District authorities approached the issue with ambivalence. The city's labor needs muted public expression of the fear of a growing free black community. Most of the black codes were not regularly enforced and were seldom effective. Erratic enforcement of the codes allowed Washington's free black population to grow dramatically in the first quarter of the nineteenth century. By 1830 free blacks accounted for approximately half of the blacks and more than 15 percent of the District's total population.

The physical dimensions of Washington's free black community took shape in the early nineteenth century, as manumitted slaves left the surrounding countryside for the new federal city. Many lived in small shacks on alleys cut off from the street, forming isolated communities; others lived at the rear of their employer's home. In general, blacks were not segregated in restricted areas, as they were to be in the twentieth century. A significant number of black households, however, did cluster in certain sections of Washington. From the early years, blacks lived along Fourth Street in southeast Washington; in 1806 Moses Liverpool, for example, purchased a lot at K and Fourth Streets, SE. Within the next generation this area became a major center of black community life.

By 1860 free blacks had settled throughout the city's southeastern quadrant, concentrating mainly along Fourth Street between the Navy Yard on the Anacostia River and East Capitol Street. Blacks also clustered between East Capitol Street and Independence Avenue—near what is now the Library of Congress—and along Pennsylvania Avenue and Third Street. Other black residences sprang up in the then undeveloped countryside of northwest Washington south of P Street and west of New Jersey Avenue. African Americans also settled in sections of Fourteenth and Sixteenth Streets, NW, and along I and K Streets.

Nineteenth-century Washington was a walking city in which commercial and residential buildings coexisted in neighborhoods. Blacks thus often lived in the same areas as their businesses. Municipal policy, however, ensured that there would be relatively few black-owned enterprises. City authorities rarely granted business licenses to blacks, thus limiting their entrepreneurial opportunities, and the black codes further restricted their commercial activities. Yet a few African Americans—often with the assistance of whites who acted as front men for their ventures—persevered in starting small businesses as hack drivers, barbers, shoemakers, and the like.

African Americans did not allow legal restrictions to go unchallenged. In 1821 William Costin, a former slave who was by that time an influential business leader in the free black community, brought suit against the restrictions leveled at African Americans. The court ruled against Costin, but his challenge would not be the last. In 1836 Isaac Carey tested the restrictions placed on blacks by selling perfume without a license. Although he was initially fined $50, the law was struck down on appeal by a Circuit Court judge who found it "repugnant to the general law of the land."[13]

Even before the restrictions were revoked, some blacks operated profitable businesses in various parts of the city. In the spring of 1800 a free black man was reported to be keeping a small shop near the Eastern Branch (now the Anacostia River) ferry. According to one contemporary observer, the shop did a reasonable business, and the shopkeeper had become a property holder—one of the earliest of a sizable propertied class of blacks that was already growing in the first decade of the nineteenth century. Another African American, Joseph Moor, began life as a slave but, by the early decades of the nineteenth century was running a grocery shop in Georgetown that reportedly did a brisk business. Jesse Garner's oyster house, at the rear of the Washington Hotel at Fifteenth Street and Pennsylvania Avenue, NW, was successful enough to allow him to open a second shop, this one specializing in shoe care and boasting a service unsurpassed "by any in America."[14]

African Americans operated several oyster houses in the District through-out the antebellum period. Ralph King's establishment was on Pennsylvania Avenue, across from Brown's Hotel, and Stevens's Oyster House was not too far away. Blacks also operated several restaurants downtown, among the most popular of which was the Epicurean Eating House, run by Beverly Snow. A scattering of hack stands, fruit stores, and other small shops rounded out the black business presence in the mid-nineteenth-century center city.

Many free African Americans managed to enter into the sales field, some in more innovative and less enduring ways than did black storekeepers. A num-ber of black vendors opened stands at the race grounds in Georgetown, occu-pying booths from which they hawked food and drink to the throngs of white pleasure-seekers frequenting the track. Other enterprising blacks peddled their wares along the avenues or in front of public buildings. Baked breads, pies, and cakes, as well as shellfish and, in winter, hot-roasted nuts, were especially pop-ular items. One could make a reasonable living from selling apples in season, and fresh cider often sold for as much as $3 a barrel.

The federal government also opened a few service jobs to free blacks. Be-ginning with Thomas Jefferson's presidency, a substantial number of black ser-vants attended the chief executive and most other officeholders. The White House domestic staff included several blacks, as did staffs of most other gov-ernment buildings. In addition, a few blacks secured jobs as government mes-sengers. These positions not only paid comparatively well, but they also put the messengers in regular contact with well-placed men—an important factor in a paternalistic racial environment. Such contacts were useful in a society that provided little protection to blacks save that which derived from the good will of influential white benefactors.

For black women at the time, the District offered a few limited opportu-nities in sewing, nursing, and, as black schools were formed, teaching. Anne Marie Hall, the first of her gender and her race to teach in Washington, was the forerunner of a long line of black women who provided education for the city's African American children. Some federal jobs became available for black women as well, the best being those as personal attendant or dressmaker to one of the prominent women in Washington society. Again, contacts made in those positions could prove to be extremely useful. Elizabeth Keckley, one of the best-known black women to fill such a position, served Mary Todd Lincoln during the 1860s.[15]

The vast majority of black women had few choices beyond taking in wash or hiring out as domestic labor. Still, the wages such work provided always con-stituted a critical contribution to the household economies of cash-starved free black families. Unlike middle-class whites, women in black society routinely worked outside the home—and not simply for "extra income." In most African American communities throughout the nineteenth century, women's wages accounted for between one-third and one-half of household incomes. Although the legal restrictions imposed on all women at the time applied to black women as well, their centrality to the black economy gave them significant political influence within their communities.

As more African Americans migrated to Washington, settled into homes, and found employment, they established a number of community institutions. One of the earliest and most important of these was the church. Initially, Washington's blacks and whites worshiped in the same churches, as was the custom in Virginia and Maryland. This pattern prevailed in slaveholding societies, where religious meetings held by slaves and unsupervised by "respectable" whites made planters uneasy. Slaves worshiped with their master's family. Personal servants were often allowed to sit with their owners in the family's pews. Other slaves and free blacks were relegated to special sections of the church, generally the gallery or the rear. Free blacks, however, who unlike most slaves had the freedom to choose their place of worship, found such arrangements increasingly unsatisfactory: whites' religious services seemed stiff and comparatively emotionless; the sermons were often irrelevant to blacks' lives and problems; the music was generally unfulfilling; and blacks had no opportunity to influence church policy or to hold church offices.

One particularly galling issue was the refusal by some white ministers to take black children into their arms when administering baptism. Such insults, combined with the humiliation of being segregated during services and a desire for more autonomy, encouraged many blacks to seek independent places of worship. Mt. Zion Negro Church in Georgetown was founded in 1814 with the support and under the guardianship of the Washington Foundry Methodist Church's white congregation. In 1820 several black members withdrew from the largely white Methodist congregation at the Ebenezer Church, on Fourth Street near Virginia Avenue, to form the first autonomous, formally organized, black congregation. They called their new church the African Methodist Episcopal (AME) Church. There, in addition to conducting religious services, they established their own Sabbath school.

Shortly thereafter the congregation purchased a building at the foot of Capitol Hill to house what became the Israel Bethel Colored Methodist Episcopal Church. That church—one of the first independent black institutions in the city—was ministered to by David Smith, a migrant from Baltimore. Smith's tenure began in turmoil. Several of Washington's black Methodists, newly freed and accustomed to white preachers, found it difficult to accept a black minister and threatened to disrupt his ministry. Fortunately, Smith received support from a number of prominent members of his congregation, and the church prospered to become an important member of the Baltimore Conference of the AME. Indeed, black Methodists became central to the religious life of black Washington and established several of the city's most influential congregations. In 1839 another black defection from the Ebenezer Church led to the establishment of Wesley Zion Church, which also employed a black minister and became the spiritual home for many prominent blacks.

The most enduring black house of worship—one still serving the community today—is the Fifteenth Street Presbyterian Church. John F. Cook, one of the city's most important black leaders before the Civil War, founded the church in frustration over racial discrimination in the Presbyterian church. In 1843 he was ordained as Washington's first black Presbyterian minister. Cook, a self-educated ex-slave, was a skilled shoemaker and a former messenger in the federal lands office. He had been freed from slavery as a boy, when his aunt Alethia Tanner bought the freedom of his mother and her five children with proceeds from the sale of her vegetables. Tanner's determination to secure the freedom of family members and John Cook's efforts to sustain his aunt's commitment reflect the aspirations of thousands of black Washingtonians before the Civil War.

Churches such as Fifteenth Street Presbyterian and Wesley Zion functioned as more than religious institutions. They also served as community-service agencies and clearinghouses for employment—which were particularly important to ex-slaves who were new to the District and in need of shelter, food, and work. The churches supported the earliest black education centers through their Sunday-school programs and provided the rooms in which the first black schools met. The churches were also social gathering places where members tended to community affairs, addressed shared problems, and aired grievances. Pulpits became political platforms and, more important, the training ground for black leaders. Black churches were also critical as shelters and fund-raising organizations for the activities of the antislavery movement and the Underground Railroad. Recent migrants and those struggling to survive in freedom knew the churches as special places for both material aid and moral and emotional support. Without the churches the black odyssey to Washington would have been immeasurably more difficult.[16]

The establishment of schools represented another major achievement of the emerging black community. When local government established the public-school system in the winter of 1804, the children of free blacks were not

John Cook Sr., an early leader of Washington's free black community. (Courtesy Moorland Spingarn Research Center, Howard University)

permitted to attend—even though their parents contributed to the support of public education through their taxes. In the District's first years only the private efforts of white benefactors and the free black community supported education for young black people. Early black schools were informal, based in private homes, church basements, and storefronts.

Realizing that black children would receive no education except through private efforts, three black men—George Bell, Nicholas Franklin, and Moses Liverpool—bought land on Capitol Hill and in 1807 built a school. Though modest in appearance, the small wooden building housed the loftiest of dreams—it was the first black school in the city. Illiterate themselves, the pioneering black leaders hired a white teacher to manage instruction.

So eager were parents to ensure an education for their children that within four years three other schools were opened. In 1809 an Englishman, Henry Potter, opened a school for black children at Seventh and F Streets, NW. The school was subsequently moved to Thirteenth Street, between G and H Streets, NW. During this period, Anne Marie Hall, a black woman from

Prince Georges County, Maryland, opened an African American school on Capitol Hill. A graduate of a predominantly white school in Alexandria, she was a capable instructor and the first black teacher in the District. Mary Billings, another English educator, taught in a white school but allowed black students to attend her classes. When white parents objected, she opened a separate school for black children in Georgetown in 1810 and, in 1821, a second school for blacks in Washington.

Education for African Americans became a major community cause. Mutual-aid societies, founded by blacks to address problems of poverty, health care, burial benefits, and aid to widows and orphans, also provided support for education. The cost of education, however, was high, and many early efforts failed. For example, the Resolute Beneficial Society, headed by William Costin, funded the opening of a black school in 1818, but the school closed its doors four years later owing to lack of funds. The society's educational venture was saved in 1823, when former slave Henry Smothers opened a tuition-free school for black children at Fourteenth and H Streets, NW. Enrollment grew rapidly to more than 100 students during the school's first few years of operation. John W. Prout succeeded Smothers as principal in 1825, renamed the school the Columbia Institute, and continued to offer free education to black students.

Nine years later John F. Cook, an ex-slave and a former student of Prout, became headmaster. Under his leadership the school enrolled both males and females—although in separate departments—and offered a broad curriculum. The institute, one of the best-established and long-lived of Washington's early black educational institutions, continued after Cook's death in 1855, guided by his son, John F. Cook Jr. In 1859 the school moved to the basement of the Fifteenth Street Presbyterian Church.

Several other schools also provided educational opportunities for black children during this period. James Enoch Ambush started a school in the basement of the Israel Bethel Church on Capitol Hill. He remained there for ten years before beginning another venture to build a second school in southwest Washington, where many blacks then resided. In addition, he founded the Wesleyan Seminary to train black ministers, an effort that lasted until after the Civil War.

Black leaders also established several schools for girls during these years. The first, affiliated with Holy Trinity Church in Georgetown, opened its doors to about thirty-five students in 1827. One of the school's administrators, Maria Becraft, was a particularly remarkable woman. The product of a local education, she was only fifteen years old when she had started her first school for black girls in Georgetown, and only twenty-two when Holy Trinity's pastor, Father Vanlomen, placed her in charge of his seminary's female students.

The most prominent black women's academy before the Civil War was a seminary started by Myrtilla Miner, a young white teacher from New York State. Through her black acquaintances in Rochester, New York, and her first-hand observation of slavery while teaching in Mississippi, Miner became committed to education for blacks. The school she single-handedly pioneered in 1851 grew to be one of the finest examples of women's education in Washington, and was visited by various dignitaries who praised its achievements.

By the Civil War at least fifty-two schools, supported primarily by the black community, a significant number under the circumstances, offered educational opportunities to black children. Always short of funds, most of the schools folded after a brief period of operation. A few, however, such as the Columbia Institute, survived through a combination of talented teachers and community resolve. These schools provided free blacks with the opportunity to learn to read and to write, as well as to go beyond basic education if they chose. The schools became an additional magnet that drew free blacks to the District from Virginia and Maryland. Like most migrants seeking to better their lives, African Americans viewed education as the key to achieving their dreams.[17]

Although Washington's free blacks established institutions that reflected their aspirations and addressed their needs, not all issues received a formal institutional response. Informal arrangements often provided the "safety net" for black Washingtonians. More often than not, individual families took in newcomers, sheltering, feeding, and clothing them until they were established enough to support themselves. Black families cared for relatives who had come to the District with little more than the clothes on their backs, and the same was done for nonkin, who sometimes were complete strangers.

As in most other black communities, taking in boarders became a widespread practice among Washington's free blacks. This was not only admirable but also extremely practical. Because most black women worked outside the home, a boarder could provide child care. Significantly, a substantial number of boarders were young female migrants who exchanged child care and domestic assistance for room and board. Additionally, because most black households were in constant economic peril, boarders who could contribute even a small amount of money toward their upkeep quickly became an integral part of the household economy. For a poor community and equally poor migrants unfamiliar with the city, the informal institution of boarding became an essential system of mutual support.

This informal response to shared needs became central to black Washingtonians' role in the abolition movement and the Underground Railroad. In the years before the Civil War the national abolitionist movement focused on the District of Columbia, viewing it as the one place where federal authority clearly had the power to outlaw slavery. In the southern states defenders of slavery and states' rights argued that the federal government had no jurisdiction over states' internal matters. Even in the federal territories to the west, settlers disagreed over whether the federal government had authority to interfere with what slaveholders saw as their property rights. Such arguments, however, were inapplicable to Washington, where the consensus was that Congress held sway. Abolitionists argued that if the federal government could be persuaded to end slavery—or at least the slave trade in the District—it would carry significant symbolic and practical value.

In the 1830s black and white activists began to send hundreds of petitions to Congress demanding action to abolish slavery and the slave trade in Washington. The abolitionist debate raged in both the House of Representatives and the Senate. In 1850, as part of a group of bills known collectively as the Compromise of 1850, Congress finally outlawed the slave trade in the District. Although slaves were still held, slave auction blocks and holding pens disappeared from Washington in the decade before the Civil War.

For black Washingtonians, removal of the slave trade from the District had profound significance. If they could not prevent their friends and relatives from being enslaved, they could at least be assured that the trade in human beings would not be conducted in their home city. Beyond this symbolic significance, abolition of the slave trade also lessened the possibility that they, their families, or their friends might be kidnapped and sold south by the slave traders who had thronged to Washington before the trade ended.

Yet ending the slave trade in Washington was only a partial victory, for slavery itself remained. Black Washingtonians understood the difficulties of conducting antislavery activities in a slaveholding city. Local authorities took steps to curb such activities among blacks. Even free blacks could not speak out against slavery in Washington as they might have done further north, where by the 1850s the practice had virtually disappeared.

Nonetheless, black Washingtonians did play a crucial role in the antislavery movement through their involvement in the Underground Railroad, which surreptitiously and at great risk carried thousands of slaves to freedom. Situated as it was in the upper South, the District became one of the most important stops on the underground route north. Basements of black churches, homes in Georgetown, and African American–owned stores all became "stations" on the Railroad. In one instance, blacks sheltered Maryland runaway

Anna Maria Weems for several days before she disguised herself as a carriage boy and stole away to Philadelphia to join her mother, who was free.

William Still of Philadelphia, one of the most important underground agents in the country and, later, author of the classic *The Underground Railroad*, viewed Washington as a critical area of underground activity in the East. Another abolitionist reported that "the road to Washington was doing . . . a marvelously large business."[18] In 1848 one underground operation almost won the freedom of seventy-seven slaves who, with the aid of District blacks and Philadelphia abolitionists, nearly made it north aboard a schooner called *The Pearl*. The plan was foiled, however, by the betrayal of Judson Diggs, a free black hack driver whose class-related jealousies and unrequited romantic attachment to one of the women in the escape party prompted his treachery.[19]

Overall, blacks were particularly valuable as Underground Railroad workers because fugitive slaves did not know agents by sight and therefore trusted fellow blacks more than white workers, who were total strangers. In fact, whether blacks were officially attached to the Underground Railroad or not, they were likely to be contacted by fugitives seeking aid. One runaway who passed through Washington from North Carolina reported that fugitives trusted no one except "colored people who never failed to take us in and to share what little they had."[20]

Most of those who provided such assistance were not affiliated with any formally organized group. They were people whose hatred of slavery ran deep and whose commitment to freedom needed no public declaration. A slave discovered aiding a fugitive had much to lose. Harsh discipline might include a severe lashing and, even worse, sale to the lower South and separation from family. Nonetheless, for Washington's black community, sheltering slaves was part of its commitment to mutual aid and freedom.

The opportunity for District blacks to strike most directly against slavery arose during the Civil War. Although the War Department had rebuffed their first efforts to join the U.S. Army, black men persisted. Abraham Lincoln, who came to office in 1860, had made it clear that the war was not against slavery but a struggle to preserve the Union. But African Americans in Washington and elsewhere knew better. Fighting, which had commenced in the spring of 1861 and dragged on into a second year, resulted in massive U.S. losses on the battlefield and forced a reassessment of war aims. Federal officials then reversed their unwillingness to accept blacks for military service in the U.S. cause.

African Americans had participated in every war in American history, yet skeptics still asked, "Will the Negro fight?" Black leaders, including Frederick Douglass, who migrated to the District after the war, responded with a recitation of the service blacks had rendered during the Revolutionary War, the War of 1812, and the Mexican American War. Douglass challenged President Lincoln to enlist black soldiers and "free the sable arm that it might strike a blow for freedom."[21]

Once Lincoln charted the new direction of the war effort, events moved swiftly. In April 1862 Congress passed the District Emancipation Act, which freed all slaves in Washington, D.C. This "compensated" emancipation provided an average of $300 to slaveholders for each slave freed. Although African Americans disliked the fact that the order implicitly acknowledged the legitimacy of slave ownership, they embraced it nevertheless because it brought freedom.

Within a year black troops were being recruited, and black Washingtonians stepped forward to offer their service. Local black leaders John F. Cook Jr., the Reverend Henry McNeal Turner, and Anthony Bowen acted as recruiters for the First U.S. Colored Troops, made up of recruits from the District. The Reverend Mr. Turner was later commissioned as the regiment's chaplain. The group trained at Analostan Island (now Theodore Roosevelt Island) in the Potomac River and served in Norfolk, Portsmouth, and Yorktown, Virginia. In 1864 the regiment was tested at Sandy Point and Petersburg, Virginia, where it sustained substantial casualties but acquitted itself with honor, proving skeptics wrong yet again.

The abolition of slavery in the District and the service of black Washingtonians in the war effort brought to a close an important chapter in the city's history. By 1860 Washington's black migrants had established a community that provided for their mutual support, sustained the local fight against slavery, and became part of the national abolition effort. The Civil War brought further far-reaching changes to the District. The black population grew rapidly during the war and even faster during the postwar period of Reconstruction. A migration that had originated in Virginia and Maryland before 1860 now expanded, bringing African Americans from all over the South, and from the North and the Midwest as well.

Black Washington by the late nineteenth century had become more cosmopolitan, yet patterns established in the early years of settlement remained important. Although black community life became more complex and more diverse, and the black odyssey took on more formidable dimensions, the hope for future generations continued to be defined by the spirit of community that had sustained black Washingtonians from the beginning and reflected their dreams for an America that would some day fulfill the promise of its capital city—a city of magnificent intentions.

James Oliver Horton

1. For a detailed analysis of the origins of Africans brought to the Chesapeake region, see Elizabeth Donnan, ed., *Documents Illustrative of the History of the Slave Trade to America*, vol. 4, *The Border Colonies and the Southern Colonies* (Washington, D.C.: Carnegie Institution of Washington, D.C., 1935); and Alan Kulikoff, *Tobacco and Slaves: The Development of Southern Cultures, 1680–1800* (Chapel Hill: University of North Carolina Press, 1986).

2. Olaudah Equiano, *The Interesting Narrative of the Life of Olaudah Equiano or Gustavus Vassa, the African* (London: Dawsons, 1789), 70–71.

3. See *Virginia Journal and Alexandria Advertiser*, 26 May 1795.

4. Dorothy Provine, "The Economic Position of Free Blacks in the District of Columbia, 1800–1860," *The Journal of Negro History* 58, no. 1 (January 1973): 61–72.

5. William Still, *The Underground Railroad* (Philadelphia: Porter and Coates, 1872).

6. Letitia W. Brown, "Residence Patterns of Negroes in the District of Columbia, 1800–1860," 1969–1970, 66–79, Records of the Columbia Historical Society, Washington, D.C.

7. Still, *Underground Railroad*, 391–92.

8. See Louise Daniel Hutchinson, *The Anacostia Story: 1608-1930* (Washington, D.C.: Smithsonian Institution Press, 1977). There is an ongoing debate among historians about the significance of the decline of urban slavery during this period. Richard Wade, *Slavery in the Cities: The South, 1820–1860* (New York: Oxford University Press, 1964), argues that slavery was in a sharp decline in most urban areas of the antebellum South. Claudia Goldin, *Urban Antebellum South, 1820–1860: A Quantitative History* (Chicago: University of Chicago Press, 1976), uses statistical data to argue that slavery was not in as great a decline as Wade suggests. Evidence indicates, however, that Wade's argument is most accurate for the District.

9. *First Annual Report of the Board of Managers of the New England Anti-Slavery Society* (Boston: New England Anti-Slavery Society, 1833), 48.

10. Solomon Northrup, *Twelve Years a Slave: Narrative of Solomon Northrup* (1854; reprint, Baton Rouge: Louisiana State University Press, 1968). See also Michael Shiner and his family in Keith Melder et al., ed., *City of Magnificent Intentions: A History of the District of Columbia* (Washington, D.C.: D.C. History Curriculum Project, Intact, 1983), 12.

11. Charles F. Adams, ed., *Memoirs of John Quincy Adams, Comprising Portions of His Diary from 1795 to 1848* (Philadelphia, 1874–75), 6:478.

12. District laws were no more restrictive than those of several states to the west, and actually less restrictive than some. At various times Ohio, Indiana, Illinois, and the Michigan Territory passed legislation requiring that free black migrants post a personal cash bond. Some of these early restrictions were repealed before the Civil War, but in several states they became more severe. Indiana and Illinois changed their laws to outlaw entirely black migration into the state. Iowa and Oregon followed suit.

13. For the Costin suit, see F. Regis Noel, "Notable Suits in Early District Courts," *Records of the Columbia Historical Society* 24 (March 1920). The court decision quoted in the Carey case is in Provine, "Economic Position of Free Blacks," 66.

14. Letitia Woods Brown, *Free Negroes in the District of Columbia, 1790–1846* (New York: Oxford University Press, 1972).

15. Elizabeth Keckley, *Behind the Scenes, or, Thirty Years a Slave and Four Years in the White House* (New York: G. W. Carlton and Company, 1868).

16. John W. Cromwell, "The First Negro Churches in the District of Columbia," *The Journal of Negro History* 7, no. 1 (January 1922): 64–106.

17. On education for African Americans in the District, see Emmett D. Preston Jr., "The Development of Negro Education in the District of Columbia, 1800–1860," *The Journal of Negro Education* (Spring 1943); and Lillian Gertrude Dabney, *The History of Schools for Negroes in the District of Columbia, 1807–1947* (Washington, D.C.: Catholic University Press, 1949).

18. Still, *Underground Railroad*, 477.

19. See John Henry Paynter, *Fugitives of The Pearl* (Washington, D.C.: Associated Publishers, 1930); and Daniel Drayton, *Personal Memoir of Daniel Drayton, for Four Years and Four Months a Prisoner . . . in Washington Jail* (New York: American and Foreign Anti-Slavery Society, 1854).

20. Quoted in John W. Blassingame, ed., *Slave Testimony* (Baton Rouge: Louisiana State University Press, 1977), 143.

21. Quoted from Douglass's speech, "The Reasons for Our Troubles," delivered on 14 January 1862 in Philadelphia. See *Douglass' Monthly*, February 1862.

ADDITIONAL READING

Buttle, Thomas C. "Published Resources for the Study of Blacks in the District of Columbia: An Annotated Guide." Ph.D. diss., George Washington University, 1982.

Borchert, James. *Alley Life in Washington: Family, Community, Religion, and Folklife in the City, 1850–1970*. Urbana: University of Illinois Press, 1980.

Brown, Letitia Woods. *Washington from Banneker to Douglass, 1791–1870*. Washington, D.C.: National Portrait Gallery, Smithsonian Institution, 1971.

Clarke, Nina Honeemond. *History of the Nineteenth-Century Black Churches in Maryland and Washington, D.C.* New York: Vantage Press, 1983.

Green, Constance McLaughlin. *The Secret City: A History of Race Relations in the Nation's Capital*. Princeton, N.J.: Princeton University Press, 1967.

———. *Washington*. Princeton, N.J.: Princeton University Press, 1962–63. Vol. 1, *Village and Capital, 1800–1878*.

Kapsch, Robert J., William C. Allen, and Henry Chase. "Building Liberty's Capital." *American Visions* 10, no. 1 (February 1995): 8–15.

Powell, Mary G. *The History of Old Alexandria, from July 13, 1749, to May 24, 1861*. Richmond, Va.: William Byrd Press, 1928.

Rohrs, Richard C. "Antislavery Politics and *The Pearl* Incident of 1848." *Historian* 56, no. 4 (summer 1994): 711–24.

3.

"The Green Streets of Washington"
The Experience of Irish Mechanics in Antebellum Washington

Margaret H. McAleer

In 1816 a sign above a Washington shop read: "Peter Rodgers, saddler, from the green fields of Erin and Tyranny, to the green streets of Washington and liberty." Besides attracting customers and announcing a trade, the sign expressed the proprietor's view of his immigration experience and celebrated American political culture.[1]

Irish immigrant mechanics such as Peter Rodgers figured prominently in Washington's heterogeneous nineteenth-century labor force. Working alongside native-born white Americans, African Americans, and other immigrants, Irish residents proved crucial to the city's physical development and economic survival. Before the War of 1812 Irish artisans in the building trades labored to raise the nation's capital along the banks of the Potomac River. While inadequate record keeping fails to reveal the percentage of the white labor force those Irish artisans represented, contemporary accounts suggest that the Irish were a significant—and perhaps even the largest—component.

After federal buildings were destroyed by the British in 1814, Irish mechanics continued to swell the ranks of carpenters and stoneworkers. In the following decades Irish carpenters, masons, grocers, tavern keepers, and laborers outnumbered other Washington immigrants as applicants for U.S. citizenship. They weathered the trials of a fluctuating city economy, as well as the influx of impoverished Irish canal workers and the sting of anti-immigrant nativist movements. Some Irish immigrants would leave Washington in search of new opportunities. For others, however, Washington became a permanent home. As residents, they contributed to the fledgling city's development and exercised the responsibilities of citizenship.

The Irish experience in Washington begins with the creation of a permanent seat of government on the banks of the Potomac River. The new Constitution, written in 1787 and ratified in 1789, yielded to Congress "exclusive Legislation" over a district to be ceded by states and "not exceeding ten Miles square," which would "become the Seat of Government of the United States." As part of a larger political compromise in 1790, the future capital would be located along the Potomac River, "between the mouths of the Eastern Branch and the Connogochegue."[2] President George Washington was given the privilege of selecting the exact site within these general parameters. Philadelphia would serve as a temporary seat of government until 1800, when the new capital would be ready for the reception of Congress. In 1791 Washington named three commissioners to a board that would oversee the laying out of the federal city, the sale of lots, and the construction of public buildings prior to Congress's expected arrival in 1800. The records of the Board of Commissioners reveal that Irish immigrants were among the earliest settlers who worked in federal construction, bought lots, built homes, and were integral to the emerging capital city.

Early in the federal-building effort, Washington's Board of Commissioners faced serious labor shortages. The region's skilled workers proved insufficient in number to meet the demands of building a national capital. The board members were confident nonetheless that skilled mechanics, if not available locally, could be drawn from other parts of the country. On 11 April 1792 they reported that 2,000 mechanics and laborers were "on tip To[e]s to come from all parts of the union." However, the prosperity of building trades in other cities during the 1790s limited the number of artisans willing to migrate to Washington. Although mechanics did migrate from the fast-growing building trades in Boston, Philadelphia, New York, and Baltimore, their numbers fell short of the expected onslaught of 2,000 workers.

The commissioners reluctantly accepted the necessity of recruiting skilled workers from Europe. Aided by merchants at home and abroad, the board sought to entice the emigration of German and Scottish artisans, who were— as Charles Fierer, a German resident of Dumfries, Virginia, put it in a letter to the commissioners in February 1793—"distinguished for their industry and sobriety." While there is no indication that the commissioners viewed French artisans as being similarly diligent, they nevertheless attempted to secure mechanics from Bordeaux, who might be convinced to emigrate out of a sense of republican kinship. Although the commissioners successfully procured numerous artisans from Europe—especially from Scotland—national restrictions on the emigration of skilled workers extinguished the hope of a large-scale migration of European artisans. Lacking any one source of mechanics, the commissioners relied on a fluctuating mixture of native-born and immigrant white labor and African American workers.

Despite the city's labor needs, the commissioners never seriously attempted to lure artisans from Ireland. Their reluctance stems from the then prevalent stereotype of Irish laborers as unskilled, undisciplined, destitute, and—according to Fierer—"generally of [the] lowest people." Coming from a country where the majority of people were employed in subsistence agriculture, most Irish immigrants lacked craft skills to enter the artisan hierarchy. Without the resources to establish themselves as farmers after emigration, many Irish accepted jobs as unskilled laborers, joining the most economically vulnerable class of free white workers.

Only James Hoban, architect of the President's House and Ireland native, proposed recruiting workers directly from Ireland. On 3 November 1792 Hoban suggested to the commissioners that he write to the "many able Stone Cutters in Dublin, with whom I have been concerned in building." It is unknown, however, whether Hoban ever wrote such a letter or if he was responsible for the Irish stonecutters who did emigrate.

Commissioners who were reluctant to recruit Irish artisans nonetheless did welcome Irish laborers who had paid their own way. In August of the same year of Hoban's offer, the commissioners wrote local merchant William Prout about the arrival of Irish immigrants aboard one of his ships. They asked that Prout inform those who had paid their own way of "the prospect which the business in which we are engaged offers, for constant employment on every line."

After the American Revolution, Irish immigrants to the United States were more diverse than contemporaries had believed and many historians acknowledge. Although the majority of Irish immigrants lacked craft skills, skilled artisans—including carpenters and stonemasons—joined the flow of emigration to the United States. Many sought employment on the public projects in Washington, and their labor proved vital in the completion of the federal buildings projects. Contemporary observations confirm that Irish immigrants were integral to Washington's labor force. In 1809 architect Benjamin Latrobe recorded in his journal that he employed "many Irish Workmen" at the Capitol. David Bailie Warden wrote in 1816 that "nearly one half of the population of Washington is of Irish origin. The labouring class is chiefly Irish."[3]

A few Irish mechanics had immigrated to the Washington area before the establishment of the capital city. They came as indentured servants employed by the Patowmack Company, founded in 1784 to improve Potomac River nav-

"North (Senate) Wing of the Capitol," 1800. William R. Birch's watercolor depicts stone-workers—some of whom were probably Irish—in the foreground. (Photo courtesy Prints and Photographs Division, Library of Congress)

igation. By 1786 200 workers, including many Irish, had worked on the canal that bypassed Great Falls. According to Thomas Attwood Digges, the adventurer son of a Prince Georges County planter, some of these Irish indentured servants were newly released convicts. Digges had visited Ireland frequently between 1783 and 1792, where he had recruited indentured servants for his brother-in-law John Fitzgerald, a director of the Patowmack Company. In 1788 Digges alerted Samuel Huntington, governor of Connecticut, to "the introduction of the Felons & Convicts into the United States of America as *Indented Servants*." He claimed personal knowledge of at least two cargos of convicts sent to Georgetown and Alexandria in 1785 and 1786. Since he himself had been an inmate of an Irish debtor prison for nearly a year, Digges informed Huntington that "of all people in the world the Irish Convicts are the wickedest."[4]

In this 19 January 1795 letter to the Board of Commissioners, Thady Hogan expresses the hardships experienced by Irish immigrants struggling to find employment in their trades. (Courtesy National Archives)

Alexandria, Georgetown, and Washington City were landing ports for many Irish immigrants who sought employment within the immediate region. The majority of Irish immigrants living in the Washington area, however, entered the country through ports outside the District, and often had relocated many times before coming to Washington. Many immigrant mechanics who had experienced difficulty finding employment where they had debarked, because their reputation and skills were unknown, were likely to migrate to Washington where labor was in high demand. In January 1795 an Irish immigrant and skilled stonemason, Thady Hogan, wrote the commissioners that "being a stranger in the country & unsupported by any friends" had left him little choice but to accept an unskilled position in a stone quarry. Hogan was eventually hired as a skilled mason on the President's House.

Upon securing employment, Irish immigrants shared fully in the artisan experience and could be found working at all levels of skill on the public projects. James Hoban, a native of County Kilkenny, designed and served as construction superintendent of the President's House.[5] Less illustrious master artisans—such as Cornelius McDermott Roe, who contracted in 1795 to undertake the brick and foundation stonework at the President's House and the Capitol—were also employed in public buildings. The majority of Irish mechanics, however, were journeymen who had successfully mastered the craft skills of the apprentice. Journeymen were paid either by piece or by time, depending on the terms they were able to negotiate. Unlike master artisans, they lacked the means to establish their own shops, hire their own workers, or contract for major jobs.

Children of immigrants, like those of native-born parents, entered into apprenticeship agreements with master artisans to learn the "art or mystery" of a trade. The contract, while usually made between parent and master artisan, included the "free will and consent" of the minor. Less frequently, immigrants less than twenty-one years old arranged for their own apprenticeship in the absence of a parent. Neale Woods, "late from Ireland," apprenticed himself in 1801 to James Kennedy, a Washington plasterer. Woods bound himself at age nineteen to his master until the age of twenty-one, during which time he pledged to keep his master's secrets; not to waste the master's goods; never to absent himself from service without permission; to abstain from cards, dice, or any other unlawful game; to shun alehouses, taverns, and playhouses; and to remain single. Kennedy in turn agreed to teach Woods the mystery of plastering, to provide room and board, and, upon completion of the contract, to give Woods a sum of money and a "freedom suit" of clothes worth twenty dollars.

Federal construction gave Irish mechanics the opportunity to practice their trades. Building plans unfortunately exceeded the new government's bud-get. Consequently workers faced periodic layoffs and conflicts with supervisors. Because the embryonic city lacked adequate housing, workers lived in tempo-rary wooden buildings, often referred to as huts, located on the grounds of the President's House and the Capitol. Workers complained most frequently about Washington's high cost of living and the failure of wages to keep pace with inflation.

Native and immigrant mechanics' response to poor living conditions in Washington reflected a comprehensive set of republican values that formed the foundation of artisan social and political thought during the early national pe-riod. This artisan philosophy, which influenced workers in other cities as well, celebrated personal independence, civic virtue, equality, and community. "Newly arrived workers, particularly skilled ones," argue historians Ira Berlin and Herbert G. Gutman, "carried artisanal traditions from the Old World to the New, where they fused with the indigenous artisanal tradition of Ameri-can mechanics and craftsmen." These beliefs, "deriving in large measure from the common character of artisan life and work throughout the Atlantic world, celebrated independence and emphasized a man's right to the fruits of his own labor as central to that independence."[6] Washington mechanics boldly articu-lated these values, often punctuating them with political significance drawn from their role in building the federal city. Evidence of the strength of these beliefs emerged during the numerous labor conflicts that erupted during the city's construction.

One of the earliest worker disputes occurred in May 1794, when a num-ber of masons and bricklayers led by James Maitland left public employment after objecting to the hiring of superintendents whom the workers claimed were unqualified. The stoneworkers and bricklayers placed a notice in the 24 May 1794 *Baltimore Daily Intelligencer* warning other mechanics not to accept positions under such conditions, which represented an "affront to the work-ingmen of this craft." At the heart of these conflicts—even those that were largely financial—was a defense of the artisan's pride in his skill. One carpen-ter employed at the President's House objected to the Board of Commission-ers's decision to decrease the wages of all carpenters. The commissioners, he argued, had failed to distinguish between "an honest man and a Rogue."[7] Sim-ilar disputes occurred in every major U.S. city during the early national period.

In addition to disruptions caused by fluctuating economic cycles and changes within the artisan system of production, workers also turned ethnic differences into points of conflict. According to a complaint filed with the Board of Commissioners, Scottish stonemason Collen Williamson challenged his 1795 dismissal by making countercomplaints couched in ethnic hostility against James Hoban. Identifying Hoban as "an Irish carpentor," Williamson complained that when Hoban had come to Washington from Charleston, he had brought with him "a compeny of thives." After his own dismissal, Williamson warned the commissioners that nothing had stopped Hoban from allowing the project to serve as "a receptacle for all the Irish vegbons [vagabonds] that cam[e] in his way."[8]

In March 1798 Pierce Purcell, one of the alleged Irish "thives" who had come with Hoban from Charleston, claimed to the commissioners that he had been "insulted in a public manner by [George] Hadfield," the English superintendent of the Capitol. Interestingly, Purcell's letter listed witnesses by nationality: four Scots, six Irish, ten Americans, and one Englishman. His multinational defense was undoubtedly designed to deflect any contention that his support came solely from fellow Irish mechanics.

Many European workers lacked familiarity with a racially diverse system that combined free, indentured, and slave labor. In 1794 the commissioners complained to the president about Maj. Andrew Ellicott's decision to assign James Reed Dermott, who was Irish, to supervise African American workers clearing trees along proposed streets. The commissioners, addressing the impropriety of this assignment, noted that "as he was an European [Dermott] had probably never had any thing to do of this kind."[9] Occasionally, immigrant workers joined with native-born white American mechanics in objecting to job competition from black mechanics, apprentices, and hired-out slaves employed at the public buildings. In 1794 the commissioners permitted stonecutters working at the President's House to accept only white apprentices. On 15 November 1797 the commissioners, responding to complaints from carpenters, ordered that "no Negroe carpenter or apprentice be hired" at either the President's House or the Capitol.

The majority of Irish journeymen, especially single men, boarded in workers' barracks or in temporary wooden boardinghouses located on the President's (now Lafayette) Square and Capitol Hill. Many of the artisans in Washington, however, made "considerable perchases of lots in the City." To encourage these purchases, the commissioners modified building requirements to allow wooden materials and structures of smaller dimensions. They also permitted mechanics to deduct the price of lots from their wages. Benjamin Latrobe wrote in his journal that numerous workers had been "enticed hither by their own golden dreams" and that many of them "purchased lots, and perhaps built homes in which they have invested all."

Artisans' willingness to buy property in Washington reflected their commitment to the city's future. They gambled their fortunes while the precarious fate of the city discouraged more prominent investors. When informed of the poor results of the first public sale of lots in 1791, George Washington, consoling himself in a letter to the commissioners, stated that "several of your Mechanics were among the purchasers of lots, as they will not only, in all probability, be among the first improvers of them, but will be valuable citizens."[10]

Irish mechanics built their homes throughout the city in the first half of the nineteenth century. As studies of other cities have shown, residential decisions were based primarily on proximity to available employment—particularly before improvements in urban transportation. In nonindustrialized Washington employment opportunities were dispersed throughout the city, and Irish mechanics made their homes in every ward.

The affordability of housing and the strength of ethnic ties also shaped Irish residential patterns. The less affluent single Irish often lived together in boardinghouses of questionable comfort. In 1828 Washingtonian Anne Royall, renowned for her travel accounts, described "a gang of low drunken Irish" living on Capitol Hill.[11] As the Irish established families, they also tended to cluster in ethnic enclaves or buildings. In 1850 a boardinghouse in Washington's first ward housed the young families of three Irish laborers, John Mahoney, John Dunn, and James Raftery.

Evidence of how Irish immigrants in Washington defined their community is often unavailable. Undoubtedly, family life was integral to their community experience. The majority of the city's Irish workers were single men, as were those of many other ethnic groups, but many of these immigrants established families locally.

The Washington economy's unpredictable cycles of growth and contraction made it difficult for mechanics to support families. Numerous workers wrote to the commissioners with this complaint. A discharged carpenter, John Dickey, complained to the commissioners in April 1799 that he had "got no work since [his] discharge" and "that [he had] got a wife & family that never offend[e]d y[ou]r Hon[or]s."

Economic hardship occasionally splintered family units. For example, a young woman published an appeal in the 25 January 1799 Georgetown *Centinel of Liberty* for information concerning her mother Kitty M'Donald who had emigrated from Ireland in 1792 with Thomas Burl. For some unknown reason—perhaps as the result of an apprenticeship agreement—Burl's father had taken the young woman away from her mother and siblings. Then living in Philadelphia, the young woman sought information about her mother, who was "supposed to have gone to the Federal City." In another instance, Maria

Cochran, a Philadelphia resident, was apprenticed by her parents to a Washington couple in 1803 to "learn the art, trade or mistery of a Housekeeper and plain needlework," according to the apprenticeship agreement. The eleven-year-old affirmed that she had voluntarily consented to the apprenticeship, which would separate her from her immediate family until the age of sixteen.

Irish residents' interaction with other Washingtonians through the city's religious congregations, fraternal associations, charitable societies, and social clubs enriched their sense of community and aided in the process of adapting to their new environment. Historians have speculated that the Washington Artillery Company, established as a volunteer militia by James Hoban in 1796, might have been predominately Irish. Hoban undoubtedly recruited members from among his workers, a large percentage of whom were Irish. In 1799 a carpenter complained to city commissioners that Hoban had reduced his wages because he was "unwilling to be in the artillery company under Captain Hoban."[12] This complaint suggests that some men's participation was less than voluntary.

Roman Catholic priest Anthony Caffrey had emigrated from Ireland in 1794 and had established St. Patrick's Church, the first Catholic church in Washington City, at Tenth and G Streets, NW. (Georgetown's first Catholic church was founded in 1787.) As the first Catholic priest from Ireland, Caffrey must have had special significance for the congregation's Irish immigrants, who previously may have attended St. John's Church in Forest Glen, Maryland, Holy Trinity Church in Georgetown, or services in the homes of prominent Catholics. One of Caffrey's successors, English Jesuit Robert Plunkett, later lamented that he would "never be a favorite of the Irish." He confessed in a letter to Bishop John Carroll that the congregation's Irish members, after Caffrey's departure, had either "abandoned the Sacraments" entirely or had sought Irish priests elsewhere in the city.[13]

Despite a preponderance of Irish in St. Patrick's Church, Irish immigrants worshiped in a mixed congregation composed of African Americans and native and ethnic whites. Yet, a special bond must have existed between those members who shared common knowledge of life in Ireland and of the Irish immigration experience. In 1802 James Hoban founded the Society of the Sons of Erin. The society's members, drawn from Washington's affluent and "middling" Irish residents, enjoyed one another's company at largely social meetings and extended charity to needy immigrants. The majority of Washington's Irish immigrants, however, did not participate in such exclusively Irish institutions prior to the Civil War.[14]

Much evidence of an Irish tradition in Washington comes from non-Irish observers. Some who commented on the Irish community noted the persistence of Irish traditions—from the wearing of shamrocks to the gathering on St. Patrick's Day. In 1838 the local anti-immigrant newspaper, the *Native American*, reported a St. Patrick's Day dinner at which George Washington Parke Custis, step-grandson of George Washington, gave the main address. In the adaptation process, the Irish added overlays of American patriotic flourishes—such as Custis's address—to their traditional celebrations.[15]

For many observers, Irish immigrants were distinguishable by their accents and speech patterns. David Bailie Warden, an Ireland native, quipped in 1816 that Irish laborers could be identified by their lack of familiarity with the English language. Latrobe was fascinated by the "Irish bulls" uttered by Simon Meade, foreman of carpenters at the Capitol, and James Forde, foreman of bricklayers. According to the editors of Latrobe's journals, Irish bulls were expressions containing "a ludicrous inconsistency unperceived by the speaker." For example, when Latrobe asked Meade if he had gone to see a lumber merchant about a business matter, Meade responded, "Yes, sir, for he wanted to see me his self, so I *met* him running after me on the Avenue [emphasis added]."[16]

Some expressions of anti-Irish sentiment separate from labor conflicts surfaced during the city's first decades. The stereotype of the violent Irish male was particularly evident. In 1802 Irish immigrant James McGurk had repeatedly beat his pregnant wife, causing her to miscarry twins before dying. On 28 October McGurk became the first person to be hanged in the District. Following his conviction in April, a *Washington Federalist* editorial on 14 April said that "the prisoner was neither born nor educated in America" and that native-born Americans rarely committed such violent crimes; it also condemned immigration laws "that for the sake of gaining a few bawling patriots, would thus hasten the strides of vice, disturb the peace, and security of our country." In the same year a jury failed to convict Robert Brown for slander, after he had spread the rumor that fellow stonemason Thady Hogan had "stuck a pitchfork into a man in Ireland and murdered him and fled."[17]

During the War of 1812 tragedy struck Washington. On 24 August 1814 British redcoats marched into the city, looking—according to Michael Shiner, a slave at the Navy Yard—"like flames of fier all red coats," as they appeared over a hill outside the city.[18] As residents fled the city, British troops set fire to the President's House, the Capitol, and the War and Treasury Departments. In 1815, after much deliberation, Congress decided to reconstruct the federal buildings and consequently revitalized the city's building trades. In its premier 28 August 1830 issue, the *American Statesman* presented a "cheering view of the progress of our city," citing a flurry of municipal and private construction, including churches, banks, government buildings, markets, and more than 1,000 residences and shops.

Employment opportunities during the 1820s continued to attract Irish immigrants to the city. During this period, the majority of Irish immigrants applying for citizenship in Washington were employed in the building trades as stonemasons, carpenters, and plasterers. Applications for naturalization and city directories indicate that as Washington developed its own service economy, Irish immigrants found opportunities as grocers and tavern keepers, as well as blacksmiths, shoemakers, coopers, tailors, printers, weavers, dyers, and turners.[19]

Naturalization records from 1818 to 1845 contain valuable information about the Irish immigrants living in Washington, who formed the city's largest number of applicants for citizenship during the entire antebellum period. These records suggest what is later confirmed in the 1850 census—that the Irish community was the largest ethnic group in Washington. By 1850 the District's 2,373 Irish constituted nearly 48 percent of the territory's foreign population. According to naturalization applications, their average age at immigration was twenty-five. While each of Ireland's counties sent immigrants to Washington, the largest number—almost 40 percent—came from County Cork. Other frequently listed counties in descending order were Dublin, Waterford, Wexford, Kerry, Tipperary, Cavan, and Limerick. Although Irish immigrants arrived at ports from Maine to South Carolina, the most commonly listed port of entry was New York City. Significant numbers, however, arrived closer to the District, with Baltimore and Alexandria frequently listed after 1815. Fewer than ten immigrants who applied for citizenship had landed first in Washington City during this period.

The number of applications for naturalization indicates a growing political and civic consciousness within the Irish immigrant population. During this period legislation required immigrants to reside in the United States for five years before becoming eligible for citizenship. Three years before naturalization immigrants had to file declarations stating their intention to apply for citizenship. The length-of-residence requirement was designed to foster both an affection for the United States and knowledge of its political system. In an 1824 Supreme Court decision, Chief Justice John Marshall wrote that the foreign-born individual, once a citizen, "becomes a member of the society, possessing all the rights of a native citizen, and standing, in the view of the constitution, on the footing of a native."[20]

There is some evidence that Irish mechanics delayed applying for citizenship because it did not guarantee the right to vote. Before 1848 voting in the District was limited to free white males with at least $100 in taxable wealth. This requirement barred a significant number of workers from the polls. According to historian James R. Wason, property requirements excluded two-thirds of otherwise eligible voters in the District.[21]

One of several challenges to the voting regulations occurred in 1822, when supporters of Thomas Carberry's Poor Man's Party admitted unqualified voters to the polls in two wards. The implied nullification of the District's voting requirements heightened immigrant residents' political consciousness. In 1824 the number of Irish immigrants registering their intention to become citizens soared. Nevertheless, the property requirements remained until 1848, when they were abolished.

The national commitment to Washington as the seat of government remained precarious during the antebellum years. Washington's leaders endured vociferous complaints about the fledgling community's lack of amenities, as well as a barrage of petitions to Congress asking that the seat of government be located elsewhere. During the 1830s Washington weathered a decade of extreme economic and social dislocation. The building trades entered a period of decline when the first wave of public building neared completion after 1829. The average number of houses built per year decreased from 103 during the 1820s to 85 in the 1830s. Washington had failed to become the major commercial entrepôt envisioned by promoters. A group of Georgetown residents petitioning Congress in the 1830s commented that "our town, notwithstanding its local and natural advantages for trade, has been gradually declining; our population is deminished [sic]; our houses untenanted."[22]

The Chesapeake and Ohio Canal, begun in 1828, was heralded as Washington's salvation. Unfortunately, construction costs crippled the city financially, and competition from the Baltimore and Ohio Railroad proved overwhelming. The project also failed to alleviate unemployment among local mechanics after 1829, when the canal company decided to import new, inexpensive, unskilled Irish labor. Journeymen who could not find work in the building trades were thus also unable to find employment on the canal.

The arrival of Irish workers employed by the Chesapeake and Ohio Canal Company swelled the number of Irish immigrants living in the vicinity of Washington. Recruited from Liverpool, Dublin, Cork, and Belfast, these imported canal workers had signed contracts before emigrating. After their arrival, they endured food, housing, sanitation, and working conditions that were uniformly poor. Not surprisingly, throughout the canal's construction, violent riots erupted within the workers' camps.

In 1832 conditions under which immigrants were forced to live threatened the entire community's safety. A cholera epidemic enveloped the city during the summer and fall of that year. The disease's first victims were immigrants employed on the public works. An Irish priest at Georgetown College (established in 1789 as the country's first Catholic college) consoled a friend that none of his acquaintances had been afflicted: "[P]oor Irish labourers and others of that class are its more general victims." Death occurred quickly among those infected, usually within two to seven days after exposure through contaminated water and food. The same Georgetown College priest described the disease as "an instrument of much good in bringing many to their [religious] duties." The number of burials at Holy Trinity Church in Georgetown between August and December 1832 was twice that of the previous year.[23]

The city's economic decline, rising unemployment, and cholera epidemic produced a range of responses from the larger Irish community. Some churches and individuals responded with genuine concern for the newest immigrants' plight. According to historian Constance Green, in 1830 Irish schoolteacher James McLeod established a charitable organization to aid Washington's destitute immigrants. Some long-term Irish residents, however, resented the competition from the more recent arrivals, who were willing to work for lower wages. They thus turned to organizations designed to defend their interests.

Several Irish mechanics joined early labor organizations such as the Association of Mechanics and Other Working Men, founded in 1830. In an 1830 broadside the organization blamed President Andrew Jackson for the cessation of public building and rising unemployment. As they criticized Jackson administration policies, the association's members articulated the critical role of "mechanics and other working men" in society. They argued that "the wisdom and the patriotism of a nation reside with its industry," which suggests that those who contributed their labor and skill had the greatest stake in a nation's well-being. Workers thus constituted "the bone and sinew—the nerve and muscle, of the land."[24] The political consciousness of these mechanics was shaped within a city whose raison d'être was political rather than commercial or industrial.

In 1837 American-born offspring of Irish immigrants participated in the founding of Washington's Native American Association. Like nativist groups in other cities, Washington's nativists attributed pervasive social and economic dislocation to the influx of immigrants. The participation of first-generation Irish Americans in Washington's nativist movement distinguished it from that of other northern cities, where such groups were explicitly anti-Irish. As self-proclaimed nativists, these Irish Americans supported an organized critique of the city's social and economic change. By adopting the association's motto,

"Our Country, always right; but right or wrong, our Country," they also asserted their American identity.

Irish American members of the Native American Association reconciled pride in their ethnic and religious heritage with the nativist philosophy. George Sweeny, the son of an Irish immigrant who had settled in Baltimore, served as treasurer and president of the Washington association. At an 1837 meeting of the association Sweeny discussed what it meant for him to be Irish American.

> My sympathies have been, and still are strongly enlisted in behalf of that portion of them, who dwell in the land which was my father's land, and still suffer as my father suffered, under an oppressive system of laws, enacted by foreign and unfeeling rulers. . . . [But] *here* centre all the recollections of my childhood; *here* are fixed all my chances of happiness, and all my hopes for my posterity [emphasis added].[25]

What also distinguished Washington nativists from those of other cities is their view on religion. The Washington Native American Association renounced the anti-Catholic religious bigotry that characterized the northern associations. Counting among its members the descendants of Irish and German immigrants "of a variety of religious denominations," including Catholicism, Washington nativists asked, "What right have we as American citizens to stigmatize the faiths of our Christian brethren?"[26]

Washington's Native American Association withered away by the 1840s, perhaps as a result of an economic recovery brought on by improvements in transportation linking Washington with markets to the west. This apparent calm, however, was shattered during the late 1840s and 1850s. The famine in Ireland had greatly increased the annual rate of Irish immigration to the United States between 1846 and 1847; Washington's foreign-born population in general more than doubled between 1850 and 1860; and by 1860 the city's 7,258 Irish immigrants were 58 percent of the foreign-born population. The local economy was not able to absorb the increased labor force, and newly arrived immigrants were forced to take low-skill, low-paying jobs that kept them in poverty. Irish immigrants clustered in such enclaves as the Swampoodle District, which were defined as much by their poverty as by their ethnicity. The Swampoodle District, not far from the Capitol, was notorious for its overcrowding and violence.

In response to depressed social conditions, churches, charitable organizations, and individual members of the Irish community assumed responsibility for the material needs of the Irish abroad and in Washington. Earning no more than fifteen dollars per month, Irish workers employed by Georgetown College supported families and friends in need, and also sent money to Ireland after 1845 for the relief of famine victims.

In the 1850s, with an increase in the number of immigrants settling in Washington, nativism resurfaced in the form of the more violent Know-Nothing movement. Like earlier nativists, supporters of Know-Nothingism attacked drunkenness, poverty, crime, job competition, and voter fraud among immigrants. This organization, however, was also expressly anti-Catholic, thereby barring the involvement of many Irish Americans who had participated in the Native American Association in the 1830s. Some Know-Nothings dismissed the patriotism of the earlier Irish American nativists, and even went so far as to charge that Washington's Irish residents had assisted the British in the 1814 burning of the capital.

On 27 May 1854 the *Washington News* asked its readers whether "fanaticism [shall] govern this, the metropolis of the Union?" A few days later, the Know-Nothings successfully elected their mayoral candidate, John Towers. The city quickly divided into Know-Nothing and anti–Know-Nothing political camps, each holding their first public mass meetings in September 1854. Through newspaper editorials, both groups accused each other of meeting in secret conclaves and abusing political power and patronage. On several occasions Know-Nothings protested in the streets. In one infamous incident, they threw into the Potomac River a stone that had been sent by the Vatican for the Washington Monument. In March 1855 they paraded in Indian dress through the seventh ward. While anti–Know-Nothings publicly condemned the Know-Nothings in the 1 June 1853 *National Intelligencer* for introducing the "rancor of party influence" into the city, voter participation in city elections rose during this period of political turmoil, which lasted until 1859.

Irish residents suffered during nearly ten years of Washington Know-Nothingism. A 28 May 1853 *Evening Star* letter to the editor declared that Gregory Ennis's defeat in the competition for canal commissioner could not be explained "unless upon the ground that he is an Irishman by birth." On 26 July 1854 William Thompson, editor of the *Washington News*, informed his readers that he had lost his city printing contract because he was a "naturalized citizen and a (suspected) Romanist."

Several Irish immigrants lost their lives during election day rioting. On 3 June 1856 the *Evening Star* reported that the "Irish were pursued, and beaten, and pelted with stones and brickbats, with little resistance on their part," and that "Irish women were struck down while trying to draw off their children or interposing to save their husbands or brothers." Irish protestor Owen Quigley was killed after shouting, "Hurrah for [William] Magruder," the anti–Know-

The "Plug Ugly" riot in Washington on 1 June 1857, when bands of Know-Nothings attacked Irish voters. (Courtesy Prints and Photographs Division, Library of Congress)

Nothing candidate. The violence climaxed during the 1857 elections. The *National Intelligencer* reported on 2 June 1857 that "bands of ill-looking men . . . with the generic and suggestive title of 'Plug-Uglies,' arrived from Baltimore." These men proceeded to attack a naturalized citizen in the fourth ward, and compelled other naturalized immigrants "to save limb and life by a general retirement from the scene." The president called on the marines to quell the rioting, which left eight dead and twenty-one wounded.[27]

The city was scarred by the violence. Dismayed by the riot, many Know-Nothings withdrew their support from the movement. By 1859 the movement's strength had deteriorated. The ethnic violence that so disillusioned Washington residents would soon be displaced by the sectional hostility that preceded the Civil War.

"The Federal City," a poem that appeared in the 17 December 1800 *Charleston City Gazette,* invited readers to contemplate the unusual social development of a city that shared "no common fate" with other towns. While Rome "increas'd from pigmy size" to its eventual grandeur, "capitols and palaces" of "awful height" loomed along the shores of the Potomac soon after its inception. How would historians write of a metropolis, asked the poet, where "late must common people come" to a place intended for a "royal race"? An astute reader might have wondered *who* had built the capitols of "awful height" if "common people" had come only lately.

Two stores owned by Thomas E. Reardon and his son, William F. Reardon, in Anacostia in 1917. The photograph provides evidence of the persistence of the Irish community into the twentieth century. The stores are decorated for the Fourth of July and demonstrate the family's pride in their success. (Courtesy Prints and Photographs Division, Library of Congress)

Irish immigrants continued to settle in Washington in the decades following the Civil War, and evidence suggests that their community solidified and prospered. In 1872 a local newspaper, the *Irish Republican*, made a brief appearance. By 1900 Georgetown's Irish families, working in skilled and semi-skilled jobs and as small businessowners—particularly of groceries and saloons—could claim two to three generations of residence. The Reardon family exemplified the type of upward mobility that frequently occurred among Washington's first- and second-generation, native-born Americans of Irish descent. Thomas Reardon's father, Dennis, and mother, Catherine, were born in Ireland. In the 1860 census, when Thomas was two years old, Dennis was listed as a laborer. In the 1900 census Thomas was listed as a plasterer and William as an apprentice carpenter. By 1920 both father and son were listed as merchants.

As individual Irish American families prospered, so did their community life. For example, Irish workers employed by the Washington Gas Light Company, who lived in the Connaught Row section of Foggy Bottom, fielded Irish athletic teams, attended St. Stephen the Martyr Church, and, in the 1880s, established the West End Hibernian Society. By the early 1900s five chapters of the Ancient Order of Hibernians flourished in the District.[28] Some of the children and great-grandchildren of Irish immigrants continue to make the Washington area their home, perpetuating a sense of community identity established by their forebears who had built the capital city.

NOTES

1. David Bailie Warden, *A Chronological and Statistical Description of the District of Columbia* (Paris: Smith), 27. This study draws on numerous primary sources. Most of the quotations concerning the first two decades of the city are taken from the Records of the Board of Commissioners for the District of Columbia, 1791–1815, RG 42, National Archives. All the references concerning apprenticeships can be found in Indentures of Apprenticeship Records, 1801–1874, RG 21, National Archives. For statistics on applicants for citizenship (name, age, date of immigration, place of birth, place of debarkation, and, occasionally, occupation), see Naturalization Records, 1801–1860, RG 21, National Archives.

2. See Henry Steele Commager, ed., *Documents of American History*, vol. 1, *To 1898* (New York: Appleton, Century, Crofts, 1963), 141; and H. Paul Caemmerer, *A Manual on the Origin and Development of Washington* (Washington: Government Printing Office, 1939), 7–8.

3. See *The Journals of Benjamin Henry Latrobe, 1799–1820: From Philadelphia to New Orleans*, ed. Edward C. Carter II, John C. Van Horne, and Lee W. Formwalt (New Haven, Conn.: Yale University Press, 1986), 3:70, 113–14; and Warden, *A Chronological and Statistical Description*, 27.

4. Thomas F. Hahn, *The Chesapeake and Ohio Canal: Pathway to the Nation's Capital* (Metuchen, N.J.: Scarecrow Press, 1984), 25; William C. di Giacomantonio, "All the President's Men: George Washington's Federal City Commissioners," *Washington History* 3, no. 1 (Spring–Summer 1991): 55; Robert H. Elias and Eugene D. Finch, eds., *Letters of Thomas Attwood Digges (1742–1821)* (Columbia: University of South Carolina Press, 1982), 411–18.

5. William Seale, *The President's House* (Washington, D.C.: White House Historical Association, 1986), 1:39. Like many master craftsmen at this time, Hoban alternately called himself "architect" and "house carpenter." Architecture did not become a regulated profession until the late 1800s. During the eighteenth century, master house carpenters, aided by building manuals, undertook both design and construction.

6. Ira Berlin and Herbert G. Gutman, "Natives and Immigrants, Free Men and Slaves: Urban Workingmen in the Antebellum South," *American Historical Review* 88

(1983): 1194–95. See also Sean Wilentz, *Chants Democratic: New York City and the Rise of the American Working Class, 1788–1850* (New York: Oxford University Press, 1984), 92 and passim.

7. Peter Lenox to Commissioners, Records of the Board of Commissioners, Letters Received, 25 April 1798.

8. Records of the Board of Commissioners, Letters Received, 27 November 1797, and 20 February 1798.

9. Commissioners to George Washington, Records of the Board of Commissioners, Letters Sent, April 1794.

10. Records of the Board of Commissioners, Letters Received, 17 November 1792.

11. Anne Royall, *The Black Book, or A Continuation of Travels in the United States* (Washington: Printed for the author, 1829), 3:209.

12. Records of the Board of Commissioners, Proceedings, 15 January 1799.

13. Robert Plunkett to John Carroll, 10 April 1810, 6V10, Archdiocesan Archives of Baltimore, Baltimore, Maryland.

14. Morris J. MacGregor, *A Parish for the Federal City: St. Patrick's in Washington, 1794–1994* (Washington, D.C.: Catholic University of America Press, 1994), 44.

15. See Allen C. Clark, "The Mayoralty of Robert Brent," *Records of the Columbia Historical Society* 33–34 (1932): 304; and *Native American*, 18 March 1838.

16. Warden, *A Chronological and Statistical Description*, 27; and Carter et al., eds., *Journals of Benjamin Henry Latrobe*, 113–14.

17. See William Cranch, *Reports of Cases Civil and Criminal in the United States Circuit Court of the District of Columbia, from 1801 to 1841* (Boston: Little, Brown and Company, 1852), 1:75–76.

18. See Michael Shiner Diary, 1813–1865, Manuscript Division, Library of Congress, Washington, D.C.

19. Naturalization records become more complete by 1818 and provide valuable information about immigrants. As noted above, the required declaration of intent recorded name of applicant, current age, place of birth, place of debarkation, date of immigration, and, occasionally, occupation. This list of occupations is compiled from the 1822 city directory of names found among Irish applicants for citizenship between 1818 and 1823.

20. James H. Kettner, *The Development of American Citizenship, 1608–1870* (Chapel Hill: University of North Carolina Press, 1978), 254.

21. James R. Wason, "Labor and Politics in Washington in the Early Jacksonian Era" (Ph.D. diss., American University, 1963), 35. Wason explores the establishment of the Association of Mechanics and Other Working Men in 1830.

22. Quoted in Constance McLaughlin Green, *Washington: A History of the Capital, 1800–1950* (Princeton: Princeton University Press, 1962), 1:114.

23. Peter Kenney to Francis Neale, 10 September 1832, 210N1, Maryland Jesuit Province Archives; Burial Register, 1818–1867, Records of Holy Trinity Church, Special Collections Division, Georgetown University, Washington, D.C. See also William W. Warner, *At Peace with All Their Neighbors: Catholics and Catholicism in the National Capital, 1787–1860* (Washington, D.C.: Georgetown University Press, 1994), 201–2.

24. *Address of the Association of Mechanics and Other Working Men of the City of Washington, to the Operatives throughout the United States* (Washington, D.C.: W. Duncan, 1830).

25. *Native American,* 19 August 1837.

26. Ibid., 21 January 1840.

27. Kenneth G. Alfers, *Law and Order in the Capital City: A History of the Washington Police, 1800–1886,* GW Washington Studies, no. 5 (Washington, D.C.: George Washington University, 1976), 18.

28. See, for example, Kathryn Schneider Smith, *Port Town to Urban Neighborhood: The Georgetown Waterfront of Washington, D.C., 1880–1920* (Washington, D.C.: Center for Washington Area Studies of the George Washington University, 1989), 34–35, 98–99; and Suzanne Sherwood Unger, "Foggy Bottom: Blue-Collar Neighborhood in a White-Collar Town," in Kathryn Schneider Smith, ed., *Washington at Home: An Illustrated History of Neighborhoods in the Nation's Capital* (Northridge, Calif.: Windsor Publications, 1988), 55–65. See also Tom Kelly, "I Knew My Parents Were Irish as Soon as I Knew Anything," *The Washingtonian* (March 1979): 144–50.

PART TWO

Race, Ethnicity, Class, and Community Building

4.

The Days of Jubilee
Black Migration during the Civil War and Reconstruction

Lois E. Horton

For African Americans, both slave and free, the Civil War was a war against slavery. For generations, slaves gathered in remote wooded areas of plantations, free blacks congregated in grand churches of northern cities, and small groups of slave and free, meeting in homes, had sung of suffering in bondage, longing for a Moses to lead the people, and anticipating the year of jubilee.[1] Many African Americans, of course, had not waited for the year of jubilee to bring them freedom, but had struck out on their own, seeking a sometimes precari-ous freedom in the North or in the relative anonymity of the city. As the cap-ital of the Union on the border between North and South, Washington, D.C., attracted thousands of black migrants.

The Civil War and its aftermath transformed Washington from a small town into a city. Incredibly rapid population growth during the war provided the clearest indication of the changes taking place. In 1860 census takers counted just over 75,000 people. At the war's climax only four years later, the District's population was estimated at more than twice that number. The in-crease was not merely a temporary wartime effect. The next census in 1870 showed that the population remained well above its prewar level and com-prised nearly 132,000 residents.

However astounding, the District's population growth was only a surface indicator of the profound changes in the city's character and demographics. Originally carved from the slave states of Maryland and Virginia, the District had never fulfilled the hope that it would become a commercial center at-tracting industry, capital, and urban diversity to the South. Below the Mason-Dixon Line, Washington had retained its southern character, as well as slav-ery, its most southern institution.

Like most southern cities, Washington had a fairly high percentage of African Americans—nearly one-fifth of the total population on the eve of the Civil War. The District's free black population had grown steadily from 1800, but their number had greatly increased after slaveholding interests convinced the federal government in 1846 to return the Virginia portion of the District. Prohibited by Virginia law from remaining in the state longer than six months, many free blacks moved from Alexandria to Washington. Still, about 20 percent of African Americans residing in the District in 1860 were slaves.

The outbreak of war in 1861 brought immediate changes to the nation's capital. Straddling the boundaries between sectional interests, the city was cut off from its southern constituency. The District became the organizational center for northern resources in the struggle to restore the Union. Many of the South's sympathizers—including southern congressmen, military officers, and civil servants—left the city. Others packed their belongings and headed north, fleeing the threatened and virtually undefended city. The southern city now faced north, where its political and economic ties remained intact. Regiments of northern troops replaced those who had fled. In the army's wake came businesspeople, retailers, contractors, and suppliers, all hoping to fill the federal needs in the expensive task of financing and equipping the military effort. New jobs attracted thousands of people, many of them women. As troops ranged over the nearby countryside and fought early battles, many people—including slaves from the plantations—fled to the relative safety of the city.

The wartime exodus of slaves to the District created a dilemma for the government. By federal law escaped slaves had to be returned to their owners. Some fugitive slaves were from rebellious states such as Virginia, where the federal law did not apply, but others were from Maryland, a slave state still loyal to the Union. Anxious to retain the loyalty of border states like Maryland, the Lincoln administration devised a temporary legalistic solution: slaves escaping from states at war with the Union would be considered "contraband of war," or captured property, and placed under the jurisdiction of the U.S. Army. Fugitive slaves from loyal states, however, were to be returned to their masters.[2]

As increasing numbers of slaves arrived, their extreme poverty was impossible to ignore in a city already straining under the demands of war. Settling into camps near army units or into makeshift alley residences, the former slaves were a constant reminder of the undeclared but persistent reason for civil war. Abolitionists, whose cause was strengthened in Congress by the southern states' secession, renewed their demands that war aims include the destruction of slavery. Black ministers, and some white ministers, preached antislavery sermons. The abolitionist Hutchinson Family Singers gave a series of concerts around the city; and a Smithsonian Institution lecture series included prominent white abolitionist speakers Henry Ward Beecher, Horace Greeley, and Wendell Phillips. Pragmatists noted the military advantage to be gained from depriving rebellious slave states of their precious human resource.

President Lincoln and the Congress advanced slowly in the attack on slavery. Still seeking compromise between freedom and the property rights of slaveholders, they devised a plan for the compensated emancipation of slaves in the District. A law passed by Congress on 16 April 1862 established a commission to receive petitions from slaveowners, authorized the hiring of a slave dealer to estimate the worth of individual slaves, and provided for an average compensation of $300 per slave to be paid from the federal treasury. Petitions were filed, including 161 from slaves themselves; more than 3,000 slaves received their freedom, costing the federal government nearly $1 million. Obviously, if this law were to serve as a model, as President Lincoln had seemed to intend, buying the 4.5 million slaves in the South would have been an expensive proposition.

In July 1862 the federal government resolved the issue of runaway slaves in the District by granting the former slaves their freedom. Technically, Maryland slaveowners could still claim their runaway slaves, and local authorities at the District jail were notoriously sympathetic to slaveholders' interests. Any arrested African American was thus placed at risk. Nonetheless, the law prompted increased black migration to the District during the summer of 1862. Finally, in January 1863 President Lincoln's Emancipation Proclamation declared freedom for all slaves held by people in rebellion against the United States, and the Union became symbolically identified with the antislavery cause.

Before the war the District's black population was about 14,000. In Washington, as in other cities, the black community had churches, mutual-aid societies, and other organizations to provide material assistance and spiritual and emotional support to those in need. Fugitive slaves, widows, orphans, the unemployed, the sick, and the destitute were cared for primarily within the black community through formal organizations and informal assistance networks. Caring for the more than 30,000 ex-slaves who had come to the city during the war, however, severely taxed the community's resources. As the need grew, blacks and whites in Washington and throughout the North organized increased aid. Abolitionists established aid societies for freed people to provide money, clothing, teachers, and educational supplies. They also began a local Washington branch of the National Freedmen's Relief Association in April 1862. In the summer of that same year Elizabeth Keckley, First Lady Mary Todd

African Americans gathered in April 1866 to celebrate the abolition of slavery in the District of Columbia. Illustration by F. Dielman, Harper's Weekly, *12 May 1866. (Courtesy Prints and Photographs Division, Library of Congress)*

Lincoln's seamstress, led a group of forty members of the Fifteenth Street Presbyterian Church in forming a Contraband Relief Association. A federal "contraband department" established in June 1862 provided freed people with food and jobs in military support work. However, only a small percentage of the needy were helped by federal aid. It was the massive organization of both public and private relief that enabled many to survive in the District.

Among those who were drawn to the capital to aid in the relief effort were many prominent northern black leaders, some of whom had once been slaves themselves. Frederick Douglass, a former slave from Maryland and a frequent visitor to the city during the war, was an important spokesperson for black rights and made substantial contributions to the Contraband Relief Association. Black abolitionist Maria W. Stewart—author and women's rights advocate in Boston in the 1830s and, later, a teacher in New York and Baltimore—moved to Washington during the war. She had little money yet managed to set

Contraband camp of the labor crew of the Quarter Master Department, Belle Plain, Virginia. Slaves fled plantations en masse as the Union Army approached and sought to join the military effort on behalf of the war for freedom. (Courtesy Moorland Spingarn Research Center, Howard University)

up a school for black children. Sojourner Truth came from New York to care for the sick and wounded. Many white abolitionists and philanthropists also came to teach, to organize welfare, employment, and medical services, and to advocate the rights of the newly freed people.

Housing was an especially pressing problem, as Washington overflowed with people involved in the war effort. The army brought wounded soldiers to the city from the surrounding countryside and turned churches, public buildings, and squares into medical facilities, army offices, and camps. Freed people constructed makeshift housing in vacant lots from salvaged boards. Early in the war the government supplied some shelter for the refugees, including housing for six hundred in Duff Green's Row on First Street between East Capitol and A Streets, SE. When the government converted these buildings into a prison some months later, the people were moved to wooden barracks at Camp Barker on Vermont Avenue and Twelfth Street, near the Contraband Department office.[3]

The army's efforts housed relatively few migrants, and the living conditions for the vast majority in more haphazard arrangements were overcrowded and dangerous. One section of shanties, now the site of Federal Triangle, was graphically called Murder Bay. An 1863 outbreak of smallpox created concern over sanitation and overcrowding in the camps. The government tried, fairly unsuccessfully, to remove people from the city by setting up new camps in the suburbs, but the overwhelming number of people coming to the city continued to make overcrowding a problem.

In outlying camps in Virginia—such as Green's Heights in Arlington, Camp Distribution near Alexandria, and Camp Rucker near Falls Church—former slaves raised vegetables for hospital patients, cut wood for fuel, and made clothing for soldiers and themselves. One model camp, Freedmen's Village, opened in December 1863 on land that had been a part of the Robert E. Lee estate on Arlington Heights. Freedmen's Village contained small cabins converted from army barracks, a day and a night school, a church, a tailor shop, a washhouse, an orphan asylum, and a hospital.

Once the Emancipation Proclamation had tentatively committed the Union to the cause of freedom for the slaves, abolitionists began lobbying for federal guarantees of that freedom. In the opinion of black activists, such as the Reverend Henry Highland Garnet and Frederick Douglass, and white abolitionists, such as William Lloyd Garrison, Samuel Gridley Howe, and Wendell Phillips, the assurance of freedom required more than legal protection against re-enslavement. Only political rights, education, land ownership, and employment would enable freed people to become full citizens. In January 1863 Phillips recommended the establishment of a "Bureau of Freedmen" to oversee the transition from slavery to freedom.

Some two years after it was introduced, a bill to establish a Bureau of Refugees, Freedmen, and Abandoned Lands was passed by Congress to aid both blacks and whites. The bureau began operation in 1864, just weeks before the war's end. It promised federal assistance to the philanthropists and teachers already sent to the District by churches, religious associations, freed people's aid societies, missionary associations, and mutual-aid societies. The Freedmen's Bureau, under the supervision of Gen. Oliver Otis Howard, opened its local office in July 1865. The bureau was concerned with virtually all the needs of freed people and refugees. Its most extensive and lasting efforts were in the areas of health care by establishing Freedmen's Hospital and in education by setting up and coordinating many day, evening, and industrial schools. Accomplishments of the Freedmen's Bureau in the District included the founding of Howard University, with which Freedmen's Hospital was eventually affiliated.

At war's end, as the government phased out housing at former contraband camps and army barracks, it sought more permanent shelter for the freed people. Trustees of the Freedmen's Educational Fund purchased lots in the city and built tenements that they rented at an annual 6 percent return on the original investment. The trustees' acquisition of a 375-acre farm from the estate of banker James Barry in Anacostia provided an opportunity for freedmen to buy land. At Potomac City, which had been established on that land, freedmen could purchase farm plots of approximately one acre for about $150 to $200; construction materials for the A-frame dwellings could also be purchased from the government. The Freedmen's Bureau donated lumber to those who could not afford to pay. By June 1868 Barry's Farm, as it continued to be called, boasted a combination church-school building, bridges, roads, and eleven wooden houses. One year later, 150 families lived in the settlement. William Hunter, a black minister from Washington and the settlement's first landholder, helped to establish the Macedonia Baptist Church, the first church of that denomination in Anacostia.[4] Barry's Farm residents organized many churches and schools, engaged in a variety of occupations that included the skilled trades, and established profitable market gardens and stone, clay, and sand quarries. As landowners, many residents were politically active. Three of the settlement's early organizers who became community leaders were Lewis, Charles, and Frederick Douglass Jr., the sons of Frederick Douglass. Douglass himself moved to Anacostia a short time later.

The end of the Civil War did not stop black migration to Washington. Uncertainty over their future encouraged many southern blacks in the surrounding areas to seek the federal government's protection. This period's greatest increase in black population thus occurred during and immediately after the war. The number of blacks more than tripled in the decade between 1860 and 1870. In 1870 African Americans numbered more than 43,000, roughly one-third of the District's nearly 132,000 residents.[5] Population figures indicate that Washington continued to exert a strong attraction for black migrants. In the 1890s black residents numbered 75,000 in a total population of more than 230,000, and they continued to be about one-third of the population well into the twentieth century.

The development of black rights in Washington created another strong attraction for African Americans. Of the civil and political rights debated during Reconstruction, none was more important than the right to vote. In late 1863, at the thirtieth anniversary meeting of the American Anti-Slavery Society in Philadelphia, Frederick Douglass had asserted that the right to vote was a crucial safeguard of black freedom. By the next spring 2,500 black men from the District petitioned Congress for the right to vote. As a result of efforts by the National Convention of Colored Citizens of the United States and its

National Equal Rights League, led by black Ohio lawyer John Mercer Langston, a bill for black voting rights in the District was introduced in the House of Representatives. Anticipating that Congress might consider testing black voting rights in Washington, local whites held a referendum on the issue the next year. The vote was overwhelmingly against extending the franchise, reflecting whites' fears and the tensions existing between the more established white residents and the new, growing black population.

Finally, in June 1866 a joint congressional committee presented the Fourteenth Amendment to the Constitution, guaranteeing all rights of citizenship—including the right to vote—to African American men. As the amendment made its way through the states for ratification (finally accomplished two years later in 1868), Republicans worked to create more rapid changes in the District, where Congress had direct control. In December 1866, after much debate, Congress passed a bill extending the vote to African American men in the District. President Andrew Johnson vetoed the bill, but Congress overrode his veto. In 1867 African American men were allowed to vote in local elections for the first time. They quickly joined the Republican party, and integrated Republican organizations—many with black officers—sprang up in all of the city's wards. Many whites protested black voting by boycotting these local elections, with the result that more than 45 percent of the registered voters that year were blacks.

The municipal election in June was a gala affair. Black men began to wait in line hours before the polls opened. The rule against talking in the voting lines was forgotten, as women brought food to serve to those waiting to exercise their new right. This picnic atmosphere was occasionally interrupted when white voters tried to form separate lines so that they would not have to wait so long, but trouble was averted when police officers quickly put an end to the separate lines. In the evening after the elections people lit bonfires all around the city, and African Americans paraded through the streets singing and cheering the victory of the radical Republicans. To the celebrants, black participation in this victory and the political power it promised seemed the fulfillment of their long-awaited freedom. It was truly the year of jubilee.

Elections the following year, in 1868, brought African Americans into the city government, fulfilling black hopes for political power and confirming the fears of many longtime white Washington residents. In that year, teacher John F. Cook Jr., son of the late Reverend John F. Cook, was elected to the board of aldermen; Stewart Carter, a barber, was elected to the city council; and Sayles J. Bowen, a white abolitionist and longtime advocate of black rights, was elected mayor. By 1869 seven blacks had been elected to the city council, one

"The Georgetown Election—The Negro at the Ballot-Box." Illustration from Harper's Weekly, 16 March 1867. *(Courtesy Moorland Spingarn Research Center, Howard University)*

from each of the city's wards. Bowen, an activist mayor, instituted such public works as street grading and the laying of sidewalks and sewers to create badly needed improvements in the growing city and to provide jobs, mainly for black laborers. The rising costs of public improvements, coupled with accusations that Bowen's programs were designed to ensure the loyalty of black voters by giving them jobs, led to the election in 1870 of a new mayor, Matthew Emery.

Postwar-period policies created new opportunities for African Americans in Washington. These opportunities and the desire to influence the process of change attracted many accomplished black leaders to the District. John Mercer Langston, who had moved to Washington in 1868, was a member of the District Board of Health for seven years, and became a professor and dean of Howard University's law department. Alexander T. Augusta, one of the officers who had been assigned to Freedmen's Hospital during the war, returned after the war and joined Howard University's medical department. Frederick Douglass, who had moved to the District in 1870, edited a newspaper and accepted a series of presidential appointments, which included positions as U.S. marshal and recorder of deeds.

The expanding rights and opportunities of the Reconstruction period in Washington also created a more diversified occupational structure for African Americans. University professors and political appointees joined the prewar propertied class, which included the successful caterers James Wormley and William Shadd, and the Interior Department messenger William Syphax (a descendant of the white Custis family of Virginia). For many years, parades commemorating the anniversary of emancipation in the District included not only bands, infantry members, and veterans, but also wagons bearing representatives of diverse skilled trades and occupations.

Influential black political appointees aided black workers at all levels. African Americans held a variety of positions in the federal and District governments—from teachers, police officers, firemen, mail carriers, clerks, and bank tellers to messengers and janitors. Many longtime black Washingtonians made great progress during the postwar period. James Wormley, who had been born free in the city in 1820, had become a successful caterer and restauranteur by the time of the Civil War. In 1871 he opened a hotel at Fifteenth and H Streets, NW. Wormley House's elegant and gracious service achieved an international reputation, and the hotel became a center of Washington's social and political life. Wormley was undoubtedly the most famous and the wealthiest of those who had begun their catering careers delivering daily meals to their customers, but there were also many other successful black caterers and barbers who served a predominantly white clientele. With greater business opportunities and new, more dignified, and secure government jobs at all levels for African Americans, the city began to build a black middle class.

The black community concentrated special effort on all types of education, from adult literacy to primary-school and university instruction. Philanthropists' efforts and increased financial support for black public schools resulted in astounding progress in literacy and educational accomplishments for freed people. Howard University, which had dedicated its first building in 1867, offered mainly a secondary-school curriculum but also organized a general college course and a professional curriculum in theology, law, and medicine. Black literary organizations, benevolent societies, and a wide variety of churches flourished. By the 1880s it was not uncommon for black churches to have more than 1,000 members.

The end of Reconstruction entailed a shift in national attention and concern, marked in the late 1870s and 1880s by the withdrawal of federal troops from the south, the end of Freedmen's Bureau activities, and the Supreme

Court's determination that the Civil Rights Act of 1875 was unconstitutional. In the District, Congress responded to increasing expenses and the potential for black political power by instituting a territorial government in 1871, which provided for the presidential appointment of many previously elected city officials. Although conservatives argued that territorial government would be more efficient, the pace and cost of public works increased as the new government instituted an ambitious program under the direction of Alexander "Boss" Shepherd and the Board of Public Works. By the 1873 depression the territorial government was deeply in debt. The crisis was finally resolved in 1878, when Congress removed citizen control of District affairs in exchange for the promise that the federal government would pay half of the city's expenses. Thus, the city was modernized and beautified, the growth of black political power was checked, and all District residents lost home rule. Presidentially appointed commissioners governed the District for almost the next 100 years.

Although Reconstruction ended gradually, lingering in Washington until the turn of the century, the eclipse of black political power meant deteriorating opportunities for African Americans in education, housing, and employment. By the 1880s the clustering of freed people that had occurred near military camps and in alleys began to take on the character of population concentrations. One of the largest of such enclaves persisted in northwest Washington, where many new migrants had settled in the refugee camp on Boundary Street (now Florida Avenue) near Freedmen's Hospital. Other migrants concentrated near jobs on the docks and in warehouses in a swampy area along the Tiber Creek in southwest Washington. In 1897 one study estimated that approximately 19,000 people, three-quarters of them black, lived in the city's alley dwellings.[6]

As more African Americans moved into these areas of concentration, whites began to move out. As the city expanded both in area and population some attractive semirural suburbs—Brookland in northeast Washington and Petworth in northwest Washington, for example—were developed on the outskirts of the city. Zoning ordinances, banking policies, and informal agreements between real estate agents and property owners made it increasingly difficult for African Americans to move into developing neighborhoods such as LeDroit Park, near Howard University. In the 1890s, after much difficulty and some subterfuge, a few of the city's distinguished black residents, including Robert and Mary Church Terrell and Paul Laurence Dunbar, were able to move into LeDroit Park. By 1900 Washington had the largest urban black community in the country, and it was a racially segregated community.

As job opportunities declined and segregation increased, the black com-

Workers building the State, War, and Navy Department at Seventeenth Street and Pennsylvania Avenue, NW, next to the White House in summer 1884. (Courtesy Prints and Photographs Division, Library of Congress)

munity turned inward for its further development. Gradually barred from the diversity of political and patronage positions that had once been available, blacks found upward mobility generally limited to those institutions and businesses that served their own community. The segregated system assured African Americans respectable positions as, for example, public-school teachers, and added a new business elite in such enterprises as real estate and insurance to the existing leadership from the community's educational and religious institutions. By the end of the nineteenth century, civil rights laws went unenforced, and African Americans were excluded from white-owned hotels, restaurants, theaters, and even many white-owned stores.

Black migration during the Civil War and the postwar period created a community of extremes. Old families of property and respected position were joined by prominent national leaders, educators, lawyers, and businesspeople attracted by the city's unparalleled opportunities for advancement and service. Drawn to the city by freedom and the protection of the federal government, the vast majority of black migrants were ex-slaves, most illiterate, unskilled, and from nearby Maryland and Virginia.

After a hopeful beginning federal assistance was withdrawn, the vote was lost, and Washington's African Americans were left to care for their own needy and to create their own avenues for advancement. By the beginning of the twentieth century, Washington's black community constituted a separate city within the newly modernized federal city. Slavery had been abolished, and African Americans had attained a greater measure of freedom and enhanced opportunities for advancement. Yet the dream of complete freedom, of the year of jubilee, remained a dream deferred.

NOTES

1. In Old Testament Jewish history the year of jubilee occurred every fifty years. During this year land was to be left fallow, mortgaged property was to be returned to its original owner, and people in bondage were to be set free. Throughout slavery the concept of the year of jubilee had special meaning to African American Christians.

2. Constance M. Green, *Washington* (Princeton: Princeton University Press, 1962), 1:173.

3. Lois E. Horton, "The Development of Federal Social Policy for Blacks in Washington, D.C." (Ph.D. diss., Brandeis University, 1977); idem, *Washington, D.C.: From Civil War Town to Modern City* (Washington, D.C.: Associates for Renewal in Education, 1979); idem and James O. Horton, "Race, Occupation, and Literacy in Reconstruction Washington, D.C.," in *Toward a New South?* ed. Orville Vernon Burton and Robert C. McMath Jr. (Westport, Conn.: Greenwood Press, 1982), 135–51.

4. Horton, "Development of Federal Social Policy," 84–85; Louise Daniel Hutchinson, *The Anacostia Story: 1608–1930* (Washington, D.C.: Smithsonian Institution Press, 1977), 81–89.

5. Reacting to the scarcity of jobs created by the great in-migration, one Freedmen's Bureau aid program moved people out of the District in the mid-1860s, seeking to redistribute unemployed former slaves to other areas. Although freed people desperately needed employment, they hesitated to use this service for fear of being sent south into virtual re-enslavement or away from recently reunited family and friends. Those who were employed through this program—about 10,000 people—were primarily sent to New England and the Northeast to work as servants. See Horton, "Development of Federal Social Policy."

6. James Borchert, *Alley Life in Washington* (Urbana, Ill.: University of Chicago Press, 1980), 42.

ADDITIONAL READING

Battle, Thomas C. "Behind the Marble Mask." *Wilson Quarterly* 13, no. 1 (1989): 84–89.

Berlin, Ira, Joseph P. Reidy, Leslie S. Rowland, eds. *Freedom: A Documentary History of Emancipation, 1861–1867.* Series 1 and 2. Cambridge: Cambridge University Press, 1982.

Brown, Letitia W., and Elsie M. Lewis. *Washington from Banneker to Douglass, 1791–1870.* Washington, D.C.: National Portrait Gallery, 1971.

Carpenter, Frank G. *Carp's Washington.* New York: McGraw-Hill, 1960.

Dabney, Lillian G. *The History of Schools for Negroes in the District of Columbia, 1807–1947.* Washington, D.C.: Catholic University Press, 1949.

Foner, Eric. *Reconstruction.* New York: Harper and Row, 1988.

Gerteis, Louis S. *From Contraband to Freedman.* Westport, Conn.: Greenwood Press, 1973.

Ingle, Edward. *The Negro in the District of Columbia.* Baltimore: Johns Hopkins University Press, 1893.

Johnston, Allan John. *Burying Freedom: The Black Community of Washington, D.C. 1860–1880.* New York: Garland Publishers, 1993.

Landis, Kenesaw M. *Segregation in Washington.* Chicago: National Committee on Segregation in the Nation's Capital, 1948.

Leech, Margaret. *Reveille in Washington.* New York: Time, 1941.

Lessoff, Alan. *The Nation and Its City: Politics, Corruption, and Progress in Washington, D.C., 1861–1902.* Baltimore: Johns Hopkins University Press, 1994.

McFeely, William S. *Yankee Stepfather.* New Haven, Conn.: Yale University Press, 1968.

Williams, Melvin R. "A Blueprint for Change: The Black Community in Washington, D.C., 1860–1870." *Records of the Columbia Historical Society* 48 (1971–72): 359–93.

5.

"Like Moths to a Candle"
The Nouveaux Riches Flock to Washington, 1870–1900

Kathryn Allamong Jacob

Not all newcomers to Washington after the Civil War were African American, German, Greek, Chinese, or Italian. Not all were urban poor, displaced peasants, or eager young men searching for a foothold on the ladder to success. Not all were fleeing from some terror—be it pogroms, famine, or night riders. As the Gilded Age dawned in the early 1870s, a phenomenon was unfolding in Washington that would prove far more important to the city than the era's political scandals. A new group of migrants was arriving in the nation's capital, the likes of whom had rarely been seen in the antebellum city.

These were a different kind of migrant. For the most part they were white, middle-aged, second-, third-, and even fourth-generation Americans. They were not seeking to realize dreams of riches. Those dreams had already come true: some owned mines yielding more than $5,000 in gold a day. Rather than fleeing from something, they were flocking toward something—something that Washington alone among American cities held out to them in the last decades of the nineteenth century.

The term "rich newcomers" is a broad umbrella sheltering at least four subgroups: the nouveaux riches; the old rich, who were new to Washington but not new to money; a handful of wealthy intellectuals, such as the historian Henry Adams; and a few rich and ruthless lobbyists. The nouveaux riches, the most numerous of the affluent newcomers, were the group whose legacy remains the most visible in the city. From where and why had they come? How did they change the capital, and how did it change them?

Mark Twain, in Washington to witness the first of these rich strangers' arrival, lampooned them in *The Gilded Age: A Tale of Today* (1873). Twain labeled the ostentatious newcomers the "parvenus," and caricatured them as the outrageous Mr. and Mrs. Patrique Oreillé. The Honorable Patrique Oreillé had clambered out of steerage at Castle Garden as Patrick O'Riley from Cork County, Ireland, and quickly rose through the ranks of the Democratic Party to a seat in the New York legislature. To celebrate their success, the O'Rileys toured Europe, then returned to America miraculously transformed into the ultrafashionable Patrique Oreillés. Dribbling mispronounced French phrases, the Oreillés set out next to "do" Washington.

The fictional Oreillés represented the real phenomenon of the nouveaux riches, who bloomed in America in the second half of the nineteenth century. In the two decades before the Civil War there had not been five men in the United States worth $5 million. By 1890 there were 4,000 of them. Millionaires were becoming commonplace, but their millions were being made in ways barely dreamed of in the 1840s—in air brakes, oil, cattle, telephones, and mining—as well as places barely heard of in antebellum America—Denver; Dayton, Ohio; Butte, Montana; and Altoona, Pennsylvania.

Few of these new millionaires were content to remain in the isolated outposts and small towns where they had gotten their start. In the postwar years waves of parvenus inundated old cities, such as Boston, and boomtowns, such as Chicago. Although the advent of the nouveaux riches was a nationwide phenomenon, each city experienced it in a distinctive way. Different individuals gravitated to different cities for different reasons. Washington's newcomers were its own, drawn to the Potomac's shores—not to Boston or New York— because of reasons unique to the capital.

Washington's nouveaux riches were primarily American-born, coming from every corner of the country except the South, where new money was too rare to be exported. The oldest cities in the Northeast—Boston and Philadelphia, for example—sent to Washington their newest makers of fortunes. Even after years of assiduous courting, these parvenus still found the doors to these older cities' entrenched elites closed to them. Most nouveaux riches from the Northeast came from newer, smaller industrial cities.

A steady stream of nouveaux riches also flowed into Washington from the Midwest, from such cities as Toledo, Cincinnati, Cleveland, and especially, Chicago. The richest, most flamboyant arrivistes, or new arrivals, however, trekked to Washington from the trans–Mississippi West, overwhelming the capital with incredible fortunes made from gold, silver, copper, and lead. The glittering procession began with California forty-niners, then expanded to include the Comstock Lode millionaires and the "Bonanza Kings" of Colorado, Montana, and Nevada.

Why had these parvenus chosen to come to Washington, and why in such large numbers only after the war? Many claimed that they had come for the city's mild winter climate. Washington's winters were indeed milder than those of Boston or New York, but they were no milder in the 1880s than they had been in the 1850s, when few rich men not elected or appointed to the federal government voluntarily set foot in the capital.

Clearly, the postwar capital possessed something that antebellum Washington had lacked. Although it could claim many new attractions, one of its most striking was the physical city itself. Warm winters meant nothing to parvenus without parks and avenues along which to promenade. In the early 1870s, Alexander "Boss" Shepherd and the other city boosters, who sought to change the form of the city's government as well as its physical landscape, provided these and other luxuries in abundance in the "new Washington." As chairman of the new Board of Public Works, Shepherd created a lovely city, filled with all the right amenities to appeal to the era's restless new rich.

Reporter Frank "Carp" Carpenter described perhaps the most important carrot that Washington dangled before the nouveaux riches:

> New York is a city of things, as well as money. Washington is a city of persons. . . . With all its great men, there is more opportunity for a nobody to become a somebody than in the whirlpool of New York.[1]

The ease with which a "nobody" could become a "somebody" was one of Washington's chief attractions for the parvenus. In *The Gilded Age*, Henry Brierly assured Laura Hawkins that she need not have any connections to succeed in Washington society: "It doesn't need a crowbar to break your way into society there as it does in Philadelphia. It's democratic, Washington is. Money or beauty will open any door."[2]

Beauty alone was a weak reed on which to lean. Money, however, did open the doors to high society in the capital. Parvenus sought out Washington because of its reputation as a city where wealth, not pedigree, counted. Washington high society had more fluid criteria for admittance than that of Philadelphia, partially because the Civil War had stripped the capital of its old, southern, elite families, the longtime arbiters of taste and gentility. There was no longer a Cerberus to guard the gate to the capital's high society.

A stable population is essential for the perpetuation of social elites, while rapid turnover is deleterious. By the 1870s the entryway into Washington's high society was a revolving door, with men and women of unknown backgrounds whirling in and out with each election. Carpenter described the effect of this constant state of flux:

> I know many people who rank here far higher than they could in their own state. I could point out some who are even ostracized in their home towns but who, in Washington, move about on the topmost layer of the upper crust. . . . Washington seldom bothers itself about the skeletons in its inhabitants' closets. Lucifer himself will be welcomed if he will dress well, keep his hoofs hidden in patent leathers, and his tail out of sight.[3]

It was the hope of exploiting this porousness that drew to Washington people who knew they could not successfully storm the gates of high society elsewhere.

To urban amenities and a highly permeable society must be added still another factor that increased the postwar capital's allure: the federal government's increasing power and prestige. The Civil War brought new vigor and vastly expanded scale to the federal bureaucracy. Whereas once Americans had felt the federal government's presence only when their mail was delivered, by the 1870s they experienced it daily through pensions, patronage, patents, claims, schools, and even free seeds from the new U.S. Department of Agriculture. Spokespersons for labor, temperance, African Americans, Native Americans, and women converged on Washington to try to channel these new powers toward their own ends. Others were attracted not by the government's potential to do good but by its power to make the poor rich and the rich richer. The nouveaux riches, for whom power was a potent lure, fell into the latter category. With few exceptions, these parvenus were not philanthropists.

The federal government's increasing international prestige was evident in the new foreign legations opening in Washington during the 1870s, another development of great interest to those parvenu mothers anxious for their daughters to marry titled Europeans. Each highly publicized match—and there were many—ensured that more hopefuls would follow.

The vanguard of the *arrivistes*, led by old friends and the comrades-in-arms of Ulysses S. Grant and the rich Republicans who had contributed to his 1868 victory, began to arrive in Washington in the late 1860s. Even if the capital's streets were still canals of mud, the capital's high society, they reasoned, was certain to be more glamorous than what they had known back home; one met few diplomats in Salinas, California.

One of the first arrivals was Gen. Edward Fitzgerald Beale. The residents of Lafayette Square, the stronghold of the remnants of the capital's antebellum elite, watched with interest in 1872 as the old Decatur House was reopened with a spectacular party, where the salads were served on dishes carved from ice. This lavish spread was Beale's way of informing all of Washington that he and his family had arrived from California. It was actually a homecoming of sorts, for Beale had been born in Washington in 1822. When his family had fallen on hard times, Beale had embarked on a military career and had seen little of the capital for nearly three decades. He had later settled in California, where he had made a fortune in land and livestock.

With Grant, an old friend from army days, in the White House, it seemed the ideal time for Beale to return to his hometown and to satisfy his wife, who was anxious to introduce their children into society. He purchased Decatur House as the site of their debut. To his neighbors' horror, Beale ordered the exterior of the handsome old house redesigned in the prevailing Grant-era style, and soon heavy sandstone trim defaced the simple Federal-period façade.

The Beales never regretted their decision to move to Washington. General Beale's lavish contributions to Republican war chests paid off quickly with an appointment as American minister to Austria-Hungary's glamorous court. Like many nouveaux riches to follow, the Beales had come to Washington partly for the sake of their children. All three younger Beales thrived in the capital, demonstrating the fluidity of Washington's postwar society. At their father's death in 1893, Mary, the oldest daughter, was married to Russian diplomat George Bakhmeteff, who had courted her in Vienna. Truxtun Beale was in Greece, where—through his father's influence—he was serving as American minister. He was also engaged to marry Harriet Blaine, daughter of the late Secretary of State James G. Blaine. Beale's youngest daughter, Emily, was married to John R. McLean, one of the richest and coarsest of the newcomers who had arrived in Washington in the 1880s.

While the Beales were settling into Decatur House, a move was afoot in the western part of town that would permanently alter the city's look and feel. Leading the way was another flamboyant westerner, William Stewart. Stewart had been born in upstate New York in 1825, caught gold-rush fever in 1850 and headed west to California, where he had become a miner, a lawyer, and a millionaire before his thirtieth birthday. Stewart then moved to Nevada, where he had entered politics and had bought himself one of the new state's Senate seats in 1864. When he, his wife, and his two daughters settled into the Willard Hotel in 1865, the press proclaimed him the richest man in the Senate.

Unlike most nouveaux riches who migrated to Washington in the late nineteenth century, Stewart took great interest in the city. It was hardly, however, an altruistic interest. Stewart recognized in Washington the opportunity to make a great deal of money quickly. He and two mining cronies, Curtis Hillyer and Thomas Sunderland, formed what became known as the "California Syndicate" and invested $600,000 in cheap land at ten cents a foot near the city's northwest limits. Snickering at their gullibility, Washingtonians dubbed the isolated wasteland the "Honest Miners' Camp."

The "Honest Miners," however, had the last laugh. Stewart had made friends with "Boss" Shepherd, who had leaked to him inside information about plans that called for the city to grow to the west. To Washingtonians' surprise, the Board of Public Works began to pour money into civic improvements on the city's western frontier; streets were paved and lit, sewers were laid and covered, and a modern bridge was built, linking the area with Georgetown. Within months property values in northwest Washington skyrocketed. By 1875 land in the West End was selling for $3 to $5 a foot.

While crews of laborers planted trees and graded roads, "Stewart's Castle," an enormous red brick, Second-Empire mansion arose beside what would soon become Pacific Circle and later Dupont Circle. When the British government announced plans to build a new legation opposite Stewart's Castle, the area's high social status was guaranteed.

The massive turret of Stewart's Castle shone like a beacon for the nouveaux riches who followed, guiding them to building lots on the circle and its tributaries: Connecticut, Massachusetts, and New Hampshire Avenues. So many large, expensive mansions sprang up in the West End that by 1890 Stewart's Castle looked like a dull red dwarf amid glittering white marble Amazons. The glamorous West End quickly eclipsed the neighborhood around the White House as the center of wealth and fashion. The old historic townhouses of Lafayette Square held little charm for parvenus in thrall of five-story porte cocheres. The Beales, among the first of the nouveaux riches to settle in Washington, were among the last who chose Lafayette Square as their headquarters.

The glories of the "new Washington" were broadcast across the nation by reporters covering Grant's second inauguration in 1873. In each interview, "Boss" Shepherd extended an invitation to America's rich men and women to visit the capital and to see for themselves its gracious ambience. Even as a severe financial depression settled over the nation, the trickle of rich newcomers that had begun to seep into Washington at the close of the war became a steady stream.

The nouveaux riches wrought changes in Washington's high society that were as dramatic as their part in the city's physical transformation. Both changes were widely noted by contemporaries. In 1873 Mary Clemmer Ames, the Washington correspondent for the *New York Independent,* commented on the "new Washington": "The old, provincial, southern city is no more. From its foundations has risen another city, neither southern nor northern, but na-

In February 1876 the New York Daily Graphic printed this engraving of President Grant attending a reception in his honor given by his friends Alexander "Boss" Shepherd and Mrs. Shepherd in their corner house of Shepherd's Row. (Courtesy Historical Society of Washington, D.C.)

tional, cosmopolitan." In 1874 the Nation noted that Shepherd's improvements had begun to attract to Washington a "class of winter residents who formerly held it in great contempt." Privately, E. L. Godkin, the Nation's editor, wrote to a friend that:

> Washington seems to be becoming more and more of a resort for people who want to amuse themselves in the winter in a mild climate, and is greatly changed in all respects. . . . A great many new houses have gone up, and a general air of smartness and enterprise has come over the place.

Reporter Emily Briggs informed her readers in 1876 that "a new set of people are pressing forward to blaze in the social sky as stars of the first magnitude."[4]

While the city's boosters were delighted that so many arrivistes had accepted their invitation to winter in the capital, not all Washingtonians shared their enthusiasm. At the end of the Civil War Benjamin French, the Commissioner of Public Buildings and a thirty-year Washington resident, happily anticipated the day when the city would ease back into "its old jog trot way of life."[5] Neither French nor his neighbors had yet grasped just how completely the war had changed their town. The "jog trot" days were gone forever. As the dust kicked up by thousands of dispersing soldiers settled, it was clear that the capital's old, southern, residential elite would no longer call the social tune. Their numbers, fortunes, and reputations had been seriously eroded by the war. They would be outnumbered, outspent, and ignored by the rich newcomers. Few of the old houses that had sparkled before the war would reopen after it ended. Mrs. A. A. Parker's mansion and Mrs. Ogle Tayloe's home on Lafayette Square were among those that remained shuttered and dark.

Not surprisingly, the old Washington elite, whom Twain dubbed "the Antiques," took a dim view of newcomers' usurping their role as high society's leaders. To one Antique, the new Washington was a horrid place full of "veneer furniture and plated spoons," a place where "vulgar people who amass fortunes by successful gambling in stocks, pork, or grain can attain a great deal of cheap newspaper notoriety for their social expenditures." Washington society, complained another, was becoming infected "by a demoralizing haste to be rich, a vulgar, consuming passion for display." Mourned another in 1878, "Ill-gotten and well-gotten wealth have usurped the leadership of society."[6]

Despite such complaints, in the 1880s the stream of nouveaux riches flowing into Washington swelled with parvenus from all over, especially the Midwest. Many of these nouveaux riches shone like holiday sparklers—spectacularly but briefly. Others, however, endured. Among those whose stars remained undimmed a decade later were the McLeans of Ohio and the Leiters of Illinois.

Washington's attraction for the McLeans was twofold: the political power concentrated there appealed to self-made millionaire Washington McLean, who, unlike most nouveaux riches, was an ardent Democrat; and its high society's reputation for easy acceptance appealed to his wife, who had had little luck in buying her way into Cincinnati's elite circles. In 1880, as his interest in Ohio politics waned and his interest in national politics grew, McLean decided to move to Washington, leaving his son, John Roll McLean, in charge of the *Cincinnati Enquirer*. Like his father, however, John soon found that Washington held a greater fascination than did Cincinnati. On one of his early visits to his parents' new home, he fell in love with Emily Beale. Their marriage in 1884 represented the merger of two of Washington's richest parvenu families.

John Roll McLean was typical of those nouveaux riches for whom entertainments were a means to an end. He viewed social contacts as useful tools for

Mrs. John R. McLean (née Emily Beale) in the gallery of McLean House at McPherson Square in 1909. Her marriage to John McLean in 1884 represented the merger of two of Washington's richest parvenu families. (Courtesy Mrs. Daniel Bartlett to the Historical Society of Washington, D.C., Goode Collection)

acquiring and extending the power he hoped to wield in Washington. He thus encouraged his wife to cultivate the capital's social and political elites. For the social campaign they planned to wage, the McLeans wanted an "important" house. They hired New York architect John Russell Pope to design their Florentine Renaissance–style villa, which would cover an entire side of McPherson Square.

His combination of lavish spending and the blackmail and bribery he employed in both politics and journalism made John Roll McLean a power to be reckoned with in Washington; he became director of the American Security and Trust Company and the Riggs National Bank, president of the Washington Gas Light Company, cofounder of the Old Dominion Railway, owner of the *Washington Post*, and a major land developer.

The Leiters were among those nouveaux riches whose reasons for coming to Washington were uncomplicated. No ulterior motives lay behind their extravagant parties. They came simply to be a part of the glamorous high society of the nation's capital. Levi Leiter, who had been born in Hagerstown, Maryland, in 1834, had headed west at the age of nineteen to seek his fortune. In Chicago he and two other store clerks, Marshall Field and Potter Palmer, had opened what became that city's preeminent department store. In 1876, when she realized that her husband was worth $3 million, Mary Teresa Leiter decided that they and their three daughters should enter Chicago society. She worked indefatigably for causes popular with the city's social elite, and Levi contributed to them generously, but their efforts met with limited success.

In 1883 Mrs. Leiter announced that henceforth her family would be wintering in Washington. The capital's high society fulfilled all Mrs. Leiter's expectations: no apprenticeship was required, no millions needed to be spent on charities, there was no background check. By their second season the Leiters were listed among Washington's premier entertainers. In 1891, when they built a fifty-five-room, white brick mansion in the West End, Mrs. Leiter was dubbed "the Duchess of Dupont Circle."

During the 1890s the nouveaux riches continued to migrate to Washington. Many of this newest flock of rich newcomers, however, were birds of passage. Earlier arrivals, such as the Beales, Stewarts, McLeans, and Leiters, built or bought grand homes in the city and returned winter after winter. The newest parvenus, however, were a different migratory breed. They were members of an emerging, itinerant, national elite who chose from a long menu of cities the spot where they would alight each winter. Many rented elegant houses, dazzled the capital for a single season, and were never seen again.

Even the Panic of 1893 did not deter parvenus anxious to experience a Washington "season." Such "pork towners" as railroad-car tycoon George Pullman and other midwesterners continued to arrive from Chicago each winter. Julia Foraker, wife of wealthy Ohio Sen. Joseph Foraker, claimed that the 1890s were also the years when "the rich, spectacular New York-crowd-with-the-names came over, took big houses, gave extravagant parties, and exotically quickened the pace."[7]

During the late 1880s and 1890s the number of "Bonanza Kings" in the capital also continued to grow. California forty-niner George Hearst unabashedly purchased a Senate seat in 1886. He wanted it partially because he thought his wife, Phoebe, would enjoy Washington society. He bought her a large, almost-new mansion just off Dupont Circle, and then spent a fortune transforming the exterior from the colonial-revival to the Romanesque style she preferred.

The richest of all the westerners was Tom Walsh, the "Colorado Croesus" who had been born in Ireland in 1850. Walsh had been building railroad bridges in Massachusetts when he caught "gold fever" and headed west in 1876. In the summer of 1896 Walsh's two decades of bad luck changed; he struck gold. His Camp Bird Mine was soon producing $5,000 worth of the precious metal daily.

In 1898 Tom Walsh announced that he and his family were moving east to Washington. His doctors had advised him to seek a lower altitude, but almost any eastern city had a lower altitude than the Rocky Mountains. More likely, he and his wife had chosen Washington after hearing reports from old mining friends, such as the Hearsts, of the ready acceptance that awaited rich, generous Republicans in the capital.

Invitations to the White House were waiting when the Walshes arrived in town. President McKinley named Tom Walsh a commissioner to the Paris Exposition. Later, as Walsh sailed home from France, he laid plans for a Washington mansion commensurate with his escalating social status. When completed in 1903 at a cost of $900,000, 2020 Massachusetts Avenue contained sixty rooms—including a gilded apartment on the third floor for King Leopold of Belgium (whom Walsh had met in Paris), should the monarch make good his promise to visit.

During the 1890s Washington matured into a full-fledged city. In 1902 the Washington *Star*, in its fiftieth anniversary issue, assessed all the changes that had taken place in the capital during the preceding half century. Among the aspects that had undergone the most dramatic changes, it concluded, were the physical city itself—its streets, buildings, density, and skyline—and its high society. The *Star* attributed the chief responsibility for both transformations to the nouveaux riches, who had begun to migrate to Washington in the years after the Civil War. Washington's West End embodied both of these changes. Who would have guessed that the isolated banks of Slash Run, dotted with slaughterhouses and farmers' patches, would emerge as the city's most fashionable neighborhood, with mansions costing nearly $1 million crowding around a busy traffic circle, which had until very recently been just a hypothetical spot on L'Enfant's original design for the city? "Boss" Shepherd's improvements, the California Syndicate's promotion, William Stewart's castle, and the relocation of the British legation had combined to make the West End the most attractive place in town to the nouveau riche migrants. By the turn of the century, noted the *Star*, the "storm center of high society," the densest concentration of fashionable families, was located in the elegant blocks around Dupont Circle. The Antiques and their sedate houses on Lafayette Square, once the "eye of the social storm," had become relics of the past.[8]

Much more had changed about Washington's high society than just its "storm center." The old southern residential elite had been displaced by rich newcomers from other parts of the country. Dismissed as "antiques," "dying snails," and "cave dwellers," the old aristocrats were relegated to carping about the vulgarity of their replacements. The *Star*'s anniversary issue articulated what the beleaguered "cave dwellers" already knew: in 1902 the leaders of Washington's high society were more likely to be northern-born than southern-born, nouveau riche rather than "old rich," and recent arrivals rather than longtime residents. Of the group of women that the *Star* singled out as the leaders of turn-of-the-century Washington high society—a list that included Mrs. Leiter and Mrs. John Roll McLean—all were *arrivistes*.[9]

A small village in 1850, to which few came who did not have to and which offered little ambience, Washington by 1900 was making strong bids for inclusion on the social calendar of the national high society that was beginning to interlace the country from coast to coast. More society reporters were assigned to cover the Washington season than ever before. The *Club Fellow*, a scandal-mongering tabloid that billed itself as the "National Journal of Society," added Washington to the list of cities and spas whose rumors it spread.

The nouveaux riches helped change the look, the image, and the actual urban geography of late nineteenth-century Washington. For the most part, they viewed Washington as a site that existed solely to give them pleasure while they were in residence. They did not show as great a concern for other aspects of the city; nor did they put down roots in the capital or come to think of themselves as Washingtonians. Their view of and interest in the city was selective. Not only were they blind to the city's alley dwellings, filled with the families of freed men and women, they also managed to nudge out the poor with whom they had first shared the West End. In the 1870s the Stewarts in their castle and the British in their new legation looked out on the crude shanties of servants and laborers, mostly African Americans and immigrants from Ireland, Great Britain, and Germany. It was these West Enders who would provide the hands to build and the domestics to staff the other mansions soon to surround them.

During the 1880s, as huge homes filled the lots around Dupont Circle and its major arteries, the poorer West End residents were forced out by the rows of expensive brick and stone houses built by speculators on the lettered and numbered streets in between. By the 1890s the entire neighborhood had become so expensive that nearly all the African Americans and European immigrants had fled. The rich West Enders remaining were no longer confronted by the shanties in which their domestics, many undoubtedly also newcomers to the city, lived.[10]

The condition of the city's public education system meant little to the nouveaux riches, most of whom were in their fifties or sixties, with children ready to enter society, not elementary school. In the severe winters of 1878–79 and 1893–94, it was a committee of longtime residents that raised money to buy food, fuel, and clothing for the poor. The rich newcomers saw no obligation to support the Washington City Orphan Asylum, the Guardian Society, or any of the capital's other charitable institutions.

Washington's fledgling cultural institutions saw few parvenu dollars. A national symphony foundered for want of support; there would be no Drew or Stanford Universities, nor a Johns Hopkins Hospital in Washington. Today, the most widely recognized name of a Gilded Age arriviste is McLean, memorialized by a suburban development of expensive homes in Virginia. Among the few exceptions was Phoebe Apperson Hearst, widow of Sen. George Hearst, who founded the Parent-Teacher Association, established kindergartens in Washington, provided funds for the building of the National Cathedral School for Girls, and helped preserve Mount Vernon. Hearst Hall at the National Cathedral School and Phoebe Apperson Hearst Elementary School are testaments to her involvement with the capital city.

The nouveaux riches' general lack of concern for the city did not go unnoticed by longtime Washingtonians. Outsiders' disregard for the city's health and welfare had been an irritant since the 1800s, when members of Congress—who would descend upon the capital for a few brief months and then flee, leaving behind urban ills of their own creation—had been perceived as the chief culprits. At the century's end Bishop Henry Y. Satterlee of the Washington National Cathedral expressed the pent-up resentment of the capital's longtime residents (who made up a large portion of his Episcopal congregation) when he denounced from the pulpit those newcomers who

> while they bring wealth, magnificence, and luxury to the capital of the country, are, as a rule, actuated by no sense of civic, moral, or religious obligation regarding the welfare of the community, and it is a very serious question whether the

material advantages they bring are any compensation for the atmosphere of care-less irresponsibility which they create.[11]

While the answer to Satterlee's question was clear—the nouveaux riches were concerned primarily with their own pleasures and with each other—many Wash-ingtonians nonetheless benefited from their presence. The nouveaux riches pa-tronized local florists and caterers for their extravagant parties. They hired lo-cal domestics, gardeners, grooms, and footmen to staff their enormous homes.

Those Washingtonians who benefited most from the advent of the arriv-istes in the city were those in the building trades.[12] While nationally prominent architects such as H. H. Richardson, Stanford White, and John Russell Pope were contracted by several parvenus to design their mansions, local architects enjoyed increased patronage as well. None profited more handsomely than did Adolf Cluss, who in addition to municipal projects for the new Washington, designed Stewart's Castle, Shepherd's Row (a handsome group of large homes that included one for Alexander Shepherd and one for Cluss himself), and Portland Flats, one of the city's first luxury apartment houses. Local builders such as Robert I. Fleming and Charles A. Langley also profited. The building boom gave a boost to Washington's brick industry, as demand grew for locally produced, high-quality ornamental bricks, which had formerly been imported from Baltimore and Philadelphia. It also fueled diversification in the building trades, creating demand and higher pay for such skilled artisans as plasterers trained in elegant moldings and bricklayers able to execute intricate patterns.

Many parvenus employed a select group of local residents as social secre-taries as well. The new profession had rapidly taken hold in Washington, where the intricate official protocol made a "social pilot" especially helpful. Few young women were more expertly equipped to guide rich newcomers through the minefield of Washington etiquette than the old elite's young, well-man-nered daughters, many of whom also happened to be in need of genteel em-ployment. Ironically, while the nouveaux riches broke the old residential elite's grasp on Washington's high society, in a small way these same socially un-schooled newcomers proved the financial salvation of many a "cave dweller" offspring.

At the turn of the century, as the Star's anniversary issue went to press, the unusual porousness of Washington's high society and the steadily increas-ing power and prestige concentrated in the capital continued to draw nouveaux riches to the city. The Washington scene, by its members' accounts, was a de-lightful pond in which to make a social splash. In her memoirs, I Would Live It Again, Julia Foraker described Washington society's fin-de-siècle charm:

Shepherd's Row, on the northeast corner of K Street and Connecticut Avenue, NW, included three of the grandest row houses in Washington. The row was named for Alexander "Boss" Shepherd, who built it and reserved the largest house on the corner for himself, a monument to his efforts to develop the West End and to modernize the city. Next door lived German-American architect Adolf Cluss, who designed this row as well as several mansions for the nouveaux riches. Shepherd's Row was demolished in 1952. (Courtesy Historical Society of Washington, D.C.)

What is so rare as a Washington morning in the season? The sunshine, the soft, sweet air, the brilliant come-and-go. Smart equipage! Horses! And the whole distinguished, cosmopolitan world abroad! Everybody knew everybody else. There was a great smiling and waving of greetings, a great many informal levees held at brougham doors. I know little about the life of European queens [there were more then], but I doubt if any of them ever held gayer matinee courts than we Washington women of the 'nineties.[13]

Most of the new arrivals headed straight for the West End, where new mansions continued to squeeze onto the few remaining lots around Dupont Circle.

Vendor parked outside the Leiter mansion, on Dupont Circle at New Hampshire Avenue,
NW, in 1923. Unless he was one of the few immigrant workers living in the alleys behind the
Dupont Circle mansions, this peanut and popcorn vendor probably wheeled his wares to
the park from a considerable distance. Joseph Leiter, who in 1913 inherited the house, and his
wife entertained on a grand scale during the 1920s. (Courtesy Historical Society of Washing-
ton, D.C., Goode Collection)

Stewart's Castle, which had once stood in splendid isolation, was dwarfed and
crowded by far larger homes. In 1899 Stewart, his fortune squandered, sold the
castle to Sen. William A. Clark of Montana, another millionaire miner, who
razed the twenty-eight-year-old landmark in 1901, intending to construct a
neoclassical mansion on the site. (Clark subsequently changed his mind and
moved to New York.) As the rubble of the castle was being carted away, another beautiful home was going up at 15 Dupont Circle. Designed by Stanford
White, the white marble mansion belonged to Chicago heiress Cissy Patterson, who eventually owned the *Washington Herald*.

The "camp" begun by the "Honest Miners" in the early 1870s had flourished. Within a few years, the development of Washington's first exclusive suburbs would begin to lure rich newcomers further from the city, and the "storm center" of high society would shift once more; but from 1900 to the 1920s the West End would remain the hub of Washington high society and the most fashionable address in the city.

The area around Dupont Circle remains the richest legacy that the nineteenth-century nouveaux riches bequeathed to Washington. Their grand houses—the Patterson house, now the home of the Washington Club; the Walsh-McLean house at 2020 Massachusetts Avenue, now the Indonesian Embassy; the Blaine house on Dupont Circle, now a law firm; and the Heurich mansion on New Hampshire Avenue, now headquarters of the Historical Society of Washington, D.C.—are tangible, enduring reminders of the new high society they helped to create in this city that welcomed, indeed courted, them a century ago.

NOTES

1. Frank Carpenter, *Carp's Washington*, comp. and ed. Frances Carpenter (New York: McGraw Hill, 1960), 8–9. Carpenter, known as "Carp," was a syndicated columnist for the *Cleveland Leader* in the 1880s and 1890s.

2. Mark Twain and Charles Dudley Warner, *The Gilded Age: A Tale of Today* (1873; reprint, New York: Harper and Brothers, 1915), 1:194.

3. Carpenter, *Carp's Washington*, 110–11.

4. See Mary Clemmer Ames, *Ten Years in Washington* (Hartford: Worthington and Company, 1873), 72–74; Constance McLaughlin Green, *Washington: A History of the Capital, 1800–1950* (Princeton, N.J.: Princeton University Press, 1961), 1:355–56; Emily Edson Briggs, *The Olivia Letters* (New York: Neale Publishing Company, 1906), 357.

5. Benjamin Brown French, *Witness to the Young Republic: A Yankee's Journal, 1828–1870*, ed. Donald B. Cole and John T. McDonaugh (Hanover, N.H.: University Press of New England, 1989), 490.

6. Benjamin Perley Poor, *Perley's Reminiscences of Sixty Years in the National Metropolis*, (Tecumseh, Mich.: A. W. Mills, 1886), 2:527; George Alfred Townsend, *Washington: Outside and Inside* (Hartford: James Betts and Company, 1873), 684; Gail Hamilton [pseud.], "The Display of Washington Society," *Galaxy* 21 (June 1878): 762.

7. Julia Foraker, *I Would Live It Again* (New York: Harper and Brothers, 1932), 6–7, 190–91.

8. Fiftieth Anniversary Supplement, *Star*, 16 December 1902.

9. Ibid.

10. Walter Albano, "History of the Dupont Circle Neighborhood, Washington, D.C., 1880–1900" (M.A. thesis, University of Maryland, 1982). See also Linda

Wheeler, "Dupont Circle, Fashionable In-Town Address," in *Washington at Home*, ed. Kathryn Schneider Smith (Northridge, Va.: Windsor Publications, 1988).

    11. Satterlee quoted in Green, *Washington*, 2:193–94.

    12. Melissa McCloud, "Craftsmen and Entrepreneurs: Builders in Late Nineteenth-century Washington, D.C." (Ph.D. diss., George Washington University, 1988).

    13. Foraker, *I Would Live It Again*, 191.

ADDITIONAL READING

[Adams, Henry]. *Democracy*. New York: Henry Holt and Company, 1880.

Brooks, Noah. *Washington in Lincoln's Time*. Ed. Herbert Mitgang. Chicago: Quadrangle Books, 1971.

Jacob, Kathryn Allamong. *Capital Elites: High Society in Washington, D.C., after the Civil War*. Washington, D.C.: Smithsonian Institution Press, 1995.

Jaher, Frederick. *The Urban Establishment*. Urbana: University of Illinois Press, 1982.

Leech, Margaret. *Reveille in Washington: 1860–1865*. Garden City, N.Y.: Garden City Publishing, 1945.

6.

"For a Real Better Life"
Voices of African American Women Migrants, 1900–1930

Elizabeth Clark-Lewis

Mama and them was slaves who'da never come. Sister and older peoples left but they was born close to slavery so they'd let theyself be worked like slaves for better work. But us freeborns? We came to Washington, not just for work, but for a real better life. — MARY JOHNSON SPROW

Mary Johnson Sprow's remembrances at the age of ninety-four reflect the reality that many southern-born African American women faced after Reconstruction. From 1870 to 1914 few of the more than four million slaves released from legal slavery in the 1860s left the South. Many hoped that the land their unpaid labor had made productive for generations would one day be theirs. But that was not to be. Instead, freed people found themselves engulfed by the South's age-old social liabilities and economic backwardness. By 1900 they faced a new wave of violent intimidation: unremitting restrictions on their traditional means of survival—including sharecropping and tenant farming—and Jim Crow legislation that denied them political and civil rights.

African American women, trapped within the matrix of material deprivation and racial discrimination, took whatever work they could find to support themselves and their families. Four percent found work as skilled laborers and professionals. The vast majority, however, entered the domestic work force—a form of employment many of them regarded as little better than slavery. Nevertheless, they developed ways to challenge white supremacy in the South. Their resistance ranged from refusing to give deference to whites to participating in boycotts. After 1900 increasing numbers of African Americans turned their backs on the South and headed north. As part of the first generation of "freeborns," driven by a determination to improve their economic and

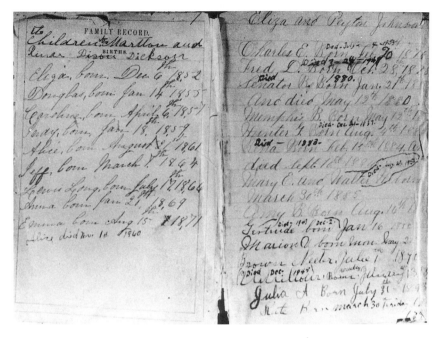

African American migrants painstakingly maintained priceless family documents. This page from a nineteenth-century Bible recorded the 1852 birth of Mary Johnson Sprow's mother, as well as the births of her nineteen sisters and brothers. (Courtesy Elizabeth Clark-Lewis)

social conditions, the eighty-two women interviewed for this study left their rural homes around the turn of the century and migrated to Washington, D.C.[1]

Early twentieth-century studies of the District repeatedly echo the belief that, as one journalist wrote in 1883, "colored people enjoy all the social and political rights that the law can give them without protest and without annoyance." Other sources, however, show the uncertainty of many African Americans as they faced the collapse of voting privileges, the dwindling of attainable economic opportunities, and daily racial humiliation.[2]

As the century turned, the press and public opinion generally attributed the progressive deterioration of African American life in the nation's capital to the failure of economic opportunity to keep pace with the "excess number" of African Americans migrating to the city. Kelly Miller, a Howard University sociologist, wondered why "Negro women from the deep South pour into Washington undeterred by the fact that jobs are difficult to obtain for colored people." In 1917 W. E. B. Du Bois listed poor pay, unjust treatment, inadequate schools, discrimination, and oppression in the South as the critical reasons for the staggering numbers of African American migrants from the South. Journalist Ray Stannard Baker, emphasizing Washington's role as the nation's capital, argued that people sought protection "near the flag."[3] Migrant Velma Davis supported Baker's interpretation. "Washington wasn't South," she explained. "It's the capital, and you had more chances for things. Jim Crow was there, but it was still not the South to us."

Davis's motives for leaving the South in 1916 reveal other reasons for female migration: personal and family considerations, which were often overlooked in the published literature. Davis recalled:

> I was sick nine years. Then my Aunt Mabel and Aunt Fannie came home for they visit and told Mama my Aunt Eva needed help with her children up here. I was trained and had worked out so I got to come. In truth, I had a cousin who was older and should have been here first. But by me being sick, I got to come first to help out my aunt and see a real doctor. Later I knew they'd put me on a job.

Like Davis, Mattie Hawkins, traveling north with family members as directed by her parents, also had migrated to the District in 1916 to assist kin. "Christmas I was told I'd go out with Sister or Cousin Rey who needed me to keep house 'cause they worked," Hawkins said. "I was gone from North Carolina before summer broke, I know."

The voices of these women reveal that self-sacrifice was an important aspect of African American female migration. Not one woman believed that her own desires had influenced migration; rather, family needs, as determined by the family's elders, had dictated the relocation. Marie Stone became visibly agitated during her interview when pressed for her own ideas and dreams related to leaving her family's Virginia farm. "Who'd have a dream? The 'me' notion wasn't thought about. . . . I was sent here to help."

White migrants, on the other hand, generally had more freedom when choosing if and where to relocate, and how to make a living once they arrived in their new city. Cathleen Uriahs of Massachusetts, whose race and education afforded her greater social mobility, was chosen to work as a typist at the Bureau of Labor in 1916. "The town is big and I spend my leisure in wonderful places, like the National Museum," she wrote with excitement in her diary. "Life, except for the summer heat, is nice for girls." In contrast, Mary Johnson Sprow wrote despairingly in her diary at about the same time that "to clean and scrub, days in and days out. . . . Work is all for a poor girl like me."[4]

Geneva Wilson, who had also arrived in Washington in 1916, had a teacher's certificate from Tuskegee Institute. She quickly learned, however, that "a kitchen was where a colored woman got work. I wished I'd stayed home, but when you're here . . . there's not a thing else for you to do. Just clean, cook, and hope for the change. . . . That didn't come 'til Roosevelt."

The transition from rural to urban living exacerbated the plight of many African American women. As one migrant lamented, "You can't grow a good potato out of bad ground and . . . dis sho is bad ground."[5] Most women described their adjustment to city life as a daily struggle. Only support from their families, extended kin, and other migrants from hometowns and home districts made their conditions bearable. Alfreda Baker, raising one dark finger for emphasis, acknowledged that: "I'd never have made it a day if my people hadn't kept me and put me to work with them. . . . That was the thing that most helped me from the first. From the first you got teachings on how to make do off a farm."

Those without such support found "making do off a farm" difficult. Athelene Walker recalled how frightened she was in her new surroundings:

> I was always lost, my stomach hurt, I could not sleep, and I was scared. I wasn't scared to be alone raising Brother's children. I did that in North Carolina. Here was different, and my talking was so bad. Everything was different, and my brother just left me. The kids took me around and helped me go here and there.

Gatha Douglass, who had received a kinder welcome, also stressed the centrality of family support to the migrant's new life:

> My sister helped me meet everyone in the house where she roomed. I met all the Virginia people living around there too. She told me how to go to the market . . . and took me on the streetcar to learn what was all around the city. . . . I bet it was two days or more of just taking me around. But then she just up and left me. It was hard.

The migrant women relied on extended kinship networks interwoven throughout their urban neighborhoods. Migrants from the same southern area tended to live close to each other, fostering socialization and mutual support. The new communities of kin and extended kin became substitutes for the family life the women had known in the rural South. Blanche Ashby smiled broadly as she related her early days in Washington:

All us from all around North Carolina was living nearby. We even went to a church full of people from Rocky Mount and all around. That Baptist church stands today! We were in the "Fredericksburg" area up from K Street. It was like home; you saw each other and helped each other. Now at a holiday or wedding— you did everything like down home. I didn't meet any people not from my home 'til I started work out [in] Chevy Chase. You just stayed with your people, at least for the first six to eight months when you got up here.

Beulah Nelson of North Carolina lived with her sister and brother in a small apartment, near Twenty-ninth and K Streets in a northwest community called "Foggy Town." She laughed deeply as she recalled their rooms "on the back with nothing to see and nothing good to smell most parts of the year. I didn't like anything but the people here who'd come from home! 'Course that's all I'd know'd!"

In addition to providing a social structure and a needed support system, the extended family network afforded the young women their first exposure to Washington employment: home-based work. Few studies explore this prevalent practice that African American migrants developed in Washington. After their arrival in the District, the initial work of more than thirty of the women interviewed was unpaid child care and household maintenance for those kin who took in the newcomers. Such home-based work sometimes included income-generating laundering or tailoring. Marie Stone described the process:

> You started working, but at your people's, not out. Now my sister was a servant in southwest [Washington] and living out, as most was. I cleaned, watched her children, and she had two people from home rooming in, so I cleaned and did for them roomers too. I got to do mending by the piece for a lady who took in washing and sewing.

Esther Lawson, who had migrated from Alabama, also had first "worked in," doing "linen piecework while at Brother's." Lawson explained that her brother's wife "worked out by the week, but I helped a washlady who lived by us and did for the childrens."

The meager earnings of all these young women went directly to the household's adult kin, continuing the pattern that prevailed in black households in the South after emancipation. "When you got up here far as money go'd," Pansylee Holmes declared sternly, "up here was just like down North Carolina. You helped out but you never saw no money you'd made. But you

Soon after she arrived in Washington in 1916, Marie Stone lived with her aunt Caroline Willis, her husband Abraham, and their four children. She did home-based work before finding employment outside. (Courtesy Elizabeth Clark-Lewis)

didn't know any better; they took all the money." Sadie Jones recalled living in an alley dwelling on Willow Tree Court and working at a neighbor's prior to her employment as a live-in servant for a white family uptown. "When you first come here you'd pull together," she said. "I helped Miss Lena, a lady who was living two doors down. But my sister got that money on Saturday when she'd come home. I guess she sent it home to Alabama. But I don't know."

Written accounts show that, apart from their local networks and their employers, newly arrived African American women from the rural South were not welcomed by the larger Washington community. Many middle- and upper-class African American residents accused the migrants of causing racial and employment problems and blamed their arrival for exploitative housing costs and the deterioration of property values within their communities. Longtime black Washingtonians generally considered the migrants to be intellectually inferior, unambitious, and crude (or "country"). Even African American businesses would not initially employ the migrants, because by District standards, they were poorly educated.[6]

The women interviewed, however, appeared to have had little awareness of the established black community's disdain. Athelene Walker squinted her eyes and looked thoughtful as she noted, "People up here made fun of you—I guess—sometime. But you wasn't allowed to be around them anyway. You didn't see or hear them much before you got to work out." Most migrants could not recall interacting with persons not "born down home" until they took outside jobs.

Southern migrants were also segregated from urban African Americans within the church—"the hard rock upon which African Americans forged and nurtured their culture," as historian Jacqueline Jones puts it.[7] They created a religious life for themselves in Washington that continued the church traditions of home but tailored them to the demands of employment. Long hours and work on Sundays thus dictated changes in worship practices, but did not lessen their importance. Official District government records disparagingly suggested that African American domestics' children "have swelled the ranks of delinquents and need to receive religious training on Sunday morning." The children were described as "delinquent, maladjusted . . . playing Konk and not in church on Sunday mornings."[8] Yet for the domestic workers and their children, not being in church on Sunday mornings did not mean not attending church at all. As Geneva Wilson explained, "Up here you'd get to church, but later in the day than down home, because nobody's servants got off 'til afternoons. . . . For a long time I didn't know churches had nothing but late Sunday and Thursday night services. That's all I went to, heard about, and saw people go to."

Migrant women also had to adjust their expectations to the reality of limited employment opportunities. From the moment they had arrived in the city, the migrant women's families reinforced the inevitability of employment as servants, acclimating them to the only jobs available to them. Expanding opportunities in clerical work that attracted white women to Washington were closed to African American women migrants, as were jobs in stores—except for those involving the most menial labor. The women quickly realized that, like their mothers and grandmothers, they would serve in "jobs they despised as much as needed." The women, with their families' assistance, could only make the most of the situation.

African American women in domestic service usually developed ways to achieve a measure of control over their lives despite the social restrictions. The first step was to master their work environment. Once they had trained sufficiently in the homes of kin, women in domestic service were generally placed by those kin in their first outside jobs. Each of the women interviewed recalled that their families had provided pre-employment information on the size of the home, the other staff members with whom they would work, and the employer's expectations of the staff. Such orientation eased the on-the-job adjustment. Velma Davis recalled that "whenever my sister and cousin were home, something about they work was talked up or complained about. Honestly, I'd been to that house a thousand times before I ever laid eyes on it. I knew everything I'd have to say, do, and be when I got there—just from what they told me over and over and over."

Family members also instructed the women migrants on any new dimensions of the household work. Five migrants who had worked for Jewish families recalled how their kin had helped them to adjust to the different cultural heritage. Zelma Powell, a devout Christian, explained

> Now long before you started work your people told you how to act when Jews hired you. You'd not do no whole lotta callin' on Jesus. That was first! Then you'd hear what they ate, they holidays, and so on. You learned all them differences long before you ever set a foot in that house. You'd know just how to do right—when you never had worked there.

Whatever the subtleties of their work environment, the women shared a vision of the "good" employer. "Good families had the money," explained Mary Sprow. "Those big houses and just everything. You'd get with them 'cause they had. Some had ten and fifteen people living in. See, these people had real money and treated us like they was used to help. Gave a tip or two and time-off pay."

The employer's social position was especially important to domestic workers for three reasons. First, domestic workers believed that through their interactions with wealthy and powerful people they could ensure employment for other southern relatives. Second, they believed that high-status employers were better able to pay salaries promptly and to provide fringe benefits, such as vacations or holiday bonuses. Third, household workers assumed that a family of significant means would have had prior experience managing household help and would, therefore, be both fair and generous.

It is thus no accident that all the women interviewed had found live-in work in the residence of a member of the Washington elite. Among their em-

African American nursemaids in Dupont Circle on a spring day in 1923. They probably lived in or commuted to this affluent area. (Photograph by Clifton Adams; courtesy Historical Society of Washington, D.C., Goode Collection)

ployers were Supreme Court justices, senators and representatives, a State Department officer, a former diplomat, and a high official at the War Department, as well as lawyers, doctors, and wealthy businesspeople. Eula Montgomery, describing her first job, revealed her understanding of the domestic worker's role in the life-styles of the well-to-do:

> He was the baby doctor for all of them congressmen and senators. He'd know them because of they childrens. . . . She [his wife] golfed with the wives of people in Congress nearly every day in summer. During cold weather they went to teas and luncheons all day for this or that charity. She was a great helper because we cooked, cleaned, and cared for all them!

Typically, Washington domestic staffs included both men and women. The men were employed as butlers, outside caretakers, chauffeurs, footmen, and

A uniformed Mary Johnson Sprow, age seventy, waits on the children's table of the Naubuck family at a Christmas party circa 1955. (Courtesy Elizabeth Clark-Lewis)

housemen (coalmen, handymen, and furnacemen). The women served as personal maids, chambermaids, parlor maids, nurses, nurses' helpers, cooks, cooks' helpers, and waitresses. In addition, some households employed nonlive-in staff, such as laundresses, tutors, and social secretaries. The women interviewed suggested that white women filled the latter two positions, which the black women considered not really "work." According to Octavia Crockett:

> Only colored people worked; did everything. Now she [the employer] sometimes had a white lady to make up her menu for her fancy parties. Or [the white employee] come there to do her invitations or Christmas cards—like that. But they didn't work. No, whites didn't do that then. I heard that before colored people came out of slavery times they used white girls as maids. But . . . I never worked with none nor saw any serving for a family.

Neddie Bass added,

> "Some people had whites [as servants], but they [the white servants] were too old to do better. Young ones? They'd I guess stay 'til a better job would come along—a store, factory, or office—somewhere would take them. But we knew we'd always do housework, and they [the employers] know'd you was there for life.

The tone of many of the women interviewed suggests that some employers had exceeded acceptable limits. "When you live in, you dress in uniform, and you must do everything but chew they food," recalled an exasperated Ann Brown. "Do this, do that, run here, run there, and when you get through—do this!" Brown had endured seven years of such badgering as she had performed the sundry domestic duties as a live-in for three families in the Dupont Circle–Massachusetts Avenue area. Nettie Edwards recalled that after working for "the mister, the mistress," and the children from dawn to late at night, the mistress had the power to keep the servants up "to all hours, worrying everybody to do this or that. And why not? She'd sleep 'til noon if she wanted to—it was you that had to be up by six-thirty."

The women interviewed also agreed that there was one striking difference between white southern households and those of Washington: many of them had received their primary training in Southern homes where the man of the house had directly supervised the servants' work and personal space. In the District, however, the women discovered that the male head was an absentee manager. Velma Davis recalled her confusion upon observing that the mistress's husband was "never home. He'd leave everything to her mainly. He'd be served and not say much. Down home they order you *and* her around. But not up here. The men? They's just there. You learned that quick."

The migrants also quickly learned that native-Washingtonian African American domestic workers had distinct advantages. Because their entire families were nearby, natives had more choices than the newcomers. The Washingtonians could—and often did—leave unpleasant employment situations without wreaking economic havoc upon their families. Migrants generally did not have this option. Dolethia Otis reported that Washington-born domestics would "get so they wouldn't take what she [the mistress] dished out. They'd leave. They had people who'd let them come on home and take a week or two to get new work. We couldn't. Once you started work you knew people in Tennessee was dependin' on those pennies you earned. You dared not quit!"

All the migrants interviewed also believed that African American women born in Washington received a superior education. Such educational advantages enabled them to become exceptions to what Neddie Bass believed white employers "knew": that black domestics would be their household servants for life. Because of native Washingtonians' education, potential employers viewed them as more acceptable for jobs as cleaning persons in the various government agencies and in local businesses. Ora Fisher, originally from North Carolina, commented:

I remember when they first started taking coloreds at the laundries or to work cleaning government buildings. Every one of them that got on came from here. They had been to school more, that was the reason. They sure couldn't work no better than us, the world knows. I know it was because they had more grades in they school up here. Most went up to [grade] six. At home they couldn't get three most of the time!

Mathilene Anderson, nearly one hundred years old, echoed Fisher's observation.

By the war [World War I] nobody in Georgetown hired a girl unless she came from down South. They knew as jobs got opened up Washington girls would leave. They could get cleaning at the Army hospital or anyplace, and they'd leave a family and never look back. . . . Pretty soon people'd only hire someone born and trained-up in the South. Them people knew you'd be there for good right along with all your people.

Despite the potential for competition, however, the migrant women consistently remarked on the absence of hostility between themselves and the native Washingtonian household workers. "Everybody got along because we was working," commented one woman. Perceived differences were food for observation rather than for antagonism, observed May Gibson of Mississippi.

We'd get together and talk about growing up on a farm and life down there. They people born up here couldn't say a thing. They didn't know about that. So they'd listen. That was the only thing I remember different about them. They didn't know about down home food too much either. But how could they? They didn't grow up down there like the rest of us [staff members] just talking late at night in the kitchen.

Knowledge of rural life appears to have been the sole interpersonal distinction the migrants made between themselves and their "citified" co-workers. Marie Stone laughed as she recalled that "a few of them had nice gardens in northeast or southwest [Washington]. But they didn't know nothing about a farm with tobacco." Other women related with pride their ability to help native coworkers put in a garden.

The annual return home that domestic workers held sacrosanct, and that forced concessions from employers dependent upon their services, illuminates the transformation of traditions forged by the migrant experience. When southern-born women became Washingtonians they did not sever ties with their place of birth. This survival strategy in turn changed the city's urban culture.

The migrant household workers interviewed delighted in telling how they had collectively compelled employers to accept the premise that work could never interfere with their annual visits back home. This change in work relations was documented in accounts of the District of Columbia Federation of Women's Clubs. In November 1916, for example, the Washington *Evening Star* reported that the organization's home-economics committee had announced a program to reward faithful domestics, now that servants were like "migratory birds" whose trips home "complicated and disheartened the household."[9] The federation urged clubwomen to give their employees such fringe benefits as post-vacation or holiday travel bonuses in order to encourage their prompt return. Many migrants thus claimed that their custom of going home every year was responsible for instituting vacations for African American household workers in general.

The women interviewed enumerated several other mainstays of survival in their new place of residence. The first was active participation in local organizations connected to home. Beginning in the early twentieth century, "home" groups formed by the women migrants helped them to understand and to cope with changes in their employment and social lives. The women who had joined Virginia's philanthropic Royal Association, for example, formed pennysavers clubs, which provided sickness and death benefits and other aid to members. Mary Johnson Sprow proudly pointed out that these women had made some of the first deposits in the Industrial Bank of Washington, an African American–owned institution established at Eleventh and U Streets, NW, in 1934. The "lowland suppers" of another migrant organization featured food sent directly from South Carolina. All the money collected at such mutual-aid fundraisers went to buy flowers for funerals or to assist with the burial expenses of migrant women from South Carolina.

In some cases the Washington-based organizations helped the home community. The Mites, a women's club whose members had come from Alabama, still sponsors one of the Washington area's largest homecoming suppers. Pro-

Marion Ricks (left), Marie Stone (center), and Julia Taylor (right) were guests at Geneva Wilson's 1956 "homecoming social" sponsored by the Mites Club. (Courtesy Elizabeth Clark-Lewis)

ceeds traditionally supported not only the club's infirm and unemployed members but also Alabama's Tuskegee Institute. Another group, whose members were from Mississippi, formed more than seventy-five years ago and still holds Mississippi fish dinners; the earnings assist young Washingtonians bound for college in that state.

To finance these rejuvenating "down home" visits, many small churches today have "third-Sunday clubs" that raise travel money for families from Virginia. Since the early 1920s two South Carolina organizations, the Georgetown Club and Sumpter (or Semper) Fidelis, have organized popular group-travel plans for the summer and Christmas holidays.

The rural southern traditions—including many culturally based spiritual beliefs—that sustained migrant women in Washington were carefully and strictly preserved. Weida Edwards noted, "I came from Florida knowing how to use a root to keep everything away that'd hurt me." Similarly, at "Carolina Day" celebrations, still an important part of many church calendars in the Washington area, participants continue to follow stringent gender-specific rules for preparing food. Many women from "down Carolina" can delineate the reproductive problems women encounter if they slaughter meat or enter a neighbor's home before noon on New Year's Day. Adhering to beliefs that ranged from "broom" etiquette to "root" energy, migrant women meticulously followed myriad southern folkways and safety tenets to address and to avoid problems encountered in their new urban environment.

From an existence begun on the bare fringes of Washington life, migrant women persevered and progressed to become an integral part of the fabric of the city. Neddie Bass proudly reported that "many a bird has been cooked by women from down home to build up Brownstone Baptist. . . . We built, from the ground up, half the D.C. churches. And the other half we keep open, warm and moving up." Indeed the impact of these migrant African American women is still apparent in today's Washington—a place where the chain of migration from the rural South to Washington continues into the next generations. Washington remains a city of communities of kin and region. Fannie King summed up migrant women's experience:

> Work, I guess, was the same. You just learned how to act different here. Having family and church and being around people from home . . . that's what helped you get set and straightened out, and let you [give] help . . . to others.

NOTES

I thank Helene Fisher and Ida Jones for contributing to the completion of this essay. I owe a special note of appreciation to Richlyn Goddard for her generous support, particularly when this project expanded to become a book, *Living In, Living Out: African American Domestics in Washington, D.C., 1910–1940*.

1. This essay is based on eighty-two interviews conducted with women who had migrated from the rural South to Washington, D.C., between 1900 and 1940. Portions of the research based on these interviews can be found in: Elizabeth Clark-Lewis, *Living In, Living Out: African American Domestics in Washington, D.C., 1910–1940* (Washington, D.C.: Smithsonian Institution Press, 1994); idem, "Duty and 'Fast Living': The Diary of Mary Johnson Sprow, Domestic Worker," *Washington History* 5, no. 1 (spring–summer 1993): 46–65; idem, "Freedom Bags," prod. Stanley Nelson and Elizabeth Clark-Lewis, Filmmakers Library, New York, 1990, videocassette; idem, "'This Work Had a' End': African-American Domestic Workers in Washington, D.C., 1910–1940," in Mary Beth Norton and Carol Groneman, eds., *To Toil the Livelong Day: America's Women at Work* (Ithaca, N.Y.: Cornell University Press, 1987); idem, *The Transition from Live-in to Day Work* (Memphis: Duke University, University of North Carolina, Memphis State University, and Spelman College

Women's Centers, 1985); and idem, "From 'Servant' to 'Dayworker': A Study of Selected Household Service Workers in Washington, D.C., 1900–1926" (Ph.D. diss., University of Maryland, 1983).

For contemporaneous studies of African American employment, see U.S. Bureau of the Census, *Negro Population in the United States, 1790–1915* (Washington, D.C.: Government Printing Office, 1918), 574; Abram Harris, "Negro Migration to the North," *Current History* 20 (September 1924): 421; and "Negro Migration," *The Crisis* 14 (May 1917): 65.

Although women constituted the largest migrant group, they are rarely included in discussions of migration or the "migrant problem"; and studies of the "servant problem" tend not to probe the experiences of African American women, despite the voluminous literature indicating that as employed persons they were concentrated in two occupational categories: "servants" and "laundresses not in laundries." For further information on the female migrant culture, see David Katzman, *Seven Days a Week: Women and Domestic Service in Industrializing America* (New York: Oxford University Press, 1978), ix, 292–94; Joseph Hill, *Women in Gainful Occupations, 1870 to 1920,* Census Monograph 9 (Washington, D.C.: Bureau of the Census, 1929), 59, 90, 96, 105, 117; and U.S. Bureau of the Census, *Negro Population.*

2. *Washington Sentinel,* 22 December 1883; Constance McLaughlin Green, *Washington: A History of the Capital, 1800–1950* (Princeton, N.J.: Princeton University Press, 1967) 2:101–10; and Mary Church Terrell, *A Colored Woman in a White World* (Washington, D.C.: Ransdell, 1940), 113–19.

3. Kelly Miller's reprinted works include *The Everlasting Stain* (New York: Arno Press, 1968); *Race Adjustment* (Miami: Mnemosyn Press, 1969); and *Out of the House of Bondage* (New York: Schocken, 1971). See also W. E. B. Du Bois, "The Migration of Negroes," *The Crisis* (June 1917): 63–65; Ray Stannard Baker, "The Negro Goes North," *World's Work* (July 1917): 314–19; and Ray Stannard Baker, *Following the Color Line* (New York: Harper, 1964): 113 and passim. For statistical information on migration, see U.S. Bureau of the Census, *Negro Population,* 502–51.

4. Diary of Cathleen Uriahs, n.d., Collection of Uriahs Family, Buffalo, N.Y.; Diary of Mary Johnson Sprow, 1916–1917, Collection of Elizabeth Clark-Lewis, Washington, D.C.

5. Quoted in Jacqueline Jones, *Labor of Love, Labor of Sorrow: Black Women, Work, and the Family from Slavery to the Present* (New York: Vintage Books, 1986), 185.

6. See Carter G. Woodson and Lorenzo Green, *The Negro Wage-Earner* (New York: Russell and Russell, 1930), 237.

7. Jones, *Labor of Love,* 165 and passim.

8. Board of Children's Guardians, *Children's History* (Washington, D.C.: Committee on the District of Columbia, 1893–1913), 4:1518, 3:1060.

9. See "Domestic Longest in Service of One Family Will Get $10.00" and "Servants Entered for Long Service Honors," *Evening Star,* 3 November 1916. See also Phyllis Palmer, "Housewife and Household Worker: Employer-Employee Relationships in the Home, 1928–1941," in Norton and Groneman, eds., *To Toil the Livelong Day,* 185, 193, and passim.

7.

*Gemeinschaft und
Gemütlichkeit*
German American
Community and Culture,
1850–1920

Mona E. Dingle

German immigrants and their descendants have contributed to Washington's social and economic life since the city's inception. Present in limited numbers before the District's formation in 1791, the German population swelled and peaked in the half-century beginning in 1850. Although German Americans had been assimilating into the English-speaking population for almost a century, a distinctly German community existed in the decades during and immediately following the fifty-year peak in German immigration. This community was defined by organizations and activities brought from the homeland and by German American patriotism for their adopted country.

The immigrants who arrived in Washington before German unification in 1871 came from a number of principalities and villages and from different religious backgrounds: Protestant, Catholic, and Jewish. Although reconstructing social relations that had existed among the various groups is difficult, evidence suggests much interaction—especially in early business, commercial, and philanthropic activities. Each group eventually established its own churches or synagogues in response to the community's changing population, and segmentation by religion and social background increased.

In the second half of the nineteenth century, Washington's native-born and immigrant German population was significant in numbers. The District's German community, however, was small in comparison with that of other cities. Germans represented 10 percent of District population, compared with 25 percent or more in Baltimore and Chicago. The community's relatively small size and the absence of either a large concentrated German enclave—as in Baltimore—or a large industrial laboring class—as in Chicago—probably hastened adaptation for Washington's German immigrants. Additionally, the lack of home rule or political representation in Congress during most of this period deterred the development of a German political bloc that elsewhere sent representatives to city councils, state legislatures, and even the Congress.

Nevertheless, between 1850 and 1920 Washington's German community—actually a series of overlapping communities—developed a distinctive identity based on acceptance of mutual responsibility, love of the German language, and nostalgia for the activities and institutions of home. The feeling of community and the acceptance of mutual responsibility, or *Gemeinschaft*, was manifest in the care accorded the entire group, especially orphans and the elderly. The community also consciously continued the somewhat boisterous social activities transported from Germany and cultivated a distinctly German sense of humor, combined in the German word *Gemütlichkeit*. The German community was at its height at the turn of the twentieth century, but thereafter began to decline for a variety of reasons. This essay traces the development of institutions that marked the period of greatest German visibility in Washington, focusing primarily on the Protestant Germans.

Even before the Revolutionary War, Alexandria, Georgetown, and Bladensburg, Maryland, had small German communities. Some of the Germans residing in Georgetown had fled Pennsylvania during the French and Indian Wars (1754–63). Among the earliest German Georgetowners were armorers John and Henry Yost, who had a contract to supply weapons to the Continental Army during the Revolutionary War. Other Germans in Georgetown and Alexandria were engaged in such trades as shipping, road building, tanning, and brewing.

There was one abortive attempt during the colonial period to establish a German community in the area that would become the District. In 1768 Jacob Funk (or Funck) acquired 500 acres of land in what is now the Foggy Bottom neighborhood. Funk divided part of the land into lots for building purposes. This area, which ran north from what was then the northern bank of the Potomac (now filled in as Constitution Avenue) to H Street, and from a line between Eighteenth and Nineteenth Streets to Twenty-third Street, was divided into 287 lots and named Hamburgh. To increase the attraction for German purchasers, Funk reserved two lots for German Protestant congregations.

More than half of the purchasers (judging by their surnames) were Germans, who bought land in one- or two-lot segments; but several buyers, including the English landowner Robert Peter, acquired larger segments. The only recorded building in Hamburgh during the colonial period, however, was a house erected for Funk himself, and it is not known whether he ever actually lived in it. German landowners apparently preferred to remain in the settled communities of Georgetown, Alexandria, and Bladensburg rather than to pioneer in unsettled territory.

In the late 1780s, as it became apparent that the lower Potomac River was a major contender for the permanent U.S. capital, George Washington had his agents attempt to buy up lots in Hamburgh and Georgetown before speculators could drive up prices. Thomas Jefferson's original plans for the federal city called for constructing all major government buildings in or near Hamburgh. After the precise location of the District was determined, however, L'Enfant's plan placed the major buildings to the east of Hamburgh.[1] No government buildings were thus constructed within the Hamburgh boundaries (the White House was erected just to the east).

Residential building in Hamburgh was slow. Christian Hines, who had lived in the area as a young boy in about 1800, later recalled that there had been fewer than a dozen houses in Hamburgh at the turn of the century, and apparently only one had been inhabited by a German. The German community of Hamburgh thus never developed as Funk had planned.

German immigration to Washington increased after 1790, when a skilled labor shortage caused the government to advertise for German and Scottish laborers to work on the Capitol. Hines noted that an old farmhouse or barn near Twenty-fifth Street, NW, had served as a rooming house for some of the first German workers, and various businesses along Pennsylvania Avenue and F Street had had German proprietors. Later immigrants came to work on the canals and the railroads, as well as on government and residential buildings. Some may have been directed to the city by the German Society of Baltimore, which had begun offering free employment placement at that major port of entry in 1845. By 1850, however, there were only 1,415 German-born residents living in the District, barely 3 percent of the total population of just over 51,000.[2]

Although religion was not a major factor in German workers' decision to immigrate to Washington or to other cities in the nineteenth century, the early German settlers were religious, and the development of German-language churches became an important activity. In 1833 a group of German Protestants living in Washington and Georgetown took possession of two Hamburgh lots, which Funk had originally set aside for religious purposes, in order to build the Concordia German Evangelical Church at Twentieth and G Streets. Protestant churches in many German states at this time had been united in state churches, and Concordia followed this model, serving both Lutheran and Reformed (Calvinist) congregants. As Washington's first German church and the

This rare photograph of the original Concordia Lutheran Evangelical Church at Twentieth and G Streets, NW, was taken before 1890, when the church was razed to make way for a grander church to accommodate the German community's growth. (Courtesy Historical Society of Washington, D.C., House Collection)

first German church in the District to offer regular services on an ongoing basis, Concordia was central to the German Protestant community's development for many years.[3] (Indeed, Concordia remains today the only visible remnant of German intentions to develop Foggy Bottom.) Although few Germans lived in its immediate vicinity, the church drew both Georgetown residents to the west and the German residents who were increasingly settling to the east.

German Catholics and Jews also built religious institutions during the antebellum period. In 1845 a group of Catholics organized St. Mary's German Catholic Church at Fifth and H Streets, NW, in a neighborhood where Germans were beginning to congregate. Although Irish Catholic churches had existed before this time, the Germans had shown some reluctance to worship in them. Moreover, their English-language services presented problems for German-speaking newcomers. German Jews in 1857 chartered the Washington Hebrew Congregation, which several years later acquired its own building.

German churches left other imprints on the cityscape, including their cemeteries. Limited lot sizes for religious institutions and restrictions on the location of burial plots, as well as high nineteenth-century death rates, required that burial grounds be located some distance from the sanctuaries themselves. Concordia Church established a cemetery at Fourth and G Streets, NE, which was subsequently abandoned for the larger Prospect Hill Cemetery on North Capitol Street and Lincoln Road. St. Mary's German Catholic Church established a cemetery in the Lincoln Road area after its burial grounds at North Capitol and O Streets became inadequate.

For the city's German-speaking residents, religious institutions provided social as well as spiritual support. They offered new arrivals a German-speaking environment, help in learning English, information about places to live and to work, and financial assistance. Church benevolent societies aided the ill or indigent: the Evangelical Society of Concordia Church was organized shortly after 1833, and St. Mary's German Catholic Church organized St. Joseph's Liebesbund in 1845.

Before the Civil War District public schools mainly served children of low-income whites and received little public support. To meet the demand for German children's education and religious instruction in the German language, the early German churches established schools, which remained in existence for varying periods of time. The Evangelical Society of Concordia Church created a German school in 1842; and St. Mary's followed suit in 1853. Later, some churches organized literary and musical societies and published German-language newspapers.

After 1850 German immigration increased rapidly, spurred in part by the failure of the 1848 revolution in Germany to bring about democratic reforms. Some political activists emigrated in fear for their personal safety, others in disappointment that reforms had not been realized. Most of the new wave of German immigrants settled in cities such as Baltimore or Chicago, where large German communities already existed. Some, however, made their way to Washington. In the ten-year period between 1850 and 1860, the District's German-born population more than doubled to 3,222, or 4 percent of the city's population.

The Germans who lived in Washington during the 1850s were generally antislavery, and many were prepared to fight for the Union cause. The refugees from the 1848 revolution, the "forty-eighters," believed strongly in economic and political freedom, and were neither slaveowners themselves nor dependent upon the plantation economy. The Eighth Battalion of D.C. Volunteers, organized in 1861 for the defense of Washington, included a company of German sharpshooters. Other German residents fought in the war on far-flung battle-fields. Although immigration decreased sharply during the Civil War, German migration into Washington from other parts of the United States grew in response to new, war-related employment opportunities.

Once the Civil War was over, German immigration to the United States resumed its growth. After slowing during the depression of the 1870s it reached a peak of 960,000 in the five-year period of 1881 through 1885. Immigration subsequently declined as industrialization and social legislation within Germany created new employment opportunities there. Nonetheless, by 1900 the District had 5,866 German-born residents and 11,913 German Americans with at least one German-born parent, or 8 percent of the total population of 219,000. The Germans who came to Washington during this period benefited from the presence of friends and family and the support institutions that earlier settlers had created.

The German American community of the second half of the nineteenth century was transformed by both the characteristics and the sheer numbers of the new immigrants. German immigrants generally had a trade, although most started with limited resources. German men were often trained as carpenters, woodworkers, machinists, model makers, brewers, butchers, jewelers, printers, leather workers, and tailors. Others had operated inns, taverns, or shops in their homeland, and tried their hand at small businesses in Washington. German women had fewer choices. Some established themselves as seamstresses or milliners, a few were teachers, and many worked as live-in servants before getting married.

Although many young men immigrated alone, extended families sometimes came together. Some came directly to Washington after landing in Baltimore or New York. Others traveled extensively in Europe and in the United States before settling in the District. Brewer and real-estate investor Christian Heurich, for example, had completed his formal schooling in Germany at the age of fourteen, after which he had apprenticed for two years in brewing and butchering. He had then spent seven years alternately working and traveling about Europe on foot, before coming to the United States in 1866 to join his sister in Baltimore. There he had worked briefly for a brewer, then traveled to the Midwest, shipped out as a sailor on a ship captained by his brother-in-law, and worked again as a brewery employee in Baltimore, before investing in a Washington brewery. Heurich's career proved unusually successful. He died a rich man at age 102. His life in some ways, however, typifies the Protestant German American immigrant pattern for Washington.[4]

Most immigrants initially lived in crowded quarters. The generous lots of

Portrait of Christian Heurich. (Courtesy Historical Society of Washington, D.C., House Collection)

L'Enfant's original plan for a grand federal city had been subdivided, and the houses built on them frequently combined a business with living quarters for a husband, wife, several children, and various other relatives. Children remained at home until they married, and servants frequently lived with the families they served. Unmarried employees were often housed in their places of employment. Single persons who resided with neither relatives nor employers lived in boardinghouses.

Many German households employed German servants (whose passages had sometimes been prearranged), although both Irish and African American servants were also found in those homes. Wives assumed full responsibility for household management. In 1880 Christian Heurich lived in his Twentieth Street brewery with his first wife, a female servant, a nephew from Germany, and twelve other male employees of German birth or parentage. Between 1892 and 1895 Heurich built a large brewery near the Potomac River and a mansion on New Hampshire Avenue near Dupont Circle. For both projects he relied

119

Christian Heurich's brewery in 1883. (Courtesy Historical Society of Washington, D.C., House Collection)

heavily on the work of German builders and artisans. Heurich's new brewery complex included living quarters for employees. At the family home, Heurich's third wife (he was twice widowed) managed a staff of both German and African American servants. The living arrangements for the domestic staff reveal the social relations of the time. German women servants lived on the house's top floor, while African American servants lived out in the community. The two groups also ate at separate tables in a basement room near the kitchen.[5]

It was relatively easy in the late nineteenth century for an artisan or merchant to set up a business with minimal capital. Heurich had begun his entrepreneurial career in 1872, when he and a partner had taken over a brewery and tavern on Twentieth Street at a cost of $1,500 for the furnishings and $150 per month for rent.[6] Several of Heurich's brewery employees eventually went into business themselves as restauranteurs or barkeepers. With houses designed to double as workplaces, carpenters could work from their homes without difficulty. Small retail businesses could be carried out on the ground floors of two-

Kloeppinger's Bakery, at Sixth and G Streets, NW, in 1900. Standing in the doorway are Will Kloeppinger (left) and Chris Stolpp (right) (Courtesy Historical Society of Washington, D.C., Ockershausen-Kloeppinger Collection)

story dwellings. Butchers could rent stalls in the Centre Market or in one of the other city markets. Although married women were expected to be full-time homemakers, many undoubtedly also assisted in their husbands' businesses.

Opportunities for German artisans and merchants were not confined to the German community. The federal government's growth and the city's expansion and modernization after the Civil War created opportunities within the larger community. Carpenters and woodworkers were in demand both to work on public buildings and to construct housing for government functionaries and new or part-time residents—including the millionaire western miners and eastern financiers, who had come to participate in the Washington social season or to lobby the government. These affluent newcomers created markets for German jewelers, butchers, bakers, and clothing and housewares merchants. Innkeepers, too, provided a necessary service for the transient population.

As the economy grew, successful shop owners and businesspeople built near Dupont Circle or acquired second stores along the developing business corridors of Pennsylvania Avenue, Seventh Street, and, later, F Street, NW. The fancy-goods establishment that was opened in 1860 on Seventh Street, NW, between H and I Streets by young Gustav and Max Lansburgh, sons of an early cantor at the Washington Hebrew Congregation, developed into one of Washington's leading department stores, serving the community for nearly a century. Other German-owned department stores included Saks and Company, located on Seventh Street from 1867 to 1932, and the Hecht Company, at Seventh and F Streets from 1896 to 1985, and now at Twelfth and G Streets, NW.

The carpenter August Grass became a successful cabinetmaker, with an establishment near Dupont Circle, and John G. Meyers and Adolf Cluss were among the Washington architects whose services were in high demand. In addition to investing in expanding their own establishments, successful German businesspeople also invested in Washington's rapidly appreciating real estate. Heurich, for example, invested his brewery earnings in rental real estate, enabling him to maintain a lavish life-style even during Prohibition, when his brewery closed.

While some German businesspeople became wealthy, and some German workers opened their own businesses, others remained employees. Washington was not the site of the industrial and shipping activities that employed much immigrant labor in other cities. Nevertheless, workers in such local businesses as breweries were beginning to organize to improve labor conditions around the turn of the century. They were challenging the relationships established by businesspeople—often those who were self-made. As early as 1883 Heurich's wholesale customers were boycotted for selling his beer because he had purchased supplies from a nonunion company. Heurich reluctantly agreed to purchase from union suppliers providing his own brewery workers remained unaffiliated with a union. Heurich justified his position later, commenting, "I did not come to America in order to be a slave."[7] His facilities eventually unionized, but conflict between brewers and organized brewery workers, drivers, and machinists continued up to the eve of Prohibition.[8]

The German immigrant community included not only employers, entrepreneurs, artisans, and wage workers, but also those who pursued the learned professions. For example, when the increase in the number of churches and the limited number of American-trained ministers and priests led to a prolonged shortage, the gap was filled by eligible European-trained German immigrants. German community leaders included, in addition to businesspeople, a limited number of teachers, lawyers, civil servants, and writers. Frank Claudy, a turn-of-the-century Pension Office employee, wrote poetry and translated Goethe's *Faust* from German into English. Christian Strack, editor of the German-language *Washington Journal* for twenty-five years, conducted research on early Germans in the Washington area. Simon Wolf, the Jewish activist who had come to the United States at the age of twelve, had read law in Ohio before becoming an influential lawyer, as well as a recorder of deeds and justice of the peace for the District.

German businesspeople and intellectuals appear repeatedly on contemporary lists of officers and boards of churches, charitable institutions, and clubs, which expanded in number and increased activities in the second half of the nineteenth century. Neither income level nor religious affiliation was a major discriminatory factor. Small businesspeople sat with the wealthy, and—except in the case of religious institutions—Jews and less religious freethinkers served with Christians.

Formal German community leadership was overwhelmingly masculine. Although ladies' auxiliaries were active in raising funds and caring for the poor, women's representation on governing boards was rare, and many organizations excluded female participation altogether except at social functions. Quite exceptional were the inclusion of one woman on the building committee for the Concordia Church parsonage in 1847, and of two women, representatives of Concordia's Ladies' Auxiliary and Sewing Circle, on the committee overseeing the building of the new German Orphan Asylum in Anacostia, which was dedicated in 1890. In 1887 Grace Reformed Church received a proposal to appoint four or more deaconesses—mainly to take care of ladies' aid duties—but no action was taken.

As the German population increased and expanded into southwest Washington and Capitol Hill, and north along Seventh Street, new churches were organized. They in turn served as a nucleus for further population growth. Some churches were also founded as a result of differences between existing churches on doctrinal, organizational, or language issues. The spawning of new institutions provides an indication of the German population's growing diversity. For example, at the time of Concordia's organization in the early 1830s, the desirability of conducting services in the German language was unquestioned. As early as 1843, however, St. Paul's Lutheran Church at Eleventh and H Streets, NW, was organized as an English-language church. Dissatisfied with the merger of Lutheran and Reformed churches, a group of German Lutherans in 1851 established the German-language Trinity Lutheran Church of the Un-altered Augsburg Confession, which was to maintain all rites practiced by Mar-tin Luther himself. In 1867 German Calvinist congregants organized the First Reformed Church. In the mid-1870s St. Stephen's Reformed Church (later Grace Reformed Church) was organized, and Grace Lutheran Church split from Trinity Lutheran Church. Both St. Stephen's and Grace Lutheran sub-stituted English for German-language services. By 1894 there were fifteen Lutheran and Reformed churches in the District. In 1868 St. Mary's German Catholic Church organized a daughter church, St. Joseph's Church in north-east Washington, a few blocks from the Capitol. In 1886, however, St. Joseph's became an English-language parish, leaving St. Mary's as the only parish church for Washington's German-speaking Catholics.

As the nineteenth century ended, religious institutions—although their numbers and activities grew—were less important as agents binding the non-Jewish German community. The concentration of secular mutual-interest as-sociations in the community increased, as was also true of the larger American society. Germans readily formed associations based on birthplace, occupation, special interests, and entertainment. Community activities brought a vast ar-ray of organizations together for celebration or philanthropic work. Some or-ganizations that had been church-affiliated at their origins severed those ties. Many groups increasingly welcomed people from other ethnic backgrounds as members or as charity recipients.

The German American community was particularly committed to caring for orphans and the aged. For example, the German Orphan Asylum was or-ganized in 1879 as the German Protestant Orphan Asylum at the instigation of the Ladies' Aid Society of the Concordia Church. The church's pastor, Mar-tin Kratt, was named president. Controversy ensued when Kratt purchased a permanent site for the orphanage in Anacostia in 1880 and signed for a sub-stantial mortgage. Orphanage supporters then demanded and received Kratt's resignation, but subsequently decided to honor his commitment, raising funds to construct the facility. In 1882 a new charter was issued for the German Or-phan Asylum Association of the District of Columbia. While St. Mary's Church continued to support a Catholic asylum, the German Orphan Asylum took in orphans without regard to religion.

Among those supporting the German Orphan Asylum was Simon Wolf, the lawyer and Jewish activist who was instrumental in clearing the title to the Anacostia land and in obtaining federal support for the asylum's construction and operations. Christian Heurich was also a major supporter. Additionally, in 1900 Christian Ruppert bequeathed $5,000 to the asylum in exchange for sufficient land on which to construct the Christian and Eleanora Ruppert Home for the Aged and Infirm. According to the terms of Ruppert's will, all indigent white Washington residents were eligible for admission, although preference was to be given to Germans.[9]

Other newly organized groups combined fellowship and common interests with mutual-support activities. Among the German localities represented by separate associations were Bavaria, Baden, and Hesse, as well as German Switzerland. Butchers, brewers, and bookbinders also had their own organizations. In addition, Germans organized building associations, savings banks, and insurance companies, which initially served mainly German customers. In 1861 a group of German businesspeople organized the Oriental Building Association to provide a secure haven for savings and a source of low-interest housing loans, particularly for low-income Germans. Organizations with similar aims, the German American Building Association and the Northern Liberty German American Building Association, were later established.

The peculiarly German entertainment associations included the singing societies (*Gesangvereine*), the gymnastic societies (*Turnvereine*), and the marksmanship societies (*Schützenvereine*). At first these groups organized for competition on a local and regional level. Later, some acquired their own halls or parks, with facilities for a wide range of recreational activities for German men, women, and children and, in some cases, for non-Germans as well. Since many families lived in cramped quarters, the availability of halls and parks for recreational purposes was particularly important to the community. Most of the activities involved beer-drinking—frequently on Sundays—which placed the German community in ongoing conflict with prohibitionists and Sunday blue law advocates.

Numerous German singing societies appeared sporadically. Those with the longest existence are the Washington Sängerbund, the Arion Society, and the Germania Männerchor. These were all-male societies at their inception, although they sometimes sang with female groups. The Washington Sängerbund was organized in 1851 by the choir director and several choir members of Concordia Church but had no official church connection. Members simply wished to sing German secular songs. The society participated in local singing contests, as well as in those in Baltimore, Philadelphia, and New York. After the Civil War the Washington Sängerbund's activities expanded along with the German American population. The society occasionally sang with the Euphonia Damenchor and in 1881 admitted women as members of a *Gemischtechor*.

The Washington Sängerbund met regularly above Dismer's Restaurant at

Dismer's Restaurant, at 708 K Street, NW, circa 1885. This was the first home of the Washington Sängerbund, which met at this German-owned restaurant from 1874 to 1893. Note members peering at the photographer from the windows of the second floor hall. (Courtesy of Mrs. Gretchen Onachila, reprinted with permission from Frank H. Pierce, The Washington Saengerbund: A History of German Song and German Culture in the Nation's Capital [Washington, D.C.: Washington Saengerbund, 1981])

708 K Street, NW, from 1874 until 1893, when it acquired its own hall at 314 C Street, NW. The hall ultimately included dining facilities, a bowling alley, and a ballroom. Major activities had to be held in even larger facilities. Membership came to include about fifty active (singing) members and more than eight hundred others—including many of Washington's business leaders and intellectuals. German men and women participated in educational, literary, and musical evenings, and German children enjoyed their own masquerade balls. Typical German activities included the *Narrensitzungen* (fools' sessions), in which otherwise dignified businesspeople and intellectuals dressed in ridiculous clothing, employed extravagant props, and poked fun at fellow members through elaborate skits or narratives.[10]

A gathering at Schützenpark, a popular and important meeting place for Washington's diverse German community at the end of the nineteenth century. (Courtesy Historical Society of Washington, D.C.)

Turnvereine, another typically German transplant, evolved from the gymnastic, educational, and political societies introduced into Prussia by Friedrich Ludwig Jahn in the early nineteenth century. In the United States the *Turnvereine* attracted refugees from the 1848 revolution who were still active in political and military matters as well as gymnastics. American *Turnvereine* tended to comprise a larger proportion of working-class members than did other German social organizations. Before the Civil War the *Turnvereine* attracted the unfortunate attention of nativist organizations, such as the Know-Nothings, that opposed all "foreign" and immigrant institutions. In the late nineteenth century the "American Turners," as they came to be called, were active in promoting social legislation to benefit the working class, and also in teaching gymnastics and German in the schools. Like the Washington Sängerbund, the Columbia Turnverein had its own hall and competed in singing as well as athletic events.[11]

Schützenpark, on Seventh Street Road (now Georgia Avenue) above Morris Avenue (now Hobart Street), was headquarters for the activities of the marksmanship society (Schützenverein). In addition to facilities for marksmanship competitions, Schützenpark housed a hotel, a band pavilion, dining facilities, and a bowling green. It was also the site of the annual summer *Schützenfest* and the German Day celebration early in October, as well as a variety of other special events.

On all major occasions—whether regular annual activities, special celebrations, or new-building dedications—major German organizations banded together, frequently marching to the Schützenpark or to a dedication site. Associations also frequently assisted with fund-raising activities for other German organizations. The Deutscher Centralverein, formed by seventeen smaller associations for the celebration of German Day in 1890, became a permanent union, eventually encompassing most of the city's German clubs. The Washington Sängerbund, however, remained separate.

German Americans were proud of their heritage and wished to pass it on to their children. Those who were able to do so visited their homeland and made financial contributions to citizens there. Although he left most of his property to the local church, Father Matthew Alig of St. Mary's German Catholic Church from 1845 until his death in 1882 also left a remembrance to his native German church. Christian Heurich made no fewer than twenty-one trips to Germany from 1882 to 1914, usually combining trips to Haina and Roemhild, his boyhood homes, with sojourns at fashionable spas and other travels. He donated a public bathhouse to Roemhild in 1912, and at various times made contributions for memorials, fire departments, kindergartens, and orphanages in Roemhild and Haina.

German Americans thus retained their ties to the German language and culture. Loyalty, however, was often to a principality or a village—a Nassau or a Baden, an Augsburg or a Haina—rather than to the emergent German Empire. Older German Americans had come to the United States before the empire was created, and some of the more recent immigrants had left in protest against the policies of Bismarck's Germany.

Grateful for the New World's opportunities, Germans were frequently the most demonstrative of patriots. Christian Heurich referred to Germany as his mother and the United States as his bride, but added that if forced to choose, he would select his bride.[12] Many older German residents were loyal members of the Veterans of the Eighth Battalion of D.C. Volunteers of 1861. A number of German organizations marched in Lincoln's funeral procession and in Garfield's inaugural parade; the Washington Sängerbund performed at President Taft's twenty-fifth wedding anniversary and, with other *Gesangvereine*, enthusiastically welcomed Theodore Roosevelt to a *Nordöstlicher Sängerbund* banquet in Baltimore. Taking particular pride in Germans who had made contributions to American democracy, they erected in Schützenpark a statue of Baron Friedrich Wilhelm von Steuben of Revolutionary War fame, and promoted the placement of his statue in Lafayette Square. The Washington Sängerbund serenaded and conferred honorary membership on Carl Schurz, a refugee from the 1848 revolution who later became a Civil War hero, Missouri senator, cabinet officer under President Hayes, and journalist.

Germans in Washington apparently accepted that business transactions required English. Consequently German American businesspeople spoke English in business dealings and belonged to the English-speaking Board of Trade and various lodges. Initially, major celebrations by German organizations included speeches or sermons in English as well as German. There was no language barrier to exclude citizens of other ethnic backgrounds from participating in celebrations at Schützenpark. Irish clergy joined in ground-breaking ceremonies at St. Mary's Church. German clubs admitted English-speaking members who shared an appreciation for German entertainment and humor; one of the most popular members of the business-dominated Washington Sängerbund was the British-born labor leader Samuel Gompers. By the end of the nineteenth century many German organizations' records were kept in English. Indicative of that trend, in 1883 the *Washington Journal,* by then the only surviving German-language newspaper, changed from daily to weekly publication.

Most children of German immigrants were fluent in English. Some spoke German only at home with their parents. As the District's public-school system improved after the Civil War, German parents enrolled their children, causing a number of private German schools to close. Public schools also began to offer German classes, in response to American universities' new language requirements for entrance and graduation. The revised 1892 curriculum for District high schools, for example, required four years of German for science students. Only later were other modern languages introduced into the curriculum as electives.

Despite, and even because of, these signs of cultural success, the German American community in the late 1800s began a period of decline—a decline that was hastened after the outbreak of World War I. One major factor was the changing demographics: German immigration to the United States declined sharply after the mid-1880s. The children and grandchildren of immigrants who had come in earlier years lacked the special attachment to the German language and institutions felt by those who had grown up in Germany. Tastes in entertainment differed as well. Although incomplete, records of the Washington Sängerbund reveal few instances of membership by two generations of the same family. Furthermore, the early tendency toward occupational concentration began to diminish. Some sons still entered their fathers' businesses, but many entered the professions, becoming lawyers or civil servants rather than butchers, brewers, and carpenters. The federal government's expansion after the Civil War and into the twentieth century encouraged that trend.

The German community also became increasingly dispersed geographically. German immigrants or, more frequently, their children, moved from cramped quarters in the early sites of German settlement to more comfortable areas in northwest and northeast Washington, and later, to suburban Maryland. Interethnic marriages became more common. Old church affiliations were broken. Suburban Protestants frequently joined Episcopal churches if Lutheran churches were not convenient, and English-language Lutheran churches received non-German members. Trinity Lutheran Church of the Unaltered Augsburg Confession, at Fourth and E Streets, NW, closed its school in 1902, citing the movement of most of its congregants to new neighborhoods. Washington's 1914 city directory reveals a relatively small proportion of German names in the formerly German neighborhood around the church.

The late nineteenth-century temperance movement also contributed to the transformation of the German American community. For many Germans, beer drinking had been an important element in social life as well as a source of direct and indirect livelihood. Because of Washington's unusual status as a federal enclave under direct congressional control, pressure for prohibition was stronger than might otherwise have been expected in an eastern city with an active German population. National temperance groups brought their campaigns to Congress, and congressmen from conservative southern and western states reflected the beliefs of their constituents.

Moreover, as occurred throughout the city's history, congressional control over the District led to legislation that did not necessarily reflect residents' views. Alcohol license fees were increased; and restrictions were placed on areas where alcoholic beverages could be sold, on the number of licensed establishments, on Sunday sales, and on sales by clubs to nonmembers. The Schützenpark closed after beer sales there were prohibited because of its proximity to the Soldiers Home. When sale of alcoholic beverages was completely prohibited in the District after 31 October 1917, both the activities and the finances of various German organizations were greatly diminished. The end of the manufacture and sale of beer led to the Washington brewing industry's demise. The closing of legal bars and saloons also obstructed one of the most common routes to entrepreneurship for German Americans.

Political developments in Germany and responses to them in the United States also affected relations between the German community and the larger American society. Germany was no longer a loose federation of states after the 1870s, but rather a centralized power with proven military might as a result of the Franco-Prussian War, and thus increasingly feared by other European powers. Most Germans in the United States had cheered the unification of Germany in 1871, although some had expressed disapproval from the outset at the role of Bismarck and the Prussian monarchy. Functionaries of the unified German nation began cultivating ties with Germans living in the United States, and the German-American Bund, formed in 1900, encouraged its members to form closer ties with the German Empire.

The Bund, political at its inception, promoted the maintenance of the German language and culture, while paying lip service to American patriotism. Its praise for German virtues and its criticisms of America were frequently strident. The Bund's affiliates included an organization of German army veterans, many of whom retained their loyalty to the German Empire. Washington's chapter became a member of the Deutscher Centralverein and hosted the 1911 Bund convention. Leaders of Washington's German community, however, divorced themselves from the Bund's more extreme views. The Washington Sängerbund, for example, refused to participate in the 1904 dedication of a statue of Frederick the Great attended by Prussian army officers. Nevertheless, the Bund's expressed views on the superiority of German culture negatively influenced some Americans' attitudes toward the German community.

The approach of war increased tensions between the German and the non-German communities in Washington, as it did elsewhere in America. Although the United States remained nominally neutral until 1917, the government's sympathies and that of the dominant press were clearly with the Allies and against Germany. Washington's German Americans protested arms exports to the Allies, and the German American press attempted to correct what it considered misrepresentations of the German army's progress in Europe. Such efforts only fanned the larger American society's doubts concerning German Americans' loyalty. When the United States entered the war, prejudice against German Americans—and everything German—burgeoned. The U.S. government imposed legal restrictions on German American activities, particularly on those of resident aliens and their families.

German Americans who had previously recognized no conflict between patriotism for the United States and pride in their heritage were saddened by the wartime divisions. At World War I's outbreak in Europe, Christian Strack, former editor of the *Washington Journal*, was writing a comprehensive history of Germans in the Washington area. Unable to confront the conflict between the United States and Germany, he burned all his papers, collapsed, and died shortly thereafter. Christian Heurich, who spent the war years in his Washington home and his Maryland farm, found himself falsely accused by the press of sending radio messages to the enemy, constructing foundations for cannons to bombard the Capitol, and even tunneling between his townhome and that of Edith Galt (then being courted by Woodrow Wilson) in order to assassinate the president. Heurich's younger daughter, a public-school student who had previously attributed no special significance to her German parentage, reported many years later that she had believed her schoolmates were avoiding her: "Well, they'd run away and say, 'You can't play with her, she's a Hun!' "[13]

The German Americans in Washington, as elsewhere, responded to accusations of disloyalty by lowering their visibility and giving up all use of the German language in public places. German-language sermons were no longer delivered in St. Mary's and Concordia Churches, and the Washington Sängerbund decreased its activities and substituted English for German titles of its activities. Some Germans anglicized either the spelling or the pronunciation of their names. Demand for German-language courses in the schools declined sharply, and in 1918 they were eliminated from the curriculum.

In late 1917 the District became one of the areas declared to be out of bounds for enemy aliens, or all unnaturalized immigrants from hostile nations, as well as their wives—even if American-born. While not all longtime residents who had neglected to apply for U.S. citizenship were forced to leave, some newly arrived Germans were sent to the Midwest. One incident of forced removal involved Father John R. Roth, a priest at St. Mary's German Catholic Church since 1911, who was forced to exchange positions with a priest in Buckeystown, Maryland. Additionally, the charter that Congress had granted to the German-American Bund was revoked at this time.

After the Allied victory in Europe formal restrictions on Germans in the United States were lifted, although prejudices were not so easily overcome. Concordia Church resumed German-language sermons, and Father Roth returned to St. Mary's. The Washington Sängerbund resumed some of its canceled activities, but attendance was low. It was soon forced to sell its hall in the early 1920s and to suspend all activities at the decade's end. A woman who had been a young child in the mid-1920s reported many years later, "[W]hen I went around to the Clubhouse, there was a *Sängerbund*, a few elderly men who sang and rehearsed there."[14]

Although the German American community ceased to be the distinct entity it had been before World War I, its descendants continue to live and to work throughout the Washington metropolitan area. German contributions to nineteenth-century Washington's built environment are still visible in the Eastern Market, the Smithsonian Institution's Arts and Industries Building, and the Sumner and Franklin Schools—all designed by Adolf Cluss—and in row houses built by Cluss and August Getz. Heurich's mansion is open to the public as a house museum that demonstrates the skill of German builders and artisans, and the life-styles of prosperous German families of the pre–World War I period. Older families have joined with more recent arrivals in such organizations as the Washington Sängerbund and the German Heritage Society, which have been organized or revived since World War II. These and other examples remind us of the distinct German community that once existed in the nation's capital.

NOTES

1. Priscilla W. McNeil, "Rock Creek Hundred: Land Conveyed for the Federal City," *Washington History* 3, no. 1 (spring/summer 1991): 39.

2. On the earliest German population, see Heinrich Christian Strack, *"Die ersten Deutschen in nachmaligen District Columbia," Deutsche historische Gesellschaft für den District Columbia* 1, no. 1 (1905): 19–55; no. 2 (1905): 11–46; and Christian Hines, *Early Recollections of Washington City* (Washington, D.C.: Chronicle Book and Job Print, 1866).

3. Until German churches were organized in the capital, celebration of religious holidays or personal rites required a trip to Baltimore—a major journey in those days. Baltimore, with its older and larger German population, continued to serve as the regional headquarters for the major German churches, and relations between the Baltimore and Washington churches remained close. See also Concordia Lutheran Evangelical Church, *Centenary Jubilee of Concordia Lutheran Evangelical Church, Washington, D.C., 1933* (Washington, D.C.: *Washington Journal* and Typographers, 1933). On the history of the German Catholic church, see Saint Mary's Church of the Mother of God, *History of St. Mary's Church of the Mother of God, Washington, D.C., 1845–1945*, 2nd. ed. with centennial celebration and additional historical information (Washington, D.C., 1946). Names of many churches underwent minor changes during the period this chapter covers.

4. See Christian Heurich, *Aus meinem Leben, 1842–1934; von Haina in Thueringen nach Washington in den Vereinigten Staaten von Amerika; Lebenslauf und Errinerungen* (Washington, D.C.: 1934); Milton Rubincam, "Mr. Christian Heurich and His Mansion," *Records of the Columbia Historical Society* 60–62 (1962): 167–205; and Candace Shireman, "The Rise of Christian Heurich and His Mansion," *Washington History* 5, no. 1 (spring/summer 1993): 4–28.

5. Karla Heurich Harrison, interview by Sarah Heald, 30 December 1987, Washington, D.C., House Museum Research Collection, Historical Society of Washington, D.C., Washington, D.C.

6. Heurich, *Aus meinem Leben*, 23.

7. Ibid., 33.

8. Labor relations turned particularly bitter when organized brewers, firemen, and drivers struck the major Washington brewers in 1915, the year after the effective date of the Jones-Works Bill, which severely restricted the sale of alcoholic beverages in the District. Brewery contracts permitted the firing of workers to the extent that the Jones-Works Bill reduced business, and workers demanded repeal of that provision. Drivers also demanded a continuation of their guaranteed income and the hiring of union helpers instead of the nonunion workers, most of them African Americans, who had been previously employed. When the brewers hired nonunion workers to replace the strikers, union members organized a boycott of "scab" beer and picketed taverns selling it. The strike was finally settled on 10 March 1916, almost a year after its beginning and less than two years before complete Prohibition in the District; the *Evening Star* reported mutual satisfaction between brewery owners and workers but did not report the terms of the agreement. See *Evening Star*, 23 March 1915 to 11 March 1916. The story of the relations between African American and white workers in the competition for scarce jobs, evident in this labor dispute, has yet to be researched.

9. See German Orphan Asylum, Washington, D.C., *Illustrated History of the German Orphan Asylum, Washington, D.C., Fiftieth Anniversary, 1878–1929* (Washington, D.C.: *Washington Journal*, 1929), and *The Christian and Eleanora Ruppert Home for Aged and Indigent Residents of the District of Columbia* (n.p., n.d.).

10. Frank H. Pierce, *The Washington Saengerbund: A History of German Song and German Culture in the Nation's Capital* (Washington, D.C.: Washington Saengerbund, 1981).

11. When a group returning from a *Turnverein* gymnastics festival in Kentucky in 1856 was attacked, police arrested the victims rather than their attackers. The Turnerbund (national headquarters of the *Turnvereine*) administration cited the fear of such attacks as a reason for moving the 1856 national convention to Pittsburgh from Washington, which in 1854 had elected Know-Nothing mayor John Towers. A large dissident group from the Turnerbund met in Washington without incident, however. At the outbreak of the Civil War the two *Turnvereine* then located in Washington organized the company of German volunteers that participated in defending the city. On 19 and 20 April 1861, Southern sympathizers, angered by the Turnerbund's support of the Union cause, attacked and vandalized the Turnerbund national headquarters and its printer's offices, which were both located in Baltimore. See Henry Christian Anton Metzner, *History of the American Turners*, rev. ed. (Indianapolis: Executive Committee of the North American Gymnastic Union, 1911).

12. Heurich, *Aus meinem Leben*, 33.

13. Karla Heurich Harrison, interview by Walter Camp Jr., 30 July 1985, Washington, D.C., in House Museum Research Collection, Historical Society of Washington, D.C., Washington, D.C.

14. Quoted in Pierce, *The Washington Saengerbund*, 82.

8.

Washington's Jewish Community
Separate But Not Apart

Hasia R. Diner and
Steven J. Diner

In September 1852 *The Occident*, a national Jewish newspaper published in Philadelphia, reported that "the Israelites have bought a piece of land for a syn-agogue . . . a congregation organized in the Capital of the United States."[1] In many respects it was an unremarkable event. As Jewish immigrants from cen-tral Europe flowed into the United States in substantial numbers after 1820, literally hundreds of small Jewish communities sprang up in towns and cities across the country. A small group of Jews would arrive in a community, strug-gle to build the first tenuous institutions, and manage to carve a respected place for themselves in the life of the larger community. In Washington, as else-where, Jews from central and, later, eastern Europe built a dazzling array of communal institutions that set them apart from other Washingtonians as Jews; at the same time they climbed out of their poverty to relative comfort and sought to prove their loyalty to their new American home.

Washington's Jewish community was nonetheless different from other Jewish communities, just as Washington differed from other American cities. With an economy based largely on the federal government's presence, the cap-ital never became a major trade or industrial city and, therefore, did not attract massive numbers of European newcomers. Jews who made their way to Wash-ington were not the garment workers, cap makers, cigar rollers, and machine operators who flocked to New York, Boston, Philadelphia, Baltimore, and Chicago. The unionism and radicalism that swept through the Jewish working classes in other cities barely reared its head in the federal city. Before the 1930s most of Washington's Jewish newcomers, seeking to become shopkeepers, mi-grated to the capital from other American cities. To conduct business, one had to know English and to understand American ways to a greater degree than one did to operate a sewing machine in a factory where Jewish bosses and fellow Jewish workers spoke Yiddish. Thus, most Jews in Washington were further down the road to Americanization than were those in other cities. After the 1930s successive generations of educated, American-born Jews came to Washington to work for the government or in the private professional sector.

Jewish immigrants in the federal city faced a distinctive situation in other ways as well. Because the city was home to large numbers of African Americans, Jews in Washington confronted issues of slavery, rigid segregation, and racism earlier and more concretely than did their coreligionists in the North. Politically, District residents also differed from other Americans, particularly after 1874, when they lost self-government. For the next hundred years, no local officeholders or political bosses appealed to Jewish or any other ethnic voters. If Jews sought political help, they had to turn to Congress. On several occasions, for example, Congress intervened in deciding who could declare that meat sold in Washington butcher shops was kosher. And Washington's Jews, by virtue of their residency in the nation's capital, took on political tasks for American Jews as a whole. For Washington Jews, local and national politics were intertwined.

The first Jews who made their way to the District did not concern themselves with community building or service to the Jewish people. Lone individuals, such as Isaac Polock, who had arrived in Washington in 1795, came to seek economic opportunity. Polock, a land speculator from Savannah, Georgia, has been credited with building the Chain Bridge as well as the first six nongovernment buildings near the President's House.[2]

Other Jews trickled into Washington. The most notable were Capt. Alfred Mordecai—a military officer assigned in 1839 to the U.S. Army's Ordnance Board, who later would become a hero in the Mexican-American War—and David Levy Yulee and Charles Lewis Levin, members of Congress from Florida and Pennsylvania respectively. The 1847 Washington city directory listed some twenty-five Jewish residents, most of whom were immigrants from Bavaria.

In 1852 twenty-one members of Washington's small Jewish community met at the home of H. Lisberg, on Twenty-first Street and Pennsylvania Avenue, to found the Washington Hebrew Congregation. Under the leadership of Capt. Jonas Phillips Levy, another hero of the Mexican-American War, the founding members, representing most of Washington's Jews, decided to organize formally and submitted to Congress a petition for a congregational charter. Congress responded that "all the rights, privileges and immunities heretofore granted by law to the Christian churches in the City of Washington, be, and the same hereby are, extended to the Hebrew Congregation of the said city."[3]

Although the number of Washington's Jewish residents grew slowly, by 1861 there were enough Jewish children to warrant a school. The Washington Hebrew Elementary School educated most Jewish children in Hebrew, English, and German until the beginning of the next decade. Washington's Bavarian-born Jews continued to speak and to read German, and some felt themselves a part of Washington's small German community as well. The city's first German-language newspaper, *The Columbia,* was launched by a Jew, Max Cohenheim.

Like many German Jews elsewhere, members of the Washington Hebrew Congregation soon embraced the Jewish "Reform" movement, which sought to modernize and to Americanize Jewish worship and religious practices. The *haftorah,* the weekly prophetic reading, was intoned in German rather than in Hebrew, and English-language sermons were offered from the pulpit (there were no sermons in traditional Jewish worship). By the decade's end, the congregation had ended the traditional practice of segregating women in the balcony, and had used a pipe organ at Sabbath services on Eighth Street between H and I Streets, NW, despite the fact that orthodox Jewish law prohibited such practices. These and other innovations proved too much for the congregation's religious conservatives, who subsequently split from Washington Hebrew in 1876 to found a traditional synagogue, the Adas Israel Congregation.

The city grew rapidly during the Civil War, and by war's end some three hundred Jewish families lived permanently in the capital. Many had come because of the expansion of commercial opportunities during the years of fighting. Simon Wolf, who had emigrated from Bavaria at the age of twelve and had previously lived in Cleveland, became an important Republican politician, served as the District's recorder of deeds, and sat on the city's charity and education boards. Adolphus Solomons, a successful bookseller and printer, had been Daniel Webster's dispatch bearer and a founder of the American Red Cross.

Most Jews earned a living as independent merchants and skilled artisans, and a few as government clerks. Because Jews generally preferred to live near their shops, Jewish residential clusters developed in Georgetown at the hub of Thirty-first and Bridge Streets (now M Street), on Fourth Street in southwest Washington, and especially near the Seventh Street, NW, shopping corridor. A correspondent for New York's *Jewish Messenger* described "at least a half-dozen kosher restaurants [in the capital], all of which appear to flourish."[4] Jewish-owned boardinghouses sprang up, and one proprietor emblazoned his advertisement with the word "kosher."

Hundreds of Jewish soldiers served in the Union Army. Care for the wounded among them devolved upon Washington's Jews. Wolf pleaded unsuccessfully with the Jewish community as a whole to create a military hospital for Jews. Instead, it was the women of the Washington Hebrew Congregation who ultimately tended to the ill and dying Jewish soldiers; The *Jewish Messenger* reported, "they have looked after the interment of many co-religionists who had no other claim upon them than that of brotherhood."[5]

From the 1860s on Washington's Jews used their proximity to the center of government to express solidarity with oppressed Jews elsewhere. Representing the Union of American Hebrew Congregations (the national organization of reform synagogues) and the Independent Order of B'nai B'rith (the largest Jewish fraternal organization in America), Simon Wolf spoke out against the mistreatment of Jews in Russia and Rumania, and, with limited success, used his personal influence with a succession of presidents and secretaries of state on their behalf.

Prominent Jews also used their influence to defend fellow American Jews, interceding, for example, on behalf of Jewish applicants seeking employment with federal agencies. One young Jewish woman wanted a job with a government department but as a Sabbath observer could not work on Saturdays. With Wolf's negotiation, she won an exemption from working on her traditional "day of rest." During the Civil War, when Gen. Ulysses S. Grant ordered all Jews expelled from the lower Mississippi Valley area as war profiteers, Wolf and Solomons lodged a vigorous protest, and President Abraham Lincoln reversed Grant's order.

The ranks of the District's Jewish population began to swell in the 1880s—not with Bavarians and other central Europeans, but with Yiddish-speaking Jews from Russia, Poland, and Rumania, who soon became the majority. In 1878, for example, no more than 1,500 Jews made their home in Washington, yet by 1905 the number had jumped to 3,500 and, by 1918, to 10,000. These increases were attributable almost completely to the influx of eastern European immigrants.

Southwest Washington had been home in the pre-1890s to a small group of German Jewish merchants. By the beginning of the twentieth century, however, it housed a large eastern European Jewish community. Newcomers also settled in Georgetown's Jewish enclave, as well as on H Street, NE, and Seventh Street, NW. They established synagogues such as Ohev Shalom (1886), Talmud Torah (1889), Voliner Anshe Sford (1907), Tifereth Israel (1907), Kesher Israel (1910), Ezras Yisrael (1911), and Southeast Hebrew (1919). Each synagogue attracted not only the residents of a particular District neighborhood, but also those who hailed from a specific region of eastern Europe.

The synagogues also provided an array of social services: a *gemilath chesed*

Meyer Aaron Wolpe and his daughter in front of his store on Four and One-Half Street, SW, circa 1913. (Courtesy Jewish Historical Society of Greater Washington)

(free-loan) society, a sick fund, a widows' fund, free schooling, and burial privileges. A longtime member of Talmud Torah recalled that at a 1920 meeting someone emphasized the importance of having what he called a "Gemilas Chesed Society."

> The folks passed around the hat and raised $104.06 to fund a Free Loan Society. The folks from the Sick Benefit Fund apparently had some extra cash, and they put in $59—and a nickel—and the Ladies Auxiliary added $105.85, so they started off with $268.96 and the Free Loan was formalized.[6]

The limited resources that the *shul* (synagogue) could provide in emergencies did not always suffice. In 1907 a number of the immigrant congregations created a Hebrew Free Loan Society to provide emergency loans and to help new immigrants establish small businesses. Similarly, the Hebrew Beneficial Asso-

One of the first institutions Jews formed when they established new communities was a Chevra Kadisha, *or burial society. Members of Talmud Torah's chevra kadisha in 1928 gathered in a private home for the mandatory annual meeting. (Courtesy Jewish Historical Society of Greater Washington)*

ciation was founded by immigrant Jews to provide burials for the poor, and in 1915, the Hebrew Home for the Aged opened.

Peddling had been one of the few occupations open to Jews in eastern Europe, and it served as a stepping-stone into business for many District newcomers. The absence of large numbers of immigrants as compared with other cities, and the difficulties and discriminatory practices encountered by many black Washingtonians when they ventured into small business, broadened opportunities for these Jews. Sixteen-year-old Isaac Ottenberg, for example, had left Landau, Germany, for New York in 1866. There he had learned the bakery trade and had married. He then moved with his family to Washington in 1869, when he opened a bakery on Four and One-Half Street in southwest Washington.[7] Jacob Love had emigrated from Russia in 1905 to escape the mil-

140

itary draft. After having been smuggled across the Rumanian border, he came to Washington, where he had two brothers, and opened a shoe-repair shop. According to his son:

> Papa's first shoe-repair shop was in northwest [Washington]. After it was destroyed by fire in 1907 he opened another in northeast [Washington], at 1407 H Street. There were Jewish neighbors: Sam Brown, a tailor, next door; Abraham Levy, a dry-goods merchant, down the block next to Joe Goldman's cleaning and pressing shop; and Mr. Bortnick, who had a junkyard across the street. In the next block were Mr. Kaplan, the butcher, and Henry Futrovsky, who ran a delicatessen.

The younger Love added that during World War I his father had expanded his business, opening a shoe store next door to the repair shop. "Mom now became a shoe saleslady [and], as we children grew older, each of us had to help in the store."

Isaac Turover, who had arrived in New York in 1907 at the age of fifteen, had been born in Warsaw, and had later moved with his family to Antwerp. Having taken one manual job after another in New York, Philadelphia, Norfolk, Virginia, Portsmouth, Virginia, and Baltimore, Turover had worked as a diamond cutter, a Western Union messenger, a waiter, a steelworker, and a laborer in a cotton mill. He had developed an avid interest in chess and, as a member of a Baltimore chess club, had competed against a Washington club. According to the family story, "The [non-Jewish] captain of the Washington team [who was] a scion of a prominent Washington family" had offered Turover a job in Washington so he could play on the city's chess team. Turover subsequently got a job in a Washington lumber business, worked his way up, and soon founded a successful lumber company of his own.

Robert Silverman, at age fifteen, had arrived in New York from Pinsk, Russia, in 1900, and had found work as a cigar maker. He had an uncle who ran a grocery store in southwest Washington, and in 1912 he decided to move to the nation's capital to start a grocery business. According to Silverman's son, "He thought the [grocery] business had a future—certainly better than licking tobacco leaves all day," but he did not want to settle in the southwest neighborhood. "So he borrowed his uncle's bike and cased the city, [settling] in the country [at] Georgia Avenue and Kenyon Street, NW."

With entrepreneurial immigrants such as Ottenberg, Love, Turover, and Silverman coming to Washington, American-born, well-established Jews of German origin did not display the same hostility and embarrassment toward the newcomers as did their counterparts in Jewish communities in other cities.

Opening day at Jacob Cohen's store, at 628 Third Street, NE, in 1905. Cohen (center), a twenty-four-year-old bachelor, had opened his first independent business venture just over a year after leaving Russia. He was so proud of his new business that he hired a photographer to record the event. (Courtesy Jewish Historical Society of Greater Washington)

Additionally, in developing Jewish social services, German Jews did not conflict with the eastern Europeans, as they did elsewhere. Jews in Washington, for purposes of self-help and philanthropy, generally ignored the geographic distinctions of Europe. For example, eastern European immigrants founded the Hebrew Home for the Aged, but the German Jews provided the bulk of its financial support. Representatives of both groups served on its board of directors.

One of the early presidents of the United Hebrew Charities, founded by Washington Hebrew Congregation members to aid poor Jewish immigrants, was Minnie Goldsmith, of the prominent local Lansburgh department-store family. Despite her "elite" origins, she won the admiration of the immigrants because she displayed profound respect for their values. "Aunt Minnie," as they affectionately called her, always worked closely with immigrants in establishing and operating a host of charitable institutions. She even helped found the

The baseball team of the Young Men's Hebrew Association in 1913. Manager Eddie Rosenblum is seated in the middle. (Courtesy Jewish Historical Society of Greater Washington)

Hebrew Relief Society, an immigrant-run institution that rivaled the United Hebrew Charities.

Other city-wide institutions also developed: B'nai B'rith lodges, a nucleus of the Zionist movement, a chapter of the National Council of Jewish Women, and a tiny Hadassah women's social-service club linked specific Jewish constituencies across the city. In 1911 the Young Men's Hebrew Association (YMHA), dedicated to providing a place where all Jewish men—regardless of background and religious orientation—could meet and relax, opened its doors. Some two years later Washington's Jewish women created the Young Women's Hebrew Association (YWHA). Athletics, outings, theatricals, dinners, and dances occupied both groups.

The "Ys" demonstrated the need for a broader-based recreational and cultural center for Washington's Jews. Local Jewish leaders met with several national Jewish figures in the spring of 1921 to discuss ways to transform the Washington YMHA/YWHA and its modest, squat building on Eleventh Street and Pennsylvania Avenue, NW, into a full-fledged Jewish Community Center. The New York elite provided some of the funding to make this possible. In any other city such an enterprise would have been entirely a matter for the local community, but national Jewish leaders wanted the symbol of a strong Jewish presence in the capital. To them, the community-center movement represented the emergence of a self-confident Americanized Jewry, proud of its inheritance and its blending of cultural, athletic, and recreational programming.

In city after city, such Jewish community centers cropped up; and their planners opted for structures conspicuously placed where all could see these symbols of the Jewish presence in America. It was thus pertinent that Washington have a highly visible symbol of Jewish Americanization. Indeed, local Jews and those across the nation took pride in the fact that President Calvin Coolidge spoke at the cornerstone-laying exercises in May 1925 for the monumental building set to go up at Sixteenth and Q Streets, NW, a central location for serving the various Jewish neighborhoods yet symbolically near the White House.

The Jewish Community Center faced an attractive area of comfortable houses and tree-lined streets along Sixteenth Street. It was to District neighborhoods such as Shepherd Park, Riggs Park, upper Georgia Avenue, and upper Fourteenth Street that the increasingly middle-class Jewish community began to move, abandoning areas of first and second settlement, such as southwest Washington. As Jews moved, synagogues sold off their modest buildings and built larger, more lofty structures in the new Jewish neighborhoods.

Washington grew rapidly and changed profoundly in the 1930s and 1940s, as the Great Depression, the New Deal, and World War II vastly expanded the place of government in American life. Those two decades also witnessed the two most important events in 2,000 years of Jewish history: the Holocaust and the emergence of a Jewish national state in Israel.

Since the days of Simon Wolf, Jews had pleaded with the U.S. government to provide assistance to their sisters and brothers in distress abroad. The ravages of the First World War upon the Jewish communities of eastern Europe had given rise to the Joint Distribution Committee, a decidedly non-Zionist body, while the flowering of Zionism in America and the burgeoning Jewish settlements in Palestine propelled other American Jews to found the United Palestine Appeal. The rise of Hitler and the decision of the British to bar Jewish emigration to Palestine further heightened American Jews' international concerns. In 1937 the Joint Distribution Committee and the United Palestine

Interior of Ezras Israel synagogue on Eighth Street, NE, circa 1937. (Courtesy Jewish Historical Society of Greater Washington)

Appeal overcame their ideological differences and joined together to form the United Jewish Appeal.

Washington thus took on even greater significance in American Jewish affairs. In the late 1930s the B'nai B'rith decided to move its national headquarters to Washington, and over the course of the next decades the American Jewish Committee, the American Jewish Congress, the National Council of Jewish Women, and the Jewish Labor Committee set up national offices in the capital. A cadre of national Jewish agency officials now worked and lived in the District.

At the same time, Jews from around the country were flocking to the capital, not only for small-business opportunities but to work in the expanding federal government. Supreme Court Justice Felix Frankfurter and labor-leader Sidney Hillman, for example, played decisive roles in national affairs, and Jewish social scientists, engineers, social workers, lawyers, accountants, and bureaucrats were becoming as commonplace in Washington as Jewish grocers and haberdashers had been a generation earlier.

As the Washington Jewish community grew, organizational life became more centralized. In 1933, at the height of the Great Depression, the various synagogue charities and other social-service groups united to form the Jewish Social Service Agency. In 1937 the United Jewish Appeal initiated coordination of all local fundraising for overseas and some local purposes. The Jewish Community Council was founded in 1938 as a form of democratically elected, voluntary Jewish "government" empowered to address issues of concern to the entire Jewish community and to coordinate Jews' relations with non-Jewish Washington.

During and after World War II Washington's Jewish population continued to grow rapidly, reaching about 40,000 by 1956. In that year, the Jewish Community Council published *The Jewish Population of Greater Washington in 1956*, which noted that District Jews were concentrated in four separate areas: 22,200 in northwest Washington east of Rock Creek Park; 8,100 in northeast Washington; 6,400 west of Rock Creek Park; and 3,600 in southeast-southwest Washington. Washington Jews were relatively affluent, highly educated, and strongly involved in both the Jewish and the larger Washington communities.

As Washington's Jews moved increasingly into the American mainstream, many continued to display strong group identity, albeit in new ways. The children of orthodox parents often joined conservative or reform congregations, and they remained eager for their children to receive some degree of exposure to Jewish learning. In 1944 the Hebrew Academy, a day school offering both a secular and a Judaic curriculum, was opened on Sixteenth and Decatur Streets. Synagogue afternoon and Sunday schools were bursting at the seams with children. The Jewish Community Council provided teaching materials and other services to Jewish schools and established the Educators' Council, which attempted to standardize the Jewish school calendar year, pay scales, and credentials for teachers. The council conducted a survey of Jewish education in the District, and every autumn placed advertisements in the local press reminding Jewish parents to register their children for some kind of Jewish education. Each year the council rented out a large hall and held an assembly, bringing together all the city's Jewish schoolchildren for a special program. In 1965 the Educators' Council became an independent Board of Jewish Education.

The Jewish Community Center on Sixteenth Street remained a hub of activity for children, teens, and adults. It sponsored a rooftop day camp, athletic events, concerts, lectures, and classes, and turned over space to the D.C. Police Department, the Selective Service Boards, and other government agencies. Synagogues used rooms for classes, and the local chapter of the Poale Zion—the Labor Zionist movement—donated printing equipment to the center.

The community council eventually became the major coordinator of Jewish involvement in secular community issues. Isaac Franck, executive director of the council from 1948 to 1975, and the council's lay leaders put the Jewish community squarely behind the civil rights movement. In 1950 the council joined with other organizations in filing an amicus curiae brief in the historic 1950 Thompson's Restaurant case, which tested the constitutionality of segregation in the District's public accommodations. In 1963 Franck coordinated all local Jewish involvement in the historic March on Washington. Congregations also sponsored special Sabbath services dedicated to promoting civil rights. The council early on supported home rule and used its national parent body, the National Community Relations Advisory Council (NCRAC), to lobby for this political goal.

While Jews forged an alliance with black and white integrationists on civil rights and home rule, they also did not hesitate to pursue their own local political agenda. The Jewish Community Council and local rabbis lodged protests with the District public schools, for example, when school officials chose to begin the academic year on Yom Kippur, the Jewish day of atonement, or when they introduced Christian-oriented programs into the classrooms. The Jewish Community Council and local rabbis complained to the local press when housing and employment advertisements contained covert or overt anti-Semitic statements, and persuaded the owners of local television stations to provide airtime for Jewish programs.

Jewish Washington also remained a focal point for national and international Jewish events. For example, while American Jews everywhere could celebrate Israel's 14 May 1948 declaration of its independence, Jews in Washington could join in a joyous street celebration on Massachusetts Avenue at the U.S. headquarters of the Jewish Agency (the shadow government of preindependence Israel).

Washington's Jewish community was not without internal strains, however. Norman Gerstenfeld, rabbi of the prestigious Washington Hebrew Congregation, refused to recognize the primacy of the Jewish Community Council in the field of Jewish community relations, for example, not only because he considered himself to be *the* rabbi of the city, but also because he opposed the council's Zionist orientation. During the 1950s, under the shadow of McCarthyism, the Jewish Community Council denied membership to the Jewish People's Fraternal Order, a Communist group. Despite such tensions, the decade saw the maturation of an urban-based Jewish community that was self-consciously distinct from yet integrated into the larger local community.

Even as Jewish institutional life in Washington flowered in the 1950s,

Jews joined the general migration out of the city and into the suburbs. This relocation transformed Washington from the hub of Jewish life to the periphery, as Jewish institutions and the bulk of the area's rapidly growing Jewish population shifted to Montgomery County, Maryland. Numerous synagogues decided to follow the population into the suburban areas, where most new congregations built synagogues. When a new Jewish day school was conceived in 1975, it was considered—much to the chagrin of District Jewish parents—a foregone conclusion that it would be located in Montgomery County. Even the Jewish Community Council leadership eventually decided that while it would keep its offices in the city, its board of directors and delegate assembly would hold many of their meetings at suburban synagogues to ensure better attendance. Significantly, in 1969 the Jewish Community Center sold its Sixteenth Street building and relocated, along with the offices of the Jewish Social Service Agency and the Hebrew Home for the Aged, to a massive complex in Rockville, thus shifting the center of Jewish institutional life to the northwestern suburbs.

It is impossible to say exactly how many Jews moved from the city to the suburbs, and how quickly they did so. In the 1960s the Washington metropolitan area grew by almost a million people, and most white newcomers to the area chose to live in the suburbs, where housing was less expensive, services were thought to be better, and new highways—such as the Capital Beltway, which opened in 1965—facilitated commuting. Newcomers accounted for most of the growth of new Jewish communities in Silver Spring, Wheaton, Rockville, and Potomac, Maryland.

When their incomes allowed, Jews in American cities, like their non-Jewish counterparts, had always readily opted for better homes farther from the city's core and its older housing stock. For some longtime Washington Jewish families, the exodus to the Maryland suburbs marked just one more step in a continual quest for self-improvement that might have begun on the H Street corridor, with several stops along Sixteenth Street, then Silver Spring, and finally to Rockville or Potomac. Some undoubtedly left after school desegregation in 1954, or when their neighborhoods became predominantly black in the following decade. However, a considerable number of Jews in the changing upper Sixteenth Street neighborhoods refused to take part in the white flight. Quite a few, including journalist and civil-rights activist Marvin Caplan, helped to form Neighbors, Inc., which worked to maintain racial integration in Shepherd Park and surrounding northwest neighborhoods.

Many of the remaining Jewish-owned small businesses in older, central-city neighborhoods were destroyed in the 1968 riots that followed the assassi-nation of Martin Luther King Jr. The United Jewish Appeal, the Jewish Social Services Agency, the Jewish Community Council, and the Hebrew Free Loan Association attempted to help entrepreneurs hit by the riots, but few of the merchants had any intention of reopening in their old neighborhoods.

Despite the fact that the focus of Jewish institutional life had moved be-yond the beltway, events of importance to Jews still took place within the Dis-trict. Jews worldwide agitated on behalf of Soviet Jewry, but only in Washing-ton could a daily vigil at noon, started in 1970, be mounted by the Jewish Community Council in front of the Soviet Embassy. (After twenty-one unin-terrupted years, the daily vigil finally ended on 27 January 1991, with the dis-solution of the Union of Soviet Socialist Republics.) Indeed, the community council and other local organizations continued to play a national role in Jew-ish affairs. The council, for example, helped to argue the Jewish case that the Christmas display of a crèche on the grounds of the Ellipse violated the pre-cept regarding separation of church and state. Similarly, in 1988, when Mikhail Gorbachev came to Washington, the D.C. Jewish Community Council dropped all its ongoing activities to plan for a massive demonstration on behalf of Soviet Jewry; the event brought a quarter of a million people to the Mall.

Even as the locus of local Jewish life shifted to Maryland, with suburban Jewish organizations viewing Washington as important primarily for national political issues, evidence indicated that a significant number of Jews still re-mained strongly committed to the city. Some institutions affirmatively chose not to leave Washington. In Tifereth Israel, on upper Sixteenth Street, mem-bers who positively wanted to belong to a city congregation in a racially mixed area triumphed over those who were leaving the city and wanted their syna-gogue to go with them. Similarly, Ohev Shalom–Talmud Torah in Shepherd Park, Kesher Israel in Georgetown, and Adas Israel Congregation on Quebec Street all decided to remain in the city.

Other new city institutions were also blossoming, even as the major Jew-ish institutions moved to Maryland. In the early 1960s, when southwest Wash-ington urban-renewal officials offered land for religious institutions, Isaac Franck of the Jewish Community Council and other Jewish leaders contacted Jewish residents of the new neighborhood. Out of meetings among council leaders, Jewish homeowners and tenants, and the urban renewal agency was born a new urban synagogue, Temple Micah. After years of sharing a building with a church in southwest, in 1995 it completed construction of its own build-ing on Wisconsin Avenue, NW. Jews for Urban Justice, an activist group of the late 1960s that was committed to civil rights and economic justice, gave birth in 1971 to the Fabrangen Fellowship, a thriving, member-run congregation that opted to have neither its own building nor its own rabbi.

In 1967 the newly organized Jewish Historical Society of Greater Washington undertook restoration of the old Adas Israel building on Seventh and G Streets, NW. Built in 1876, the synagogue was the first in the District. After the congregation had moved to larger quarters in 1907, the building served as a Greek Orthodox church and then, ironically, as the Dixie Pig Carry-Out. Slated for demolition, the building, through the efforts of the Jewish Historical Society of Greater Washington, was designated a historic landmark. In December 1969 it was put on rollers and, as traffic came to a standstill, moved to the corner of Third and G Streets. In the following years the building was restored, refurbished with many of the original furnishings, and transformed into an historical museum, showing that Jews had long been a part of the city's life.

By the 1980s these modest developments had flowered into a consciously city-oriented renaissance in Washington Jewish life. The Jewish Studies Center, launched in 1979, offered a thriving program of classes in Hebrew, the Bible, the Talmud, and Jewish history and culture to adults across the city. Gay and lesbian Jews started a new congregation, Beth Mishpachah. In 1988 the Adas Israel Congregation began a Jewish elementary day school, the first Washington alternative to the five similar schools in the Maryland suburbs.

The most dramatic sign of a resurgent and assertive Jewish community in the city, however, was the founding of a new District of Columbia Jewish Community Center. Created in 1979 as an outreach branch of the Rockville center, it put together, in rented facilities across the city, a substantial program of cultural arts, Judaic learning, volunteer social-service projects, athletics, and lectures on political issues. The center also ran a summer day camp, a day-care center, and an after-school program. From cramped, rented headquarters at Dupont Circle, the center grew more rapidly than anyone had imagined and quickly became a full-service, albeit nontraditional, center with special appeal to the large number of young, single Jewish professionals in the District—most of whom did not belong to synagogues or other Jewish organizations.

At the May 1985 annual meeting, held symbolically in the old and now-abandoned building on Sixteenth Street, the District of Columbia Jewish Community Center declared its independence from the parent body in Rockville. No longer would it—or, by extension, its Washington membership—see itself as an urban outpost of a suburban community. In 1988 the center began negotiations with District officials to buy back the Sixteenth Street building, which had been sold to the city in 1969, in order to transform it once

Walter Washington (center), mayor of the District, and Isaac Franck (left), director of the Jewish Community Council, dance the hora at a May 1973 celebration of Israel's twenty-fifth anniversary. (Courtesy Jewish Community Council of Greater Washington)

again into a hub of Jewish life in Washington. Center officials signed the sales contract in the summer of 1990 and began total renovation in 1995.

It is difficult to know whether the 1980s renaissance of Jewish life in Washington stemmed from a significant growth in the District's Jewish population, or simply from a new urban Jewish consciousness. The U.S. Census does not ask questions about religion, and only in 1983 did the metropolitan Washington Jewish community undertake a follow-up to the 1956 demographic study. Certainly Jews were represented among those who had settled in old central-city neighborhoods undergoing "gentrification," but it is unlikely that those neighborhood changes caused a major increase in the District's Jewish population. In 1983, 24,285 Jews lived in the District of Columbia, representing 4.1 percent of the city's total population and a much larger proportional presence in the District than whites in general. About 15 percent of metropolitan-area Jews lived in the District, as compared with only 8.2 percent of the white population. Most of Washington's Jewish population were young adults, more of whom were single than married; 39 percent of the District's Jews were between the ages of 18 and 34, and only 49 percent of those over eighteen were married.

The renaissance of Jewish self-expression and cultural life in the city in the 1970s and 1980s paralleled a literal rebirth of political life with the advent of home rule. As Washingtonians plunged into electoral politics for the first time in a century, individual Jews and Jewish organizations quickly became a part of the political scene. The Washington chapter of the American Jewish Committee, for example, under the leadership of Rabbi Andrew Baker, began an African American–Jewish dialogue group in the early 1980s, which has met regularly since then to discuss local as well as national issues. Both the committee and the Jewish Community Council have sponsored trips to Israel for local elected officials and African American leaders.

Jews won election to the Board of Education, the District Council, advisory neighborhood commissions, and the Statehood Constitutional Convention, and have served as presidents of neighborhood associations and public school parent-teacher associations. Several prominent Jewish lawyers and businesspeople developed close ties to the city's political leadership, and District officeholders have regularly attended Jewish events. In short, as political life returned to the city, Jews extended their longtime involvement with federal issues to the new local government.

From the start, Jews built a highly self-conscious community, aware of their special visibility in the capital. Today that community is one of many centers of the Washington metropolitan area's Jewish life, yet it is self-confident and eager to assert both its Jewishness and its commitment to the city.

NOTES

1. *The Occident*, September 1852, 137.

2. Constance McLaughlin Green, *Washington: A History of the Capital, 1800–1950* (Princeton, N.J.: Princeton University Press, 1962), 1:93.

3. Quoted in Abraham Simon, *A History of the Washington Hebrew Congregation* (Washington, D.C., 1905), 12–13.

4. *Jewish Messenger*, 26 February 1864, 59.

5. Ibid., 24 January 1862.

6. Hyman Goldman, "Some Persons and Events in My Early Life in Washington, D.C.," *The Record: Publication of the Jewish Historical Society of Greater Washington* 3 (March 1968): 9.

7. For this and subsequent first-person accounts, see Jewish Historical Society of Greater Washington Oral History Project, 1981, Washingtoniana Division, D.C. Public Library, Washington, D.C.

ADDITIONAL READING

Bigman, Stanley K. *The Jewish Population of Greater Washington in 1956*. Washington, D.C.: Jewish Community Council of Greater Washington, 1957.

Blum, Nancy Moses. "The Inter-relationship between American and Immigrant Jews in Washington, D.C., 1880–1915." Master's thesis, George Washington University, 1974.

Diner, Hasia R. *Fifty Years of Jewish Self-governance: The Jewish Community Council of Greater Washington, 1938–1988*. Washington, D.C.: Jewish Community Council, 1989.

Kaganoff, Nathan M. "The Education of the Jewish Child in the District of Columbia, 1861–1915." Part 1. *The Record: Publication of the Jewish Historical Society of Greater Washington* 3, no. 1 (March 1968): 43–51.

Rosenblum, Edward. "Young Men's Hebrew Association, 1912–1923, Washington Jewish Community Center, 1923–1957: Fifty Years of Recollections." *The Record: Publication of the Jewish Historical Society of Greater Washington* 3, no. 1 (March 1968): 12–25.

Shosteck, Robert. "An Economic Study of the Southwest Jewish Community, 1855–1955." *The Record: Publication of the Jewish Historical Society of Greater Washington* 3, no. 2 (November 1968): 22–35.

———. "The Jewish Community of Washington, D.C., during the Civil War." *American Jewish Historical Quarterly* 56, no. 3 (March 1967): 319–47.

Siegel, Jonathan. "50 Years of Washington's UJA." *The Record: Publication of the Jewish Historical Society of Greater Washington* 14 (July 1987): 1–48.

Tobin, Gary A. *A Demographic Study of the Jewish Community of Greater Washington, 1983*. Bethesda, Maryland: United Jewish Appeal Federation of Greater Washington, 1984.

9.

The Evolution of Washington's Italian American Community

Howard Gillette Jr. and
Alan M. Kraut

On 13 June 1911 Italian immigrant Antonio Scafetta made the headlines. The front page of the *Washington Post* reported his death by electrocution, as he attempted to switch power for a street railway car from an overhead to an underground conduit. A native of the central Italian town of Vasto, Scafetta was one of those anonymous contributors to the city's life most often overlooked by historians.

Although scholars have established the centrality of Union Station (whose construction brought Scafetta to Washington) to the movement to beautify the city, and have begun to examine the importance of the early electric railway companies, they have left virtually unexplored the history of the Antonio Scafettas, their kin, and their descendants. Constance Green's two-volume study of Washington does not provide a single reference to Italians in the index; and Washington's public-school text, *City of Magnificent Intentions*, while mentioning the Italians' role in early transportation, leaves obscure the rest of their history. Even a historian attempting to trace Scafetta's life from the *Post* article would have been blocked at every point. Not only did the *Post* and the certificate of death misspell his name, but the city directories of the period failed to record his nearly five-year presence in Washington.

The omission of Italians from Washington history is especially ironic, because the very structures that distinguish the capital from other cities and brought its architecture international renown were often crafted by Italian immigrant artisans and built with the sweat of Italian construction workers.

Lacking a great ocean port, Washington was never the "golden door" to America for the world's "huddled masses" that Baltimore, Philadelphia, New York, Boston, and San Francisco were in the nineteenth and early twentieth centuries. Since efforts to encourage large-scale industry in Washington failed during those years, entrepreneurs were unable to assemble the basic ingredients to nurture industrial development and industrial capitalism in the Potomac's sleepy southern town. As a city whose major enterprise was government, Washington did not attract the masses of immigrant workers who fueled the growth of such industrial centers as Chicago, Cleveland, and Detroit. As it grew to become one of the nation's largest cities, however, the District did attract an ethnic population, albeit a small and relatively selective one.[1]

In his provocative study of ethnic groups in Detroit between 1880 and 1920, historian Olivier Zunz describes how industrialization profoundly altered that city. Zunz depicts Detroit prior to 1880 as a city of semiautonomous ethnic communities, each in its own enclave. Within a particular community, Zunz argues, there existed "strong intra-ethnic group channels for upward mobility." Such economic mobility experienced within the group often strengthened ethnic divisions. An Italian fruit peddler from Sicily, for example, might eventually buy a grocery store in a heavily Sicilian corner of the Italian enclave and achieve modest security, but rarely great prosperity, within the bosom of his Sicilian *paesani*. There were thus plural opportunity structures in Detroit, as each immigrant enclave held opportunities for the enhancement of its own members' economic status.

Industrialization largely erased such intraethnic channels for upward mobility. One shoe factory could eliminate the entrepreneurial opportunity for dozens of would-be, self-employed cobblers in ethnic enclaves throughout the city. Increasingly after 1910, class rather than ethnicity became the salient feature of urban life in Detroit. According to Zunz, "The nineteenth century plural opportunity structure gave way to a new single opportunity structure," based on industry. Ethnic bonds were "irrevocably weakened" by the changed structure brought about by industry.[2]

Italian immigrants who came to Washington in the late nineteenth and early twentieth centuries found a modest "plural opportunity structure" in place. As time went on, however, the community did not escape assimilation's suction, and Italian neighborhoods eventually fragmented as they did in other cities with Italian immigrant populations. Nevertheless, the District's multifaceted but nonindustrial economy may well account for the tenacity of ethnic sensibilities among Washington's Italians and partially explain the persistence of the Italians in the District's urban structure until the massive exodus to suburbia in the post–World War II era.

The rising Italian immigration to America—from 55,000 in the 1870s, to 300,000 in the 1880s, to the stunning 3.8 million who arrived between 1890 and 1920—had a limited effect on Washington. Without the magnet of industry, which attracted large foreign-born populations throughout the East and Midwest, Washington seemed an unlikely place for immigrant settlement. Consequently, the nation's capital did not develop the "Little Italys"—with their intricate matrix of personal and institutional relationships rooted in blood and *campanilismo* (localism)—found in Chicago, New York, and other heavily immigrant-populated cities. Washington was more like Toronto, where there were never enough Sicilians or Neapolitans in the same city block or neighborhood to dominate the social order. Despite new arrivals in the decades after restriction, as late as the 1940s the Italian community that existed in Washington was smaller and more internally diverse than that of most other U.S. cities. It was nonetheless rich in the cultural influences and the flavor of the old country. Occupational choices, religious affiliations and worship styles, voluntary associations, and shared customs and traditions were the ties that strengthened Italian community life in the District.

The Italian entry into the city began modestly. In 1880 Washington ranked next to last, exceeding only New Orleans among the nation's twenty largest cities, in percentage of immigrant population. *Polk's Washington City Directory* for that year listed only 277 individuals with Italian names, probably a low count but still a good approximation of the Italian presence. Of these, many were in the service trades as bakers, confectioners, restaurant owners, fruit sellers, grocers, tailors, druggists, and jewelers. A few professionals—five physicians, five music teachers, a group of four musicians, and a father-and-son legal team—completed the roster. There is no evidence of extreme poverty, high unemployment, or excessive criminal activity among the newcomers. Even an increase in population during the following decade did little to affect the community's character. Washington's small early Italian community was moderately prosperous and quietly law-abiding.

Contemporary reports support this profile. An 1890 congressional investigation of immigrant exploitation by labor brokers, known among the Italians as padrones, elicited testimony that suggests an Italian immigrant enclave smaller in scale and with fewer of the economic and social problems that existed in the large industrial cities. Italian physician Tulio Verdi, who had served as president of the District's Board of Health under President Ulysses S. Grant, testified that, unlike New York, where Italians were reportedly "compelled to huddle together as best they could," those five or six hundred who lived in Washington were "all working, all lived in comfort, all educated their children, and made good citizens." In Washington, he observed, "not an Italian was to be found in a hospital," nor did any break the law or behave badly in public.

Verdi had taken his wife, an American woman, to a ball hosted by Italian peanut sellers, tailors, and barbers, where, he reported, every man wore a clean suit and all the women were well-dressed. He felt it necessary to add that, of course, that would not have been true in New York. Both written and oral testimony confirm that social problems—such as poverty, crime, family desertion, and public drunkenness—when at all evident among Washington's Italians were handled within the community through a low-key, informal voluntarism.[3]

Washington's Italian community appears to have eluded many of immigration's concomitant social problems because, instead of a large influx of impoverished, unskilled job seekers, those who arrived were often skilled workers or aspiring entrepreneurs, attracted to the city by specific job or investment prospects that provided them with ample, though rarely high, income. This pattern differed sharply from that of other cities. Virginia Yans-McLaughlin has calculated that in Buffalo, New York, for example, 69 percent of Italian-born adult males were unskilled laborers working in outdoor seasonal occupations. First- and second-generation Italians in Buffalo rarely followed older immigrant groups up occupational ladders or competed with them for jobs in the economy's growing industrial sector. Instead, Yans-McLaughlin reports, "unskilled and uneducated sons of immigrants repeated their fathers' careers in building, general labor, and service occupations." They might seek new job opportunities driving taxis and trucks, but they did not pursue work in Buffalo's expanding steel and auto industries. A similar pattern was identified by Dino Cinel in San Francisco, where immigrants from other nations generally had better jobs than Italians.[4]

In the late nineteenth century the buildup of the capital attracted some Italians—largely those from northern Italy—who could offer special skills as craftsmen. A number of stone carvers, for example, were hired to work on the new Library of Congress building in the 1890s. These workers typically migrated to Washington after holding jobs in other American cities. Records of Italians in both the city directory and the federal census for 1900 show that a predominance of workers in service trades were suddenly in demand in the rapidly growing city. The census listed 638 employed Italian males: 58 professionals (9 percent), of whom 43 were musicians; 145 (22.5 percent) in domestic and personal service, a field led by 40 barbers; and 234 (36 percent) in trade and transportation, including 109 merchants and dealers. While 201 (31 percent) were listed as employed in manufacturing, these were concentrated in the service-oriented occupation of boot and shoe repair. The concentration of merchants reflected the influx of southern Italians for whom, as Rudolph Vecoli has reported, no sentimental attachment to the land stood in the way of their

Italian workers at the Union Station construction site, circa 1905–1907. Although the Irish predominated in the construction of early transportation improvements—including canals— Italians were recruited to help build Union Station on Massachusetts Avenue. (Courtesy Prints and Photographs Division, Library of Congress)

becoming artisans, shopkeepers, or priests.[5] As if to confirm Washington's special status, the city drew numerous immigrants who had first tried industrial work elsewhere but who took up a range of service trades in the capital.

Significant in the longterm process of building the city was the boost provided by the McMillan Commission Plan of 1902. The plan called for not only the creation of parks but also the construction of public buildings suitable to the capital of a nation propelled to international prominence through its decisive victory in the recently concluded Spanish-American War. Although the program envisioned in 1902 did not materialize until construction of the Federal Triangle in the 1920s and 1930s, the construction of Union Station between 1905 and 1907 did have an impact on the building industry. It provided work for stone carvers and a host of recent immigrant day laborers, who took up the heavy work of grading roadbeds and laying new track.

As happened in other cities, these untutored new arrivals from southern Italy drew criticism from established Italians as well as native-born citizens, and the city responded by placing them in residential labor camps. Extending from sites near Union Station out beyond the old city line into Congress Heights and Prince Georges County (both in Maryland), these camps were intended to maintain strict social control. Signs posted in Italian warned against carrying a gun, destroying public or private property, and even using profanity in the streets. Despite the concern they might have generated, these new workers did not pose the same threat to social stability that southern Italians posed in such cites as New Orleans, Philadelphia, or Chicago. Without industry or organized seasonal agricultural employment nearby, Washington simply did not attract the numbers of workers who came to other cities, and thus escaped the trials of seeing hundreds of those workers unemployed in the winter months.

True to a system of plural opportunity, Italians in Washington found ways to supplement their wages through service to their compatriots. Some set up businesses in individual homes. Railroad worker Francesco Tana's wife ran a store in their home at Sixth and Quincy Streets, NE, where fellow railroad workers could eat a quick lunch or buy groceries. Frank Croccia, a musician, followed suit, setting up a grocery store.

Although Washington appeared to lack widespread padrone activity, John Bacchini reported that his father, Charles, who worked for the National Mosaic Company for a number of years in the early twentieth century, used to be considered a padrone by local workers. As many as 150 of them would gather daily at his office in search of day work. Others have suggested that the Bianchi Travel Agency, established in the early 1920s, played a similar role in assisting potential workers with jobs as they prepared to make the trip to Washington. More generally, family networks played a role in easing the transition to the United States. Those who intended to make the journey to the New World learned through a transatlantic network of letters and visits that in Washington there were families, such as the Masinos, who could be counted on to board newcomers until they could find homes. Women such as Maria Rosa Masino served as intermediaries for non-English-speaking mothers and became known on both sides of the Atlantic for their dependable service as midwives.

In Washington, as elsewhere, immigrants preferred to live close to their jobs, which were most frequently located along commercial strips in the older, central neighborhoods near Union Station and the Capitol. Italians mixed with immigrants of other nationalities along Four and One-Half Street, SW, and along North Capitol Street, where Italian shops were interspersed with Irish saloons, dry-goods stores with Jewish proprietors, and an occasional

Frank Croccia's Groceries, Confectionery, Cigar and To-bacco store. Washington's demand for services offered Croccia and his compatriots opportunities for starting their own small businesses. (Photo courtesy Frances Croccia)

Chinese laundry. The largest number of Italians settled near Union Station in the area then popularly known as Swampoodle. Once dominated by the Irish, who in the 1920s were beginning to move to newer District neighborhoods beyond Florida Avenue, the area was affordable for newly arriving Italians. Some lived in northeast Washington in housing built by the Washington Terminal Company, the contractor that constructed and managed Union Station, while others congregated in Schott Alley, also in the northeast. These crowded and sometimes unsanitary byways attracted the criticism of early reformers, especially that of Charles Weller, the driving force of the Associated Charities.[6] However squalid the accommodations, those who lived there could find cheer in the camaraderie of other *paesani*. According to Leo Balducci, who used to frequent Washington's alleys, in the evenings men who had come from the same Italian villages sat together outdoors and socialized, playing cards, drinking red wine, and recovering from the day's work.

Although the Washington *Evening Star* may have exaggerated in a 1911

Like most immigrants writing home, this couple, Nicola and Maria Rosa Masino, wanted to provide a record of their arrival in the New World for their friends and family in Italy. The Masinos chose the Capitol as their backdrop. (Courtesy Gelman Library, George Washington University)

article that described the city as having a "Little Italy," the paper did identify the elements of an ethnic infrastructure, especially voluntary benevolent associations and businesses that were owned by and catered to the needs and tastes of an almost exclusively Italian clientele. Even as some Italians who had achieved a measure of wealth were leaving their old neighborhoods for the District suburbs of Brookland and Petworth, newly arrived Italians replaced them in the community's multiple-opportunity structures. Newcomers now patronized "the outcropping of Italian grocery stores and restaurants" mentioned by the *Star*'s reporter. Among the new businesses started by Italians were a spaghetti factory on Four and One-Half Street, SW, and "Happy" Harry Guiddott's restaurant on New York Avenue, described by the *Star* as "one of the few truly Bohemian places Washington has ever produced."

In the larger Italian communities of other cities, such as New York and San Francisco, regional loyalties caused Sicilians, Neapolitans, Abruzzese, and others to insist upon separate voluntary associations and even separate

In the early twentieth century Italians clustered near Union Station and the Capitol Grounds, where other immigrant groups had preceded them. Holy Rosary Church, at Third and F Streets, NW, lay at the heart of the community. (Courtesy Journal of American Ethnic History)

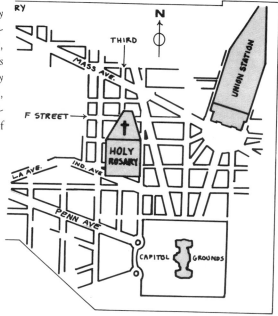

churches. However, like smaller Italian communities in Utica and Rochester, New York, or Kansas City, Missouri, Washington's Italian population was both small and varied so that ties rooted in *campanilismo*—or even in a broader form of regionalism—were insufficient to bind neighbors tightly together. There were simply not enough Sicilians, Neapolitans, or the like to constitute cohesive communities. Catholicism proved the strongest bond among Washington's Italians, and it was not until they built their own church in 1913 that the community truly found a core.

Confined in number as well as by finances, Washington's early Italians were forced to join other ethnic groups' Catholic institutions, taking mass at their churches and burying their dead in their cemeteries. Some joined St. Mary's, a German Catholic church at 727 Fifth Street, NW. Others joined churches with predominantly Irish congregants and priests, such as St. Aloysius on North Capitol Street or St. Dominic's in southwest Washington. Italians were buried in separate sections of previously established cemeteries, principally Mount Olivet and St. Mary's in northeast Washington, where Irish and Germans, respectively, had predominated.

As the Italian population grew, church leaders began to see a need for an Italian national parish such as the Germans had in St. Mary's and the Irish in St. Patrick's. Diomede Cardinal Falconio, the apostolic delegate to the United States from 1902 to 1911, expressed his fears that Washington's railroad workers in particular lacked proper religious instruction. He cautioned Baltimore's James Cardinal Gibbons, who bore responsibility for Washington's Catholic community, "that unless Your Eminence takes urgent measures, many poor souls will be lost." Gibbons responded by delegating Monsignor James Mackin of St. Paul's Church to recruit an Italian priest to head a new national parish. However, the plans met with opposition from other Washington priests who, like St. Patrick's Father William Russell, feared the competition for parishioners that would result from yet another national church. Arguing that the opportunities for Italians to worship were already quite adequate in existing churches, Russell charged that Italian workers who were building Union Station would probably be seeking work in another city upon the project's completion, and that those who remained in the city would have mastered English and would no longer demand an Italian-language service.[7]

The controversy over where the Italians ought to worship stirred bitter anti-Italian sentiments and interethnic rivalry. At St. Joseph's Church, the rector, the Rev. V. F. Schmitt, complained to Cardinal Gibbons that Schmitt's assistant, Father Ignatius Fealy, was doing all he could to attract Italians to the parish, "to the complaint of the good old stock of the English-speaking people of the parish." Fealy's dismissal two months later drew an anguished response from Italians. There is ample evidence that anti-Italian prejudice often underlay the controversy over the financial viability of a new church structure and an additional priest to accommodate the Italians. After leaving St. Patrick's to become bishop of Charleston, Russell later wrote, "If the Italians are becoming self-respecting Americans, I am sure we shall all rejoice. They have hitherto been a disgrace to the Church and a stink in the nostrils of all Americans."[8]

Not all those in Washington who resented the Italians' presence were as discreet as Russell had remained until after his departure. As their growing numbers heightened their visibility, Washington's Italians were subject to a good deal of name-calling. What was more debilitating, however, was the official discrimination they faced from a law prohibiting aliens from owning property in U.S. territories or the District. Those seeking exception to the law were forced to seek relief through individual acts of Congress.[9]

It was in this context that local Italians established their own parish. Father Nicholas DeCarlo, a native Italian who had left a Philadelphia assignment in 1912 to study biology at Catholic University in Washington, was recruited the following year to be pastor. He served his first mass as pastor of the Church of the Holy Rosary on Sunday, 14 December 1913, on a makeshift altar in a small converted house on H Street, NW.

In a spirit of cooperation more typical of smaller Italian communities, a broad base of representatives from different regions and occupations came together to establish the new parish. Recognizing the subtleties of Italian culture, Father DeCarlo encouraged each local and regional group to maintain its special identity within the umbrella of the parish by maintaining its own traditions through the celebration of local saints' days and the formation of organizations to institutionalize these customs. These groups included the Saint Gabriel Society (1923), the Confraternity of Saint Anthony (1934), the Saint Joseph Society (1936), and the Lady of Consolation Society (1945). Realizing, however, that such imported loyalties could be detrimental to community solidarity, he offered the church, as an institution, and himself, as parish priest, as promoters of cohesion. He labored tirelessly to ease the community's growing pains and his parishioners' personal struggles by serving as an intermediary, translating when called upon, placing compatriots in jobs, or assisting them with local authorities in matters of law. Some Italians worshiped in Protestant churches, including the Baptist Church of the Redeemer, which actively sought converts among Washington's Italian Catholics. Nevertheless, when interviewed, DeCarlo's former assistant, Aldo Petrini, noted of Holy Rosary and especially of the pastor that, "without [them], there would not have been an Italian community in Washington."

As testimony to the church's strength, a spate of associated secular as well as religious organizations sprang up. Under the leadership of grocer Joseph Balducci a Holy Name Society was organized in 1915. On 10 October of that same year three hundred members marched in a Holy Name Society parade down Pennsylvania Avenue. Balducci also organized the Men's Catholic Society in 1917 and served seventeen consecutive terms as its leader. Italian women organized the Women's Sodality in 1915 and the Union of Italian Catholic Women in 1918.

As the nucleus of Washington's Italian immigrant community, Holy Rosary increasingly catered to the broader secular needs of Italians. Outside Washington, in larger urban communities where industrialization was challenging the hegemony of local ethnic institutions, those needs were often served by nondenominational settlement houses, some of them originally inspired by the Protestant missionary spirit. In Buffalo, for example, neighborhood and settlement houses occupied important positions among the charita-

Parishioners gather outside the Church of the Holy Rosary, the center of Washington's Italian religious and social life, in 1934. The church stands today at Third and F Streets, NW, and retains its ethnic flavor. (Courtesy Gelman Library, George Washington University)

ble agencies. In Washington, Father DeCarlo, a strict priest of the old Augustinian order, did not encourage using the church for social work, socializing, or cultural enhancement. Younger members of the parish, however, found an acceptable means of bringing single parishioners together through the formation of a dramatic club, which offered a series of religious and secular plays during the 1920s. In 1920 the boys' club of the church-supported Christ Child Society was founded to instill in young Italian males "the principles of fair play, honesty, cleanliness, self-control, and mutual responsibility," without exposing them to the secularizing influences that might subvert their Catholic beliefs or undermine their respect and loyalty to their Italian heritage. Later, the church supported athletic teams and bowling leagues. While secular organizations emerged to offer some of the same social and recreational opportunities— including a number of *paese* (native place) clubs—these remained relatively small in number. The strongest and most persistent of these groups, the Club Fiumendenisi, in announcing the addition of a new wing to its clubhouse in 1938, reported that it had thirty-six members.

During the late 1920s and 1930s Washington's Italian community underwent subtle change. Most visibly, the federal building program, which New Dealers hoped would put many Americans back to work, attracted more Italians to construction jobs in the District. Authorized originally by the Buildings

Act of 1926, the Federal Triangle project included funds for architectural embellishment, which in the 1940s would provide work for many artisans and workers, a number of them Italian immigrants. Roger Morigi, a stone carver at the National Cathedral, recalled that for artisans like himself, Washington was the place to be. Sculptors hired to work on federal buildings reported to the architects but sometimes recommended the artisans who would execute their creations. Many became acquainted with highly skilled Italians and insisted on their employment. Large contractors, based mainly in New York, including John Donnelly, the Piccirilli brothers, Edward Adolino, and Gino A. Ratti, brought Italian immigrant artisans from jobs in other cities and put them to work in Washington.

Local companies also sprang up to provide building skills, both to the federal government and to a city stimulated by the growing federal presence. Among the contractors who early on chose to live and to work on the District's outskirts, where building materials were available along with a demand for new housing, were Louis and Frank Perna, sons and grandsons of Italian stonemasons from Calabria in southern Italy. Starting with buildings in the Tenleytown area, the Perna brothers eventually landed contracts for churches, schools, and commercial buildings. Other contractors included Vincent Tonelli, who had made his way to Washington in 1929 via the premier marble-cutting area of Barre, Vermont; Anthony Izzo, who established a highly successful bricklaying company in 1931; and George Gianetti from Tuscany, who set up an ornamental plastering firm in 1935. The 1940 *Polk's Washington City Directory* revealed that Italians dominated the cut-stone contracting business and listed nine general contractors and nine plastering contractors.

Although Italians continued to be identified in Washington for their skilled contributions to the building trades, many pursued entreprenuerial opportunities. As the Italian population swelled to 14,700 by 1937, Italians continued to sell fruits and vegetables and to repair shoes. While fewer Italians than Jews operated the small delicatessens, grocery stores, and produce stands that catered to the city's older, in-town neighborhoods, they nonetheless accounted for significant numbers. A few became neighborhood "institutions," such as Vaccaro's, which had been opened in 1906 in the 400 block of H Street, NW, and Litteri's, established at Sixth and G Streets, NW. In addition to offering traditional foods, the sound of Italian being spoken, the owners' friendly banter, and—when necessary—a generous credit policy to homesick immigrants, shopping at these and at a handful of other places helped Italians to retain identities with their community, thus fortifying ethnic identity against

James Zagami at his shoe-repair shop. Zagami had worked at a West Virginia mining camp before relocating with his family to Washington, where he took up an entirely different occupation as a shoemaker. (Courtesy Dino Zagami)

the forces of assimilation. In addition, a few Italian doctors and lawyers provided professional services to their compatriots.

Still, the seeds of change were planted in this period by the new opportunities provided by an expanding federal presence. A review of the 1940 city directory shows that Italians continued to find work as craftsmen for the government, as they had at the turn of the century, and a few found positions in the Government Printing Office and other industrially organized sectors of the government. The significant change, however, was Italians' employment in white-collar positions.

Most striking, if perhaps atypical, was the career of Ugo Carusi, who had been born in Calabria, Italy, and raised in Barre, Vermont. He had left that stone-cutting center to take a job as assistant to Calvin Coolidge's attorney general, John Garibaldi Sargent. Although he lacked a college degree, Carusi studied law at night and rose quickly in the Justice Department, ultimately becoming the highest appointee of Italian heritage in the federal government as commissioner of immigration during World War II. Gino Simi, whose father had migrated from northern Italy to take work in Washington as a stonecutter, spent a good deal of his career with the Department of Labor. Many other Italian men made government their career.

A number of Italian women, such as Anna Vaccaro, continued to work alongside their husbands in family businesses. Gilda Ruggieri, a mother of six, helped her husband sell fruit and vegetables on weekends. Some, however, broke with tradition by taking salaried jobs in the private sector, which had expanded to serve the city's growing population of clerks, salespeople, and stenographers. Others, following the expansion of opportunities in the federal government, took positions as secretaries, stenographers, and administrative assistants. Although quotas on federal hiring of District residents forced some, such as Mary Mastromarino Davis, to wait for jobs in the public sector, they were still considered worth taking. Although she waited two decades for a public position, Davis held the federal job she ultimately secured for thirty-four years. Whether daughters or wives, such working women contributed to the family welfare, helping to make it possible for their families to leave the older sections of the city for newer homes in the suburbs.

A sample drawn from occupational data in *Polk's Washington City Directory* for 1940 indicates that families that had been in Washington since the early twentieth century experienced upward occupational shifts into mid-level business and service jobs. The large Bovello family, for example, which had been dominated by musicians in the early 1900s, included in 1940 two plumbers, two salesmen, a bookkeeper, a printer, a laborer, and one music teacher among its males. Of the four Bovello women who were listed as having occupations, two were clerks and two were stenographers. Having established a coal company in Washington in the early 1900s, the Rinaldi family still maintained the business in 1940, but two of the Rinaldi men also worked as barbers, five were clerks, one was a porter, one was a tailor, one was a bartender, and two held unidentified jobs in federal departments. In addition to the two women listed as officers of Rinaldi Coal, one worked as a stenographer and another as a saleswoman.

Evidence of the confidence and self-esteem of an Italian community untroubled by the stratification born of industrial competition is provided by the formation in 1929 of the Lido Club, a fraternal organization. Three Italian-born businessmen took the lead in its organization: Massino Ferrari, vice-president of the Columbia Fruit and Candy Company; Fred Colaprico, a barber; and Ralph Cipriano, an agent for the New York Life Insurance Company. Among the club's charter members were prominent businessmen and attorneys, but also entrepreneurs who were finding their path to upward mobility in Washington's multiple-opportunity structure. Charter members also included men in the building trades, the restaurant business, and tailors. Capt. Gregory Cipriani, of the U.S. Army's Judge Advocate's General Office, and Dominick Bianchi, whose travel office served many Italians coming from and returning to Italy, were the club's first president and secretary, respectively. In subsequent years the club gained visibility in public affairs by electing as its second and third presidents two increasingly important attorneys, John Sirica in 1930 and Ugo Carusi in 1931. Sirica's family had traveled around the United States before settling in Washington in 1918.

The Second World War proved to be a difficult period for Italian communities throughout the nation. As Ronald Bayor reports, prior to the war's outbreak, "the achievements of their ancestral home enhanced the prestige of the Italians in America and inspired pride in the accomplishments of the Mussolini regime."[10] During the war, however, most flocked to the Allied cause. In Washington, Carusi was given a particularly visible role by President Franklin Delano Roosevelt: he spoke to Italians around the United States and broadcast anti-Fascist messages to Italians in Europe on Allied radio stations.

Italian loyalty was articulated in Columbus Day celebrations in the streets of the nation's capital and through cooperation with national security measures—even those that caused embarrassment and inconvenience. Some jurisdictions required that Italians without American citizenship be fingerprinted and prohibited from crossing state boundaries. For members of the Angelo Petrini family, especially Mrs. Petrini, moving back and forth across the District line from the family's home in Hyattsville, Maryland, seemed an insurmountable problem. However, the mayor of Hyattsville, ill at ease at having to trouble a member of a highly regarded Italian family, did not enforce those regulations that would inconvenience Mrs. Petrini. When aliens were required to be fingerprinted, the mayor refused to allow Mrs. Petrini to come to the Post Office and sent a clerk to her home instead.

After the war Washington's Italians joined in the great national exodus to suburbia. Some were already living in nearby suburbs such as Brookland and Petworth; now the out-migration was accelerated and extended. Some found Prince Georges County, Maryland, attractive because housing was more plentiful and less expensive than in Washington, which had become overcrowded in the war years. Other Italians left in the wake of the black migration to the city, as did whites from other immigrant and native-born groups. As the Italians left, many of their institutions followed. The Rinaldi funeral home moved first from a downtown H Street address to upper Georgia Avenue, and finally beyond Silver Spring to White Oak, Maryland. A leading black-owned company, McGuire Funeral Service, took over the Georgia Avenue location. Pressed by rising land values in Washington, the Giannetti sculpting studio moved to Maryland, near Hyattsville, in 1961. As part of a stonemason family that had located in Tenleytown in the 1920s, Frank Perna shifted his home to Bethesda and his business to Tuxedo, Maryland. Only the Church of the Holy Rosary and a few stores remained, and many of these, such as Vaccaro's delicatessen and the St. James Cafe in northwest Washington, have closed in recent years. For some 56,000 Italian Americans scattered throughout the Washington area, suburban parishes and fading memories of the flavors and aromas of the old neighborhood make visits there less frequent.

In Washington, then, the ties of ethnicity among Italians were not broken by class differences, as they were in industrial cities such as Detroit, where a single-opportunity structure prevailed. Rather, ethnic ties were gradually weakened by the more complex and subtle pressures of assimilation, wrought by cultural, economic, and demographic changes operating within a plural-opportunity structure. As individual families prospered, they moved to the suburbs, where they bought homes next to non-Italians and shopped along with them in the same local supermarkets. They no longer required Italian-language church services, and they gradually loosened their ties with—but never lost their feeling for—ethnic institutions in downtown Washington.

NOTES

This chapter is reprinted with minor modifications from Howard Gillette Jr. and Alan M. Kraut, "The Evolution of Washington's Italian-American Community, 1890 to World War II," *Journal of American Ethnic History* 6 (Fall 1986): 7–27, by permission of the Immigration History Society. The journal article contains the complete citations for this chapter.

1. Italian immigration to Washington does not follow the traditional chain-migration pattern that historians have applied to their investigations for the past twenty-five years. See, for example, John S. McDonald and Leatrice D. McDonald, "Chain Migration: Ethnic Neighborhood Formation and Social Networks," *Milbank Memorial Fund Quarterly* 17 (1964): 82–97. According to such early studies, the chains were linked by *paesani*—those with the same village of origin. First came the individual "pioneers"; next came the "birds of passage" (young unmarried men temporarily following their padrone labor recruiters); and finally the permanent immigrants arrived in complete nuclear-family groups. Today this model is criticized by some scholars as too rigid. See Donna Gabaccia, "Links in the Chain: A Case Study of South Italian Migration, 1880–1930" (paper presented at the meeting of the Social Science History Association, 26 October 1984).

2. Olivier Zunz, *The Changing Face of Inequality: Urbanization, Industrial Development, and Immigrants in Detroit, 1880–1920* (Chicago: University of Chicago Press, 1982), 401.

3. Interview with Aldo Paul Petrini, 11 May 1984, Special Collections Division, Gelman Library, George Washington University, Washington, D.C. Subsequent references in the essay to other interviews and first-hand accounts collected by the authors and participants in local history projects are also on file at Gelman Library.

4. Virginia Yans-McLaughlin, *Family and Community: Italian Immigrants in Buffalo, 1880–1930* (Ithaca, N.Y.: Cornell University Press, 1977), 46–47; Dino Cinel, *From Italy to San Francisco: The Immigrant Experience* (Stanford, Calif.: Stanford University Press, 1982), 144–45.

5. Rudolph J. Vecoli, "Contadini in Chicago: A Critique of *The Uprooted*," *Journal of American History* 51 (December 1964): 407.

6. In a caption to one of his own pictures, Weller described an Italian mother who, "in the shacks of Washington, misses the beauties of Italy." Charles Weller, *Neglected Neighbors in the National Capital* (Philadelphia: John C. Winston Company, 1909), 124.

7. John Tracey Ellis, *The Life of James Cardinal Gibbons* (Milwaukee: Bruce Publishing Company, 1952), 2:263; William T. Russell to James Cardinal Gibbons, 15 May 1916, Archdiocesan Archives, Catholic Center, Baltimore, Maryland (hereafter cited as AAB).

8. V. F. Schmitt to James Cardinal Gibbons, 13 October 1913, AAB; Mark and Cesare Peca to James Cardinal Gibbons, 15 December 1913, AAB; William T. Russell to James Cardinal Gibbons, 1 November 1921, AAB.

9. Such restrictions were passed into law 26 February 1885, 48th Cong., 2nd sess., P.L. 52. For an example of special legislation to exempt an individual, Francesco Perna, see H.R. 1729, 55th Cong., 3rd sess., 11 January 1899.

10. Ronald H. Bayor, *Neighbors in Conflict: The Irish, Germans, Jews, and Italians of New York City, 1929–1941* (Baltimore: Johns Hopkins University Press, 1978), 78.

ADDITIONAL READING

Bodnar, John. *The Transplanted: A History of Immigrants in Urban America*. Bloomington: University of Indiana Press, 1985.

Briggs, John W. *An Italian Passage: Immigrants to Three American Cities, 1890–1930*. New Haven, Conn.: Yale University Press, 1978.

Gabaccia, Donna R. *From Sicily to Elizabeth Street: Housing and Social Change among Italian Immigrants, 1880–1930*. Albany: State University of New York Press, 1984.

———. *Militants and Migrants: Rural Sicilians Become American Workers*. New Brunswick, N.J.: Rutgers University Press, 1988.

McDaniel, George W., and John N. Pearce. *Images of Brookland: The History and Architecture of a Washington Suburb*. Rev. and enl. Martin Aurand. GW Washington Studies, no. 10. Washington, D.C.: George Washington University, 1982.

Mormino, Gary R., and George E. Pozzetta. *The Immigrant World of Ybor City: Italians and Their Latin Neighborhoods in Tampa, 1885–1985*. Urbana: University of Illinois Press, 1987.

Orsi, Robert Anthony. *The Madonna of 115th Street: Faith and Community in Italian Harlem, 1880–1950*. New Haven, Conn.: Yale University Press, 1980.

Vecoli, Rudolph J. "The Formation of Chicago's Little Italies." *Journal of American Ethnic History* 2 (Spring 1983): 5–20.

10.

Greek Immigrants in Washington, 1890–1945

Christine M. Warnke

James Nicholas Kokinas, treading corkscrew trails down the wild Pelopon-
nesian Mountains of southern Greece, traveled by moonlight from the village
of Vourvara. His head was filled with dreams of a country where gold covered the
ground, a belief fostered by stories of the California gold rush. As an eleven-year-
old boy, he had gone abroad to visit New York. However, in August 1897,
when Kokinas was twenty-three years old, he left his impoverished village to
make his home in the United States. He knew his final destination by the tag
tied to his lapel: it bore the name of a village compatriot living in Washington.

Kokinas traveled by train from New York City to the nation's capital.
There he found his compatriots eager to finance his business endeavor, and for
several years he sold bananas from a pushcart at Seventh and I Streets, NW.
Eventually he joined a small-business partnership with fellow villagers. In October 1911, financially secure and convinced of the opportunities Washington
offered, Kokinas returned to Vourvara to find a wife. A year later he married
Stamatiki Lambrakis. In 1915 he again crossed the Atlantic, temporarily leaving his wife and children to seek his fortune in the United States once more.[1]

Within five years Kokinas was joined by his family. His optimistic view of
America, especially of Washington, enticed other members of his village. By
1904 the number of Vourvarans in Washington had grown so rapidly as to warrant a hometown-village society, the first of several Greek village networks to
appear in the District. The "hometown" designation, surpassed only by familial loyalty, was a crucial form of social definition for the early Greek immigrants. Villagers sought out their fellows in America; regardless of where they
ventured, the tie with the place where they and their parents had been born
remained supremely important.[2] For the thousands of single young Greek

males venturing to the United States, this cultural dictate was all-powerful.

The world that Kokinas and 16,000 other Greeks left behind in the late nineteenth century was one of devastating poverty. Crop failures, earthquakes, oppressive taxation, family debts, and political uncertainty in Greece compelled large-scale emigration. Economic conditions were already desperate in the mountainous rural region of southern Greece, where Kokinas and the majority of Greek male immigrants of the time had originated. Living conditions deteriorated further during the 1890s, when the price of currants—one of Greece's main crops—dropped drastically. Young and middle-aged males consequently sought opportunities elsewhere, particularly in Europe and South America.[3]

Between 1880 and the turn of the century, 95 percent of the Greek immigrants to the United States were men, most between the ages of eighteen and thirty-five. Moreover, Greek immigration had been so preponderantly male before 1910 that even as late as 1930 the ratio of males to females among Greek-born Americans was a remarkably high 2.8 to 1. Greek males, who during their high productive years in Greece could usually obtain jobs easily, willingly risked their futures on a chance in America.

During the early years of Greek immigration, from 1894 to 1904, those who came to Washington worked at various menial and unskilled jobs: peddling fruit, shining shoes, laboring in railroad gangs and in factories or mills, or cooking and waiting at counters in food stands owned by relatives or village compatriots. Yet they generally disdained working for wages. For them, the desire to be an artisan or a merchant, so as to control one's own labor, time, and income, generally outweighed the limited security of laboring for someone else—and for someone else's profit.

As soon as immigrants accumulated savings, they would establish their own businesses. In some cases, immigrants set up their own snack stands or shoeshine parlors; in other instances, they bought into a partnership, either paying the total cost in cash or making longterm installment payments to an employer who would eventually become a co-owner. Their financial assets included loans from supportive relatives or friends.[4]

George Alafoginis, who had founded the Bay State Beef Company in 1945, later recalled how he and his family had come to Washington and the important role that the Greek community's early business-support network had played in that decision:

When we arrived in Lynn, Massachusetts, in 1912, we didn't have a dime in our pockets. My father worked in a shoe factory and saved enough passage money to take the family back to Greece. When we returned in 1916, I sold papers and shined shoes at night, while my mother worked in a heel factory and my sister worked for a laundry. One day a village compatriot in Washington wrote my father asking him to come to the nation's capital. My father quickly wrote back saying that he couldn't, since he didn't have a cent. In the next letter to my father his friend enclosed a check for $2,500 with a note that read: 'Come down here and we will buy this business. From the profits, you can pay me back.'

In the early years Hellenic settlers found significant small-business opportunities. Fruit and candy peddling was one of many lucrative enterprises. According to Boyd's 1894 *Directory of the District of Columbia*, the first Greek immigrant to own a confectionery business was James Georgeopoulos, who operated his store at 447 Sixth and One-Half Street, SW. In 1899 Louis P. Dounis and Nicholas Skiados combined their meager assets and shared profits from their adjoining confectionery stores at 916 and 918 Seventh Street, NW. The candy-making business, which required no prior experience, minimal overhead expenses, and little up-front capital, was concentrated in an emerging Greek enclave near the center of town, in Jackson Hall and Cox Alleys (now the site of the Canadian Embassy). Using their places of residence, confectioners enlisted other household members' help, and worked through the night so that their wares would be ready to sell the following day. Obliged to work hard and fast, young men simultaneously boiled, pounded, and pulled the candy. By daybreak the peddlers filled their carts with assorted sweets and pushed them up and down the commercial corridor of Seventh and F Streets, NW.

Greek immigrant fruitsellers, such as Kokinas, traveled as far as Baltimore to obtain their produce at the best wholesale prices. Pushing fruit carts at the bustling Centre Market—at the corner of Seventh Street and Pennsylvania Avenue—the Greeks soon captured a large share of this business from their Italian counterparts. A 17 December 1904 Washington *Evening Star* article noted the change:

> The confusion in the popular mind between the Greek and Italian arises in the main, perhaps, from a confusion of their occupations. Many imagine that the guild of pushcart peddlers who carry fruit and candy on the streets is made entirely of Italians. This, however, is a mistake. The traveling candy stands of Washington are almost [altogether] in the hands of Greeks, [who] also control a large part of the fruit business of the city.

The Greek entrepreneurs also concentrated in food-counter services, shoeshine parlors, huckster wagons, barbershops, floral shops, and retail and wholesale

The Deoudes family's wholesale celery business on Fifth Street, NE. Many of the African American employees understood and spoke Greek. (Courtesy John Deoudes)

produce. Kokinas, for example, rose from peddling fruit to operating a wholesale fruit-and-vegetable business at Centre Market. Nationally acclaimed photographer George Tames had spoken of the monopoly that his father and other Greeks had over the celery market:

> They had a lock on it. The celery would come from across the country by train, and it would be auctioned off in the railroad yards. The produce was exactly the way it came out of the fields, still with dirt clinging to the roots. It was very primitive—not like today.

Tames also provided a rare glimpse into social relations between Greek immigrants and contemporary African American Washingtonians:

> The Greeks would organize a system on Market Street where the blacks and young Greek men would dump the celery in large wooden buckets of water and use

brushes to scrub off the debris. The celery was dipped, cleaned, trimmed, and the stalks removed in time to be sold that same day. Greek was spoken to such an extent that some of the blacks became proficient in it.[5]

A cluster of barbershops that had developed in the 900 block of D Street and John Marshall Place joined other downtown Greek businesses. In 1906 Anthony Panagos and William P. Loomis opened their barbershop at 917 D Street, NW. Soon thereafter Loomis teamed up with Panagos's brother, Milton, to run the same business that catered to Washington's rich and famous. James Chaconas, Peter Chaconas, George Carigan, and Milton Panagos also owned barbershops on John Marshall Place, NW. One of the earliest barbers, John Constas, ran his shop first at 803 then at 923 D Street during the day while attending George Washington University medical school at night.

The early Greek entrepreneurs also found opportunities in the shoeshine business. Scores of shoeshine parlors cropped up in big northeastern cities, including Washington. A boy who had no better options could always find work in a shoeshine parlor run by a fellow Greek. In an era when walking was still a principal means of transportation, and Washington's unpaved streets contributed far more dust and dirt than they do today, bootblacks did a brisk business. Moreover, with the high-button shoe fashionable in the early 1900s, standards of shoe presentation were heightened. Owners of Washington's bootblack establishments fared well, and for many years bootblacks and Greeks were synonymous.

By 1909 close to thirty Greek-owned lunchrooms and restaurants operated in the Seventh Street corridor downtown and on the north side of Pennsylvania Avenue, east of Four and One-Half Street. It was no accident that the restaurateurs picked this location for their operations: they also lived nearby. Washington's Greek-American community initially established itself on Four and One-Half Street and John Marshall Place, NW. Arriving by train from New York City during the late nineteenth century, the early Greek immigrants disembarked at the old Baltimore and Potomac Railroad Station between Fifth and Sixth Streets, NW, and claimed houses once occupied by German immigrants, who had prospered and moved further north along the Seventh Street commercial corridor.[6]

Unlike most Greek businesses, which catered to the general public, the *kafenea*, or coffeehouses/lunchrooms clustered in the community and served the needs of an almost exclusively Greek clientele. The Four and One-Half Street area emerged as the Greek community's social and economic nucleus, with many coffeehouses that functioned as social centers for single men lacking a genuine family environment. The *kafenion* at 214 John Marshall Place, for example, served as an informal club and refuge. As the community grew in the first decade of the 1900s, other *kafenea* surfaced. Harry Magafan, who had come to Washington in 1942 and had founded Alfa Foods four years later, explained:

> In those days the Greek immigrant men had no families and, as a rule, knew very little English. They needed a place which served Greek food and provided some form of recreation. Even upon the arrival of women to the community, the *kafenion* was strictly off limits for women because there was a lot of gambling and cussing.

The mutual support and cooperation reflected in the all-male *kafenea* also characterized the Greek immigrants' lodging arrangements. In settlement houses along Jackson Hall Alley or John Marshall Place, groups of single Greek men lived together—not only under one roof but often also in one room. Early census records confirm that few male Greek immigrants lived alone or owned their living quarters. Extreme parsimony was their operating principle, so that they could save and send as much money as possible back to Greece or launch a business.[7] Usually a half-dozen men would rent a room in a row house and share expenses. Unless the men chose to designate a cook and housekeeper among them, they also shared cooking, cleaning, and shopping chores.

Although men predominated in Washington's early Greek community, women started to trickle in by 1903. As the overall Greek male-female population grew close to one hundred by 1904, and the number of immigrants from the same village increased, early community leaders established *topika somatea*, formal hometown clubs or village associations such as Kokinas's Vourvara Society. Initially, the majority of these organizations were small—with no more than fifteen to thirty members—and were governed by a council. The clubs provided social forums for preserving and enjoying cultural traditions, and also ensured that members in need of medical assistance received financial aid. Their most important goal, however, was to guarantee a steady flow of money back home to Greece.

The Vourvara Society, the first known hometown club in Washington, admitted members from that village only. Founded in November 1904, the society adhered to a constitution with bylaws and articles of incorporation. The club operated under parliamentary procedure, and was formal in keeping its books and membership lists, preparing reports, and, in some instances, transacting business on a cash rather than a barter basis. The club served as a training ground in formal business practices for the newly arrived, who were only familiar with the traditional village-style exchange of services or labor. In this way, the newcomers adopted a new frame of reference and organizational style.

Although the Greek immigrants honored some American administrative and business standards, they still abided by their cultural proprieties. They celebrated Greek Independence Day (March 25) by wearing the traditional Greek *fustanela*. Every Greek household possessed these native costumes, and their display represented a commitment to the homeland. The Greek American community also developed a distinct social structure and, by 1906, was dominated by two *topika somatea* that sponsored picnics, dances, and musical recitals catering specifically to Greek social needs. The importance of these clubs for Greeks—lacking the supportive village networks of home and facing ethnic hostilities, including competing business groups—cannot be overrated.

The resources offered by the larger American society—the government and private charities—were of little help in sustaining Greeks, partly because language and cultural barriers kept the Greek newcomers from using them. A 1910 U.S. Immigration and Naturalization Service study of city populations, including that of Washington, showed few Greeks among the 5,756 persons assisted by Washington's Associated Charities. Instead, like other immigrant groups, the Greek American community generally depended on its own mutual-aid and benefit societies, charitable organizations, nationalist groups, and cultural clubs. Such formal and informal groups created a support network that ultimately touched virtually every Greek household in such American cities as Washington. In 1902 Andre Xenophone, president of New York's Greek Benevolent Society of Pallas Athena, acted on behalf of Greeks in Washington and tried to persuade the District commissioners to provide English-language instruction. When the commissioners denied his request, Xenophone undertook the sponsorship of a night-school class to ensure that his fellow compatriots learned English.

In Washington, as elsewhere, the main objective of the *koinotis*, or organized Greek community, was to raise funds to establish and to maintain a local Greek Orthodox church. The Washington community's effort drew the enthusiasm, cooperation, and financial assistance of almost every one of the Greek immigrants living in the area at that time—including one of the earliest female arrivals, Mrs. Louis P. Dounis. Because club activities, as well as nearly everything else in the early Greek community, were male-oriented, the church provided the only institution open to women's active participation. The increasing number of women and their fund-raising efforts on the church's behalf helped to anchor the evolving community.

The Berbakos family in front of their row house at 119 K Street, NW in 1923. Clockwise from top center, *Nick Berbakos, Mrs. Athena Berbakos, Angelo Berbakos, George Berbakos, Pete Berbakos, and Mr. Patriclos Berbakos. Mr. Berbakos owned a coffeehouse at Four and One-Half and Johnson Streets, NW. (Courtesy Nicholas Chaconas)*

The formal establishment of the Saint Sophia Greek Orthodox Church in 1904 provided Washington's Greek immigrant community with its first permanent place of worship. The earliest settlers had attended religious services conducted in a private home by a Syrian orthodox priest. Later, in 1901 and 1902, the community experimented with a series of itinerant clergymen who helped celebrate the four sacraments of baptism, confirmation, Holy Communion, and marriage. Ultimately the community organized its own church, which became the arena in which Greeks worshiped, attained social recognition, and nurtured relationships. The church also provided security, aid, and comfort to those in need, and fellowship for those facing the perplexities of life in a strange land.

By 1906 the arrival of new immigrants precipitated Saint Sophia's move to larger quarters on C Street, between Sixth and Seventh Streets, NW. A year later the community acquired a permanent priest and an even larger meeting place on the top floor of the former Adas Israel Congregation synagogue, at the southeast corner of Sixth and G Streets, NW, which had been transformed into a commercial building. In 1905 Stephen Gatti converted the ground floor into various business establishments, including a bicycle shop. For the relatively small Greek community, their top-story, sunlit, deep-windowed house of worship provided an ideal temporary home.

As the community grew, so did the church's membership and activities. Overflowing collection trays on Sundays clearly indicated that the church's faithful were engaged in gainful occupations. The community purchased a lot in 1913, and in 1921 the Saint Sophia Greek Orthodox Church community moved into a new church at the northwest corner of Eighth and L Streets.

The story of Aspasia Economon, a member of Saint Sophia, illustrates many of the changes that took place in Washington's Greek community, even within a framework of cultural continuity. Economon, who had been raised by her father, a priest, in a strict orthodox family in Thrace, came to Washington with her mother in 1920. Just seventeen years old, Economon captured the hearts of many suitors in a community where single men predominated. Several months after Economon had presented her favorite suitor with a rose plucked from a bouquet given to the visiting Greek Orthodox Archbishop, Constantine Sakes proposed, and they were married in 1922. The two made a dashing couple at hometown society black-tie balls, and their romantic union reflected the growing trend to marry for love, an American ideal, rather than for convenience, wealth, or other traditional European family considerations.

Although change and growth marked this early period of settlement in the 1910s and 1920s, Greek Americans continued to identify most strongly with their homeland and, more important, with their hometown villages. They still sent remittances back home and often made several ocean crossings back and forth. Furthermore, Greeks, like many other immigrant groups, were reluctant to establish permanent residency in the United States. A 1930 survey of twenty-four nationality groups showed that Greeks ranked last in acquisition of American citizenship. The circumstances surrounding the outbreak of World War I in July 1914 most clearly defined the ambivalent love and loyalty Greek immigrants came to feel toward their homeland over the next several decades.

World War I and questions surrounding Greece's role in it sparked heated political debates, and intolerably strained the cohesion of Greek society, both in Greece and abroad. The immediate cause of the *Ethnikos Dihasmos*, or National Schism, lay in political differences between King Constantine I and his prime minister, Eleutherios Venizelos. Constantine preferred to remain neutral; Venizelos favored the Allies. Although Venizelos ultimately prevailed and committed troops to the Allied cause, the bitterness that ensued continued for years and showed that the prime minister had underestimated the residual support that existed for the crown. Washington's Greek community, described as "one of the most peace-loving and progressive communities in America," did not emerge unscathed from this conflict.

Irreconcilable differences between the political factions finally broke the fragile community in two. In June 1918 ten members of Saint Sophia's parish, including aspiring young law-student George Vournas, founded the new parish of Saints Constantine and Helen Greek Orthodox Church and bought its first place of worship at Sixth and C Streets, SW, beyond the boundaries of the original Greek community. Despite the burdensome financial and social responsibilities each church community now had to bear, the politically motivated sentiments that pervaded every facet of Greek American community and family life precluded a reconciliation between the factions. Thus the Washington Greek community continued as two geographically and politically distinct groups.

By 1920, with the war just over, Greek immigrants faced the difficult decision of whether to stay in the United States and to make their new roots permanent, or to return to their homeland. In spite of internal divisions within their community, many Greeks had amassed sufficient capital to acquire large businesses and to start their own families.[8] Those who decided to remain in the United States also confronted other difficulties, including hostility toward foreigners in postwar America. In the southern states in particular, Greek Americans were attacked by those who, in the name of American "purity," were preaching a doctrine of bigotry and hatred against various ethnic and religious groups.[9]

Congress's passage in 1921 of immigration legislation based on nationality quotas, coupled with threats from the Ku Klux Klan, intensified concern among Greek Americans. The move toward restrictive immigration culminated in the Reed Johnson Act of 1924, which required that the number of immigrants entering the country be determined by a formula based on nationality distribution in the 1890 census. The intent to exclude immigrants who came from southern and eastern Europe was evident in the quota established for Greeks, which allowed only 100 immigrants per year compared with the 28,000 who had entered the United States in 1921.

For Greek Americans, the halt in mass migration had profound consequences—some far-reaching, others immediate. Foreign-born Greeks concluded that it was not only future arrivals who were endangered but also those, such as themselves, who had already settled in America. The restrictions thus

Greek immigrant men and women wear their village costumes and dance to native songs in front of the U.S. Treasury building during the 4 July 1918 Independence Day parade. A large banner of Victory in the background anticipates World War I's outcome in favor of the Allied forces. (Courtesy Virginia Petroutsa)

intensified the immigrants' group consciousness. Additionally, as the number of immigrant associations and the scope of their activities increased, they developed a twofold purpose: to provide sociability, insurance, and assistance; and to serve as an instrument of defense against the overt hostility of a society that rejected their members.

By 1922 the pattern of localism among Greek immigrant associations as embodied in the hometown-club concept came to an end.[10] In that year, a group of Greek American businessmen in Atlanta founded the American Hellenic Educational Progressive Association (AHEPA). A fraternal association with Masonic influences, AHEPA soon grew to become the leading Greek American lodge. It advocated American fraternal forms of organization and process, which could enable its members to transcend the divisive politics familiar from their homeland. Furthermore, except for those who wished to adhere to traditional Greek life, AHEPA met its members' need to assimilate into American society.[11]

After attempting to organize a Washington chapter for almost a year, several of the original AHEPA leaders finally succeeded in August 1924. The Washington chapter's charter members were mostly businesspeople who represented a cross section of the community's early leadership. AHEPA'S officers included V. I. Chebithes, Charles J. Demas, P. L. Doonis, George Devakos, Paul Kolalis, Steven Chaconas, Victor Kissal, George Majouris, and Constantine Lynard. During the chapter's first year the officers implemented a program of Americanization by requiring that one first obtain initial citizenship papers before induction into the chapter.

Fraternal organizations such as AHEPA offered Greeks a new set of standards by which to judge their peers and thus marked a major change in Greek community life. For the first time, Greek Americans did not accept their fellows solely on the basis of a shared ethnic or localist identity. Moreover, Washington's AHEPA focused on ingratiating itself with the larger community by inducting non-Greek honorary members. The chapter also sponsored banquets, planned annual balls and dinners, and donated food and clothing to orphanages as part of a campaign to create general goodwill outside of its ethnic membership and in the Washington business community at large.

A sense of urgency precipitated fairly rapid incorporation of Washington's Greek American businesspeople into the mainstream. By the mid-1930s many Greek Americans had successfully established themselves in small businesses and were increasingly opening larger, service-oriented operations such as wholesale meat and fresh-produce establishments, bottling facilities, bakeries, and coffee companies—a logical progression from their earlier fruit, vegetable, and food-counter ventures. Saint Sophia Greek Orthodox Cathedral's 1934 annual directory carried advertisements from several Greek American vendors, who operated under such names as the Try-Me Bottling Company, the Capital Beverage Company, Model Lunch, Christopher's Pie Company, the Columbia Wholesale Confectionery Company, and National Coffees.

Nonetheless, while Greek American businesspeople sought to avoid using difficult-to-pronounce Greek names on their storefront windows, they maintained a sense of ethnic identity by continuing to deal with compatriots for supplies, services, and various business transactions, including loans. Generally, Greek Americans conducted business in their native tongue when dealing with their peers. Peter Stathes recalled how his brother-in-law, Spiros Versis, who owned one of the largest wholesale condiment operations in Washington, made his daily rounds: "Spiros spoke good English, but he never lost his Greek accent and always maintained his native tongue. His business supplied all the Greek-owned restaurants, so it kept him in touch with Greeks

William P. Loomis wearing the traditional Greek dress, the fustanela, in 1944. Note the AHEPA logo on his hat. (Courtesy Margaret Loomis)

all day long. When he would go into a Greek restaurant, he only spoke Greek."

As the 1930s ended, Greek Americans began to experience a degree of assimilation that would catapult them into mainstream American society both socially and culturally. Italy's invasion of Greece in the fall of 1940 marked the second major watershed for the Greek American community: Greece succeeded in throwing back the invaders in October 1940, and for months thereafter Greek Americans basked in unaccustomed acclaim as the American media lauded the heroism of their compatriots in Greece.

When the United States entered World War II in December 1941, Greek American support for the war effort was highly visible and genuine. Never before had Greek and American interests coalesced so well. Between 1941 and 1944 numerous press accounts highlighted the Washington Greek community's patriotism and contributions to the war effort. Local Greek American patriotism also made national headlines when AHEPA launched a multimillion-dollar war-bond effort spearheaded by Washingtonian George Vournas. By the time the war ended, Greek Americans had comfortably "arrived" in American society.

The prosperity that followed World II brought Greek Americans yet another opportunity for upward mobility, particularly in Washington, where successful small businesspeople predominated in the local Greek American immigrant community. Discussing the restaurant business, George Dravillas, a first-generation Greek American who had prospered through the Washington real estate market, noted that:

> During the war the Greeks made a lot of money. The money they amassed was through the servicemen who came to Washington. They would get fifty to sixty servicemen for dinner in one of their restaurants down on Seventh Street, NW, and the owners would literally sweep the floor with the money the servicemen [threw] away. The men felt that since they were being sent to Japan to fight, they might as well have as much fun as they could.

Greek Americans' growing prosperity entrenched them in the middle class. They began to move away from their established neighborhoods on Fourth Street and Seventh through Eleventh Streets, NW, to more spacious, detached homes on Sixteenth Street, and eventually into the suburbs. Despite the community's geographic dispersion the churches continued to serve as social, cultural, and spiritual centers, providing the physical space essential for ongoing interpersonal relations.

Like other upwardly mobile ethnic groups, Greek Americans in Washington confronted the question of how much to adapt to the dominant Anglo-American folkways and how much to retain and to perpetuate their homeland's traditions. Such age-old cultural expressions as dance, music, and theater have bridged the divide and sustained the common bonds of an instinctively strong ethnic identity. For Greeks, dancing is not merely an enjoyable form of expression but a way of preserving a sense of self in times of hardship and cultural upheaval. For several years, Independence Day parades in Washington afforded Greek immigrant men and women, clad in native costumes, the opportunity to dance and to play Greek musical instruments. In addition, hometown societies sponsored ballroom dances throughout the year, which provided opportunities to enact all the ceremonies of life—high-spirited and solemn—through dance.

The formation of the Mandolin Society in the 1910s by a group of young Greek men who played both classical and native Greek music provided another means of preserving and perpetuating ties to the homeland. The group practiced every week through the 1920s at 516 Ninth Street, NW, above the Greek-owned New England Restaurant. In addition to exhibiting their love of music, Greek men and women demonstrated their acting prowess by performing in plays, occasionally in new works written by community members. Approximately ten to fifteen thespians would regularly meet at the Old Palace Hall, at Seventh and U streets, NW, to rehearse for community-sponsored performances. They ultimately performed *Children of Two Wars* at the National Theater.

In today's Greek American community similar traditions manifest themselves at ethnic bazaars and picnics, dances, meetings of fraternal organizations, Greek-language classes, film showings, and musical and theatrical presentations. Most important, however, are the rituals of the Greek Orthodox church. The community has five churches: two in the District (Saint Sophia Greek Orthodox Cathedral, now at Thirty-sixth Street and Massachusetts Avenue, NW, and Saints Constantine and Helen Greek Orthodox Church, now at Sixteenth and Upshur Streets, NW); two in Maryland (Saint George Greek Orthodox Church in Bethesda and Saint Theodore Greek Orthodox Church in Takoma Park); and Saint Katherine Greek Orthodox in Falls Church, Virginia. The churches serve as primary links to traditional culture and perpetuate the language and the many subtle traditions that signify Greek American community life, much as did the small Saint Sophia Greek Orthodox Cathedral community when it met above a store at Sixth and G Streets, NW, with James Kokinas as one of the congregation's twelve founders. Kokinas, who lived into his mid-nineties, sank deep roots into his new homeland. His offspring and those of the other Greek immigrants who came to Washington in the first half of the century have left an enduring imprint on the capital's business, civic, and cultural life.

NOTES

1. Much of the primary material for this essay comes from tape-recorded interviews I have conducted with first- and second-generation Washington Greek Americans. The interviews not only provide accounts of the early period of Greek immigration but also corroborate the oral histories collected in the late 1960s and 1970s by the late Pete Chipouras, a longtime Washingtonian and lawyer for the U.S. Postal Service. Chipouras had drafted an initial outline for a book based on years of gathering oral histories, but had to curtail his research after suffering a stroke in the late 1970s. The material given to me by his wife in 1986 proved to be an invaluable resource—especially with regard to the early church. The oral histories on which this

essay is based are in my possession. Several of the notable figures of Washington's early Greek American community are still alive, and one, George Vournas (born in Messenia, Greece, in 1897), contributed to the essay. Other primary sources for the essay include personal written records, business records, and accounts of Greek American business organizations, and Greek American newspapers, church records, newsletters, family albums, and personal documents, photographs, and letters.

2. See Phyllis Pease Chock, "Key Symbols and Social Categories in Greek American Ethnicity," in *Washington Anthropological Careers: Perspectives on Research, Employment and Training*, ed. Ruth Landman (Washington, D.C.: Anthropological Society of Washington, 1981).

3. For conditions in Greece, see, for example, Helen Zeese Papanikolas, *Toil and Rage in a New Land: The Greek Immigrants in Utah* (Salt Lake City, Utah: *Utah Historical Quarterly,* 1974).

4. Phyllis Pease Chock, "The Greek-American Small Businessman: A Cultural Analysis," *Journal of Anthropological Research* 37 (Spring 1981): 47–60, corroborates information obtained through the oral histories of local Greek Americans.

5. Tames recalled warm memories of his black childhood friends who lived on the same street in downtown Washington. The Greeks, he remembered,

> were very friendly with the blacks. In fact, I was envious of my black childhood friends because the first Christmas tree I ever saw was displayed in one of their homes. In those days the Greeks were very much opposed to the celebration of Christmas and gift giving. My mother made a tremendous concession one year when she placed a beautiful Christmas tree in our Victorian row house third-floor apartment window. Though we shared the house with other Greek families, many black families dwelled in the other small Victorian rowhouses on our block.

Another Greek pioneer, George Vournas, recalled that restaurants owned by the Greeks catered to the black community when other restaurants would not allow blacks to enter or to be served.

The recollections of Hortense Mims Fitzgerald, a longtime Washington educator, offer a corroborating view. Fitzgerald, whose parents had migrated from Louisiana when she had been an infant, recalled what it was like growing up in the segregated city, where "the black people's world ended [at] about Florida Avenue." She also remembered that not far from her childhood home on Massachusetts Avenue, near Union Station:

> Our neighbors . . . were mostly white. There was a little Greek girl my Mama would let me play with. Her name was Kristoula Generis. Her father ran the store on the corner of Third and H Streets. That was very grand because I could go up with Kristoula and Mr. Generis would give us candy or gum or something and you felt kind of big just walking in the store like that without any money. I was invited to their parties and I had lovely times. I can remember the tasty Greek cakes that would melt in your mouth. There were many Greek people who lived around the Greek Orthodox Church there on Eighth and I Streets.

> Kristoula, I remember, had to go to two schools. She would go to the public school for half the day and then to Greek Orthodox school the other half.

See the Hortense Mims Fitzgerald interview in Keith Melder, Kathryn Schneider Smith, et al., eds., *City of Magnificent Intentions: A History of the District of Columbia* (Washington, D.C.: D.C. History Curriculum Project of Associates for Renewal in Education, 1985), 299.

6. *Washington Post*, 7 December 1972.

7. Twelfth U.S. Census Records, Population Schedule for the District of Columbia, 1910, National Archives, Washington, D.C.

8. Greek couples tended to have large families (an average of 5 to 6 children), at least until the 1970s.

9. See, for example, Barbara Billinis Colessides, "Greek Immigration and Adjustment to the United States, 1960–1985" (master's thesis, University of Tulsa, 1988).

10. Charles Moskos, *Greek Americans: Struggle and Success* (Englewood Cliffs, N.J.: Prentice-Hall, 1980), 40 and passim.

11. George J. Leber, *The History of the Order of AHEPA* (Washington, D.C.: Order of AHEPA, 1972).

ADDITIONAL READING

Kopan, Andrew T. *The Greeks in Chicago: A Study of Ethnic Achievement.* Urbana: University of Illinois Press, 1989.

Psomiades, Harry, and Alice Scourby. *The Greek American Community in Transition.* New York: Pella Publishing Company, 1982.

Scourby, Alice. *The Greek Americans.* Boston: Twayne Publishing, 1984.

11.

From Pennsylvania Avenue to H Street, NW

The Transformation of Washington's Chinatown

Esther Ngan-ling Chow

Chinese Americans' immigration history began in 1820, when the U.S. Immigration Commission reported the arrival of the first Chinese in the United States.[1] Poverty, political oppression, and social turmoil in feudal China, compounded by natural disasters, drove many Chinese to emigrate in the mid-nineteenth century. When gold was discovered in 1848 near Sacramento, California, among the first to arrive for the California gold rush were two Chinese men, who worked as laborers in the mines, and one Chinese woman, who was employed as a domestic servant. By 1852 the then-thriving U.S. economy—marked by rapid growth of the American West, the high demand for cheap unskilled labor, and the gold rush's promise of quick riches—had attracted more than 20,000 Chinese, most of them men. Cultural restrictions, familial responsibilities, and the cost of travel from China, combined with severe hardships in the New West—which included anti-Chinese sentiment and outright discrimination—generally discouraged Chinese women from emigrating.

The Chinese men were willing to work hard for low wages under poor conditions. Initially, they filled jobs unwanted by white workers. By the mid-1850s, however, the Chinese presence became a sore point with unemployed white workers and labor unions. After Chinese laborers finished working on the Transcontinental Railroad in 1869, some were recruited to provide labor in other cities, thus creating a far-flung network of relatives and compatriots that supported subsequent Chinese migrants, who were also gradually forced eastward in search of employment.

A national economic recession in the 1870s exacerbated labor problems on the West Coast, and Chinese laborers became the scapegoats of both industrialists and organized labor. Exclusionary policies against Chinese immigrants were effected in public schools, jobs, mining industries, unions, and skilled trades. In a series of riots and massacres in the West in the 1870s and 1880s, angry whites lynched and murdered many Chinese and destroyed their communities. California constitutional provisions in 1879 actually forbade the hiring of Chinese by incorporated firms as well as by state, municipal, and local governments. By 1882 anti-Chinese sentiment led to Congress's passage of the Chinese Exclusion Act, prohibiting further immigration of Chinese laborers and barring the courts from issuing citizenship to those already in the United States. Thousands of Chinese on the West Coast who lacked support and feared for their lives migrated to the East Coast, the Midwest, and the South in search of less hostile environments and better economic opportunities.

These early Chinese Americans, following general migration patterns, went to major urban centers where jobs might be available; Washington, as the U.S. capital, was one of the major cities that attracted Chinese migrants. Chiang Kai, documented as Washington's first Chinese resident, settled on Pennsylvania Avenue in 1851. Many more Chinese, primarily originating from southern China, arrived in the District following the anti-Chinese atrocities on the West Coast.

Washington's first Chinatown developed in the 1880s on Pennsylvania Avenue near Four and One-Half Street, NW (now John Marshall Place). In 1878 there were no stores in this tiny enclave. There were, however, a few street vendors such as Kit Ah, who sold tea. By 1881 the city directory listed four Chinese laundries: Lee Ning Harry's, Shing Wong Wing's, Sing Horp's, and Sing Wah's. Washington's Chinese population in 1884 comprised about one hundred inhabitants, some of whom lived in the newly emerging Chinatown while others were scattered throughout the city. In 1892 the Toe Sing Chung Grocery Store was opened in Chinatown; two others were opened in the next two years. By 1898 the area had expanded to include six buildings on the south side of Pennsylvania Avenue between Third Street and Four and One-Half Street, NW, and a row of old brick houses on the west side of Four and One-Half Street just below Pennsylvania Avenue. Some of these buildings had stores on the ground floor with living quarters above; others had stores in the front and living quarters in the rear.

By 1903 Washington's Chinatown was bustling with its own drugstores, restaurants, barbershops, tailor shops, mercantile establishments, and fraternal lodges. According to a March 1903 *Washington Times* article, Chinatown was considered an "orderly and well-regulated community, with stores neatly kept and stocked with canned goods, preserved fruits, gifts, and Chinese foodstuffs."[2] The community gradually expanded along both sides of lower Pennsylvania

Taken in 1891, this photograph provides a rare view of early Chinatown on the south side of Pennsylvania Avenue, NW, near the Capitol. (Photograph by L. C. Handy, courtesy Washingtoniana Division, D.C. Public Library)

Avenue between Third and Sixth Streets, NW. The 1914 city directory documents the existence of the Sun Sing Laundry; Lee Ying's cigar manufacturing; the Yuen Hong Low and Tong Hing Low restaurants; the Lee Yick and Wah Chong grocery, and the import companies of Yuen Chong, Wah Yick, Kim Lai Yueng, High Yuen, Tuck Cheong, Puen Chong, and Hop Duey—all within the Chinese commercial cluster on Pennsylvania Avenue, NW.

The formation of a Chinatown in Washington, as in other major cities, was primarily a self-defense mechanism. Prevailing discrimination, racial tension, and economic hardship led early Chinese Americans to form distinctively ethnic enclaves to protect themselves from the larger, mostly hostile society. Within these closed communities they felt a sense of security and support. With better jobs reserved for whites, economic survival, not personal preference, mandated that the Chinese accept menial jobs as cooks, waiters, launderers, tailors, domestic servants, unskilled laborers, and construction workers. Ethnic businesses—most commonly laundries and restaurants—afforded financial security and autonomy for entrepreneurs excluded from other occupations.

Most of the early Chinese immigrants were men who hoped either to return to their families in China after they had made a small fortune, or to save enough money to bring their families to the United States. However, the Chinese Exclusion Act of 1882, the Geary Act of 1892, and the Exclusion Act of 1924—which remained in effect until 1943—thwarted their dreams by forbidding Chinese wives from joining their husbands and thereby preventing

An early twentieth-century Chinese restaurant (circa 1930) on Pennsylvania Avenue, NW, in the original Chinatown. (Courtesy Washingtoniana Division, D.C. Public Library)

family reunification. Additionally, mixed marriages— even those between Chinese men and American-born Chinese women—were prohibited. The legislation thus severely limited Chinese population growth and Chinese family formation. The heavily unbalanced sex ratio in Washington's Chinatown resulted in a dearth of marriageable partners for the Chinese men, the survival of only a few families, and the establishment of a primarily bachelor community. According to the *Evening Star* in 1898, no Chinese women could be seen in Chinatown.[3] By 1908 there were only two or three women, and even as late as 1927 no more than fifteen Chinese women could be seen by outsiders.

In the absence of traditional family life, Chinatown became a familiar and convenient place for Chinese men to congregate and to bolster their group identification. On Sundays, their only free day, they gathered together, enjoyed Chinese meals, obtained provisions, attended Sunday school at nearby American churches, and were updated on news about China.

Within the microcosm of Chinatown, residents set up district associations (tongs) and family associations to meet the members' needs. Still in existence today, these social institutions have served protective, charitable, and governing functions, thereby easing the immigrants' and migrants' transitions. District associations are governing bodies that settle differences between Chinese of diverse backgrounds. The first such association, the G. King Tong, was organized in 1894; the Washington branch of the On Leong Merchants Association was formed in 1912; and the local Hip Sing Labor and Commercial Association was founded in 1925. At about the same time, family associations, including the Lee Association established in 1905, were formed for those with the same surnames or from related clans. These family associations served as ruling bodies and economic cooperatives or credit unions, consolidating limited resources and power to serve the community's daily needs and to bind members closely together. In 1920 a local tong war that resulted in a Chinese waiter's death provided an excuse for city police to conduct interrogations in Chinatown and to ferret out illegal immigrants. Pressured by the police and by the Chinese community itself, which wished to avoid external interference in its affairs, the tongs worked out an informal reconciliation and have since become more cooperative.

Until stereotypes distorted society's perception of early Chinese Americans—their culture and their community—Chinese people were initially portrayed by the press as hardworking, honest, and frugal, "one of the inoffensive foreign elements" in the city. Newspaper articles in 1898 and 1903 claimed that a visit to Chinatown (the "colony of the Mongolians") to see Chinese customs, artifacts, and life patterns so different from those of other Americans was "as good as a trip to the museum." Ignorance and misunderstanding, however, resulted in the gradual tarnishing of these early images. By the 1920s Chinese Americans were often viewed as secretive, mysterious, and inscrutable.[4] The dominant press overwhelmingly depicted them as wearing black attire, smoking long pipes, and speaking strangely. Chinatown's reputation eventually dwindled to the degree that it came to be seen as dilapidated, unclean, and unsafe.

Lacking opportunities to move into the American mainstream, the Chinese maintained their own way of life and spent their leisure hours in limited social circles. This insularity tended to further Chinatown's image as mysterious and of its members as unassimilable. The press continued to report sensational tales of tong wars, gambling, opium dens, vice, crime, and violent rivalries between business groups with roots in China. Aside from limited formal dealings with whites, Chinese interaction with other races was not commonly reported. Black women were reportedly hired to do washing for Chinese launderers, however, and a few interracial marriages between white women and Chinese merchants were noted in the press.

Federal beautification plans for the city in the late 1920s and early 1930s brought tragedy to the original Chinatown, whose culture and architecture came to be viewed as a blight on Pennsylvania Avenue. In 1929, after the Chinese had lived in the area for nearly fifty years, the federal government forced the evacuation of Chinatown to make room for the construction of federal and district municipal buildings planned as part of the Federal Triangle project. The Chinese lacked the political clout to halt their community's destruction, and the 398 Chinese living in the area had no choice but to move.[5]

In an effort to find new homes for the displaced residents, the influential On Leong Merchants Association, with its New York headquarters' assistance, became involved in real estate negotiations to lease or to purchase eleven properties at Chinatown's present site, in the vicinity of H Street between Fifth and Seventh Streets, NW. This proposed relocation of Chinatown met with hostility from white property owners on H Street, who petitioned the government to keep the Chinese out, fearing that they would bring about a rapid deterioration of rental and housing values and would not attract new business to the area.[6]

Although the petition failed, the relocation of Chinatown in 1931 from Pennsylvania Avenue to its present site generated further resistance and antagonism. White residents worked out discriminatory agreements with real estate agents to prevent any heavy concentration of Chinese in the area. For example, they bought buildings that real estate agents had previously offered for sale to the Chinese, thereby hindering the latter for many years from buying property and renting apartments. This geographic confinement reduced Chinatown's capability to grow in physical space as well as in population.

Nevertheless, Chinese Americans forged ahead with renewed spirit, building better homes—in terms of space and adequate electricity—than those they had been forced to leave. In 1936 one observer, V. Ray Sawyer, estimated that 800 Chinese were living in Chinatown, in addition to others living outside the neighborhood. He reported that Chinatown was then home to thirty-two families, twelve shops, eight associations and men's lodges, and thirty-four students attending local universities and colleges.[7] Additionally, 145 Chinese laundries and sixty-two Chinese restaurants were scattered across the city.

Within this new niche, Chinese Americans formally established various social institutions that paralleled those in the larger U.S. society yet were distinct to their own ethnic group. The district and family associations remained powerful ruling bodies and judicial groups that settled disputes within the community, although their importance declined somewhat over time. The three largest family associations were the Lee, the Moy, and the Chen. These groups' major functions were generally to provide support to the needy, to take care of the sick, to bury the dead, to attend to the welfare of the elderly (especially those with no family in the area), to give credit and loans, to supply general medical services, and to help youngsters seeking educational and employment opportunities. Betty Lee Sung, author of *Mountain of Gold*, recalled that when she had been growing up in Washington, reliance on close family ties and on district or family associations for financial assistance and the resolution of familial and community grievances had been critical for her family's survival.

The desire to preserve Chinese culture, an important concern of the community, was reflected in the establishment of Washington's first Chinese school in 1931. Children could attend this school in the evening, after their American classes, to learn about Chinese customs and ways of life. Curricula included Chinese history, arithmetic, geography, brush writing, and singing. The creation of this school suggests that Washington's Chinese had finally begun to establish substantial families, so central to Chinese culture.

The Reverend C. C. Hung, who had been born in China and had migrated to Washington from Detroit, established the city's first Chinese Christian church in 1935. The hardworking parishioners pooled their meager earnings and eventually raised enough funds to construct their own building, which was completed in 1939, near Eleventh and L Streets, NW. The church provided not only spiritual but also physical and emotional support for several generations. The congregation offered its own Chinese school for children and later added the Chinatown Service Center to provide much-needed social services, outreach, and referrals.

Shau Yan Leung, who had come to the community in 1939 to complete his doctoral degree in foreign service and international law at Georgetown University, was recruited to teach at the church's new school. When interviewed in 1990 at the age of eighty-one, he recalled that the church, through its devoted members and the Reverend Hung's leadership, reached out to the needy and the isolated and mediated community conflicts. The church also sustained many Chinese in their ongoing struggle for economic survival. According to Leung:

> Earning a living was extremely hard for the Chinese. Many used all their energies and time working at more than one job to earn extra pennies to support themselves and their families here or back in China. Being excluded from the dominant society, there seemed to be no life outside of Chinatown for many Chinese.

With limited access to entertainment facilities and few opportunities to intermingle with outsiders, the Chinese turned to their own resources for leisure.

*The Chinese Community Church Parish Hall and Educational Building (left), the Rev.
C. C. Hung, pastor and principal of the Chinese Language School (upper right), and Shau
Yan Leung (bottom), a doctoral student at Georgetown University and a teacher at the Chi-
nese school in 1940. (© Washington Post, courtesy Eastern Wind, Inc.)*

They organized a music and art group, the Ching Sing Club, which gave its first
benefit concert for the church's Chinese school in 1936. The Pythian Temple
on Ninth Street, NW, now demolished, was another popular entertainment
center for the Chinese community for decades. Gambling in various forms, including a Chinese lottery, was a common recreation outlet.

 Changing political and economic circumstances, which have historically
shaped race relations, deeply affected Washington's Chinatown. During the
Great Depression, community life hinged on stark survival. Social tensions
during the depression contributed to increased racial stereotyping and lowered

regard for the Chinese. One elderly Chinese man, remembering how difficult it was to earn a living in the 1930s and 1940s, described how strained social relations had become:

> Even though [the] Chinese had some money, they could not buy a lot of things. . . . Like blacks, Chinese and [other] Asians are colored . . . and had to walk out in the streets, and the whites walked on the sidewalks.[8]

Despite the Chinese community's limited interaction with other Washingtonians, the scarcity of Chinese women as potential mates resulted in some interracial marriages. In 1943 W. E. Hogan, a graduate student, reported fifty-six Chinese/white and six Chinese/black marriages, as well as 175 common-law marriages between Chinese and non-Chinese.[9]

The international scene also dictated changing attitudes toward Chinese Americans. The Sino-Japanese War (1937–1945) evoked sympathy and support from local Chinese; Washington's Chinese community raised funds for refugees and, in unusual displays of public unity and outrage that mobilized the community's men, women, and children, held numerous political demonstrations against Japanese aggression. During World War II, with the United States at war with Japan and with anti-Japanese sentiment rampant, American whites frequently mistook Chinese for Japanese. Fear of displaced racism toward their group led many Chinese to hang American flags from their homes and businesses and to devise identification cards and emblems to show the crossed flags of the United States and China. Some Chinese Americans, pledging their loyalty to the nation, joined the U.S. military to fight against Japan. After the war, with China hailed as a U.S. ally, positive attitudes toward the Chinese reemerged. Chinese businesspeople responded in turn by hiring more white waitresses and black assistants in their restaurants and shops.

In 1943, partially as a result of improved relations with China during World War II, Congress repealed the restrictive immigration laws that had both excluded Chinese and imposed severe restrictions on those already in the country. In the two decades following the repeal of the repressive laws, Washington's Chinatown experienced a gradual population growth and community transformation.

Nevertheless, the community's evolution continued to be influenced by larger social forces. For example, in the 1960s, as the U.S. economy shifted from labor-intensive to capital-intensive industries, Chinese laundries began to decline. The convenience of automatic laundromats, the popularity of permanent press and other synthetic fabrics, and the availability of automatic washers and dryers in households reduced the demand for hand laundries. Conversely, Chinese cuisine and delicacies gained such popularity that Chinese restaurants became the predominant ethnic business.

Yet, international developments continued to affect public perceptions of Chinese Americans. Anti-Chinese sentiment escalated anew when mainland China became a communist state in 1949 and continued throughout the cold war years of the 1960s and 1970s. Although some Chinese had been living in the United States for many years, and second- and third-generation Chinese Americans spoke English as their first language, they were still often considered "foreigners" and thus distrusted. They were also frequently suspected of being communist agents, which caused great concern—particularly for those Chinese who worked for the federal government. When diplomatic relations between China and the United States improved in the 1970s, attitudes toward the Chinese became less hostile, but the continually fluctuating U.S. relations with China caused understandable wariness.

The Chinese American community grew relatively slowly throughout the 1950s, but absorbed a new wave of members in the mid-1960s, when the U.S. government expanded the quota for Chinese immigrants. Under the new immigration laws, spouses and children were able to join those Chinese with U.S. citizenship or resident-alien status for family unification. The political turmoil in China led three major groups to immigrate here in the early 1950s: families with money and education who came when the communists took over mainland China; students and displaced Chinese living or studying in other countries, but whose hopes for returning home had been dashed; and refugees who fled China for political freedom. Some, faced with economic deprivation in their homeland, were attracted by the still prevalent and exaggerated tales of America as the "gold mountain." Under an occupational-preference system, Chinese with special professional training and with skills in short supply in the United States were allowed to apply for immigrant status. Under these conditions emerged a new group of Chinese immigrants who differed from those who had come earlier. In general, the newcomers came from more diverse geographic regions in China than had their predecessors, were relatively younger, included more females, were better educated, were more skilled, and were more likely to have professional status.

This influx of new immigrants helped Washington's Chinatown regain its vitality and eventually develop into a large community that went beyond the geographic boundaries of Chinatown itself. By 1966 approximately 3,000 Chinese immigrants and American-born Chinese resided in Washington. Many of the newcomers adapted to the city with the assistance of ethnic organizations,

A grocer from the east end of the 600 block of H Street, NW, delivers vegetables to nearby restaurants on 15 March 1981. He passes the China Inn Restaurant, which had been recently renovated with a modern design. (Photograph by Tim Dillon, © Washington Post, courtesy Washingtoniana Division, D.C. Public Library)

family ties, and friendship networks that bound old-timers and newcomers together. As in the past, more Chinese lived outside than inside Chinatown. The physical community nonetheless remained a haven for recent immigrants, who preferred to live in a culturally familiar locale where they could speak their native language, readily find jobs in Chinese enterprises, and obtain supplies for daily needs.

While new immigrants were arriving in Chinatown, established families began moving out, following the urban trend toward decentralization. Second-generation families, as well as some recent immigrants, began to move to the suburbs, where family circles and new social networks provided companionship, strong support, and financial assistance that had previously been available only in Chinatown. Modern Chinese restaurants, gift shops, and grocery stores began to appear in uptown Washington and suburban shopping areas, where they provided food supplies and other conveniences for Chinese American suburbanites. Although the 1968 riots that had followed Martin Luther King Jr.'s assassination discouraged some suburban Chinese from shopping downtown, many others visited that area regularly with family or friends to stock up on supplies and to attend meetings, churches, and occasional social events.

By the 1970s, according to such observers as James V. Allred, distorted impressions of the Chinese that prevailed during the cold war period had changed to positive ones.[10] They argued that the press and public opinion generally began to view the Chinese as respectable and law-abiding, and to attribute to strong family ties the fact that few Chinese were on welfare or in jail. Other observers, however, maintained that old stereotypes (including Hollywood's portrayal of Chinese characters as sneaky, inscrutable, dangerous, and cunning—traits embodied in Fu Manchu, Charlie Chan, and various notorious "dragon ladies") were simply replaced by new ones, which, though more subtle, were just as insidious. Significantly, a young generation of Chinese Americans emerged to address those images and to urge abolition of all ethnic and racial stereotypes, regardless of how trivial they might appear.

Such activity marked the development of a new consciousness among Chinese Americans and a turning point in the history of the Chinese in Washington. The 1960s social movements that fought for civil rights advances for minorities had a ripple effect on the previously politically quiescent Chinese community. The civil rights movement awakened some Chinese to their history of oppression shared with other minority groups and increased their awareness of their own ethnic heritage's importance. Several new groups were formed and became involved in such community activities as the Chinatown History Project, the Chinatown Mural Project, and the *East-Wind Newsletter*. Other groups—such as the Organization of Chinese Americans, the Organization of Chinese American Women, and the Organization of Pan Asian Women—promoted the rights and general welfare of Chinese/Asian Americans and women. Chinese Americans also benefited from affirmative-action policies and programs in employment, education, credit, and small-business entrepreneurship.

Throughout the 1970s Chinese Americans' racial consciousness, ethnic pride, and community activism were at an all-time high. Friendly relations between the Chinese community and the city's majority black population began to develop through cooperative church and civic activities. As did African Americans, Hispanic Americans, and other minority groups, the Chinese became more active inside and outside their own community, leaving their mark on the city's evolving urban structure and culture.

A Chinese American woman poses with an American flag. (Photograph by Ray Lustig, © Washington Post, courtesy Washingtoniana Division, D.C. Public Library)

Since the early 1970s, Washington's urban-renewal and redevelopment plans have once again posed a direct threat to Chinatown's physical existence and ethnic identity. The District's blossoming tourist industry created a need for such centralized facilities as a convention hall and hotels. An ambitious redevelopment project included a sports and convention center to the west of Chinatown, new hotel and department-store complexes to the north and south, the retention and expansion of existing government offices to the east and southeast, and a Metro subway stop in Chinatown. The convention-center plan alone, which originally called for a location close to Chinatown's center, would have necessitated the demolition of many buildings and the displacement of 13 percent of the residents, and would have caused skyrocketing property values that would have made housing less affordable and more scarce. Concomitantly, the ethnic heritage that many Chinese deeply valued would gradually have eroded as a result of the shrinking of Chinatown.

When these plans for redevelopment and urban renewal were announced, Chinatown centered around a group of small shops and restaurants and housed approximately 500 residents, mainly Chinese—many of them immigrant families and the elderly—although a few whites, blacks, and other Asians also lived

A Chinese New Year parade drew a diverse crowd to the 600 block of H Street, NW.
(© *Washington Post*, *courtesy Washingtoniana Division, D.C. Public Library*)

in the community. Refugees of Chinese descent from Indochina, as well as immigrants from various parts of the People's Republic of China and from Hong Kong and Taiwan, were gradually replacing the substantial proportion of earlier southern Chinese immigrants. New immigrants, primarily from low-income groups with few skills and limited knowledge of English, continually filled Chinatown's rental apartments—no matter how deteriorated the facilities were. Many of these families could not afford automobiles and therefore preferred to live downtown, as did those who worked long hours in the neighborhood and could not afford commuting time.

In addition, the first-generation elderly, who constituted a sizable proportion of Chinatown's population, were among those who would have been hardest hit by construction of the proposed convention center. They generally lived alone, away from grown children who had moved out of the neighborhood. Self-reliant to some extent, they preferred to live in Chinatown because of its conveniences and their familiarity with its cultural milieu, in which they could speak their native language and associate with others in similar social circumstances. Many of them could also be categorized as among the urban poor; as

This 1975 photograph of a "Save Chinatown" banner near Seventh Street, NW, remains relevant twenty years later, as new plans are underway for another, larger convention center and a downtown sports arena. (Photograph by Robert Lee and Harry Chow, courtesy Eastern Wind, Inc.)

such they endured dilapidated housing, language barriers, crime, poverty, and limited health and social services.

Like the African American communities of Georgetown and southwest Washington, Chinatown seemed about to fall victim to urban growth, commercialism, and persistent underlying racism. This time, however, the community responded. Religious and community leaders, businesspeople, and activists inside and outside Chinatown formed a broad-based coalition to denounce efforts to destroy the community and launched several protest rallies and demonstrations. Although some Chinese merchants and other businesspeople, arguing that the convention center would increase economic prosperity, favored its construction, others expressed concern about the preservation of Chinese culture and the community's cohesiveness. The forces of urban renewal and high-stakes speculative development, however, resulted in purchase offers that most Chinese businesspeople found difficult to refuse. By the late 1980s only about 25 percent of Chinatown was still owned by Chinese, and the futures of many Chinese businesses were in the hands of absentee landlords.

As the Chinese lost control over their community's redevelopment, many residential buildings were replaced by commercial properties that were more profitable for developers. Although Chinese residents and merchants welcomed the arrival of the Metro station, prolonged construction delays caused inconveniences and loss of business as well as actual damage to the premises and the merchandise of some stores along Seventh Street. (Responsibility for repairs was later assumed by the Washington Metropolitan Transit Authority.) As one concerned Chinese man remarked in a *Washington Post* article, the question is not "how much Chinatown will look like Chinatown when it's all done, but how much of Chinatown will be left when it's all done."[11]

In an effort to retain Chinese residents and to revitalize Chinatown, several Chinese groups were able to secure funding from the U.S. Department of Housing and Urban Development and to begin construction, at Sixth and H Streets, NW, of a 153-apartment complex of Chinese design, the Wah Luck House (House of Happiness). Completed in 1982, it has provided subsidized housing for displaced residents and the elderly from both Chinese and non-Chinese, low- and moderate-income families.

The Chinese community also secured a modest victory when city officials agreed to move the convention center several blocks west to Ninth and H Streets, NW, to ensure the neighborhood's cultural continuity. Nonetheless, when the D.C. Convention Center officially opened in 1983, one-hundred Chinese families had been displaced and 12 percent of the area torn down. Overall, redevelopment has proved to be a mixed blessing to Chinatown residents, bringing fortune to a prosperous few but failing to meet the needs of the majority—especially the elderly and the more recently arrived immigrant families.

The elaborate, Chinese-style "Friendship Archway"—erected in Chinatown with joint financing from the District and Beijing governments and officially opened in November 1986—symbolizes the intended revitalization of the Chinatown community. Although its construction sparked intense conflict between those loyal to the People's Republic of China and those loyal to Taiwan, the archway, symbolically reaffirming Chinese Americans' identity, ethnic pride, and cultural heritage, refreshes Chinatown's image and reasserts its significance to the larger community.

Still limited in space by its fixed boundaries, Chinatown's resident population has gradually decreased since the late 1960s, although estimates by community leaders show a slight increase in recent years. According to the 1990 census, 55,250 Chinese live in the Washington metropolitan area, with 3,144 of them in the District. The problem of declining population in Chinatown is magnified by concern for cultural loss. Some older residents have complained that many young people cannot read or speak Chinese or learn about their cultural traditions, because their families have moved to other parts of the metropolitan area. Others, however, feel that residential decentralization among Chinese Americans may also indicate that the community has transcended the spatial and economic boundaries of Chinatown. With shared values, traditions, language, and life-styles, Washington's Chinese Americans, both inside and outside Chinatown, remain bound together by their ethnic identity, cultural heritage, kinship, and friendship ties.

NOTES

1. This essay is based on archival research, interviews with both community leaders and longtime residents, and participant observations in the Washington, D.C., Chinese community since the mid-1970s.

2. Chinatown Slumming Parties Are Now the Fad," *Washington Times*, 29 March 1903. See also "A Bit of the Orient on the Capital's Main Avenue," *Washington Times*, 14 December 1902; and "Through Washington's Chinatown," *Evening Star* 6 September 1908.

3. For a discussion of Chinatown's early development, see "A Trip to Chinatown," *Evening Star*, 8 January 1898.

4. E. C. Cohen, "Chinatown Has Own Spirit of Exclusiveness," *Evening Star*, 14 August 1927.

5. "Where Will Chinatown Locate?" *Washington Times*, 6 August 1929.

6. Interview with "Uncle John" by Tommy Doong in "Washington, D.C.'s Chinese Community: Chinatown," August 1975, Report, Chinatown History Project, Collection of Esther Ngan-Ling Chow, 16–18. "Uncle John," Chinese senior citizen, remembered the bitterness accompanying the community's relocation in 1931. He reported that Ninth and L Streets, NW, was another site being considered, but that most people preferred Sixth and H Streets because the latter intersection was closer to stores and transportation. White residents in the area publicly and with racist overtones announced their rejection of the new residents. See also "Chinese Invasion of H Street Irks Property Owners," *Washington Post*, 10 October 1931.

7. V. Ray Sawyer, "The Chinese in Washington, D.C.," George Washington University, May 1936 (Washingtoniana Collection, D.C. Public Library, Washington, D.C., photocopy).

8. Tommy Doong, "Interview: Mr. Y," in "Washington, D.C.'s Chinese Community: Chinatown," August 1975, Report, Chinatown History Project, 18.

9. W. E. Hogan, "A Sociological Study of Interracial Marriage by the Chinese in the District of Columbia" (master's thesis, Catholic University, 1943).

10. James V. Allred, "The Chinese Community in Washington, D.C.," Catholic University, December 1970, Washingtoniana Collection, D.C. Public Library, Washington, D.C.

11. James Wu, "Chinatown Divided," *Washington Post,* 10 January 1988. See also "Wrecker's Ball Threatens Way of Life in Chinatown," *Washington Post,* 24 April 1981; "Chinatown: Dreams for a Better Life," *Washington Post,* 24 February 1985; and "Chinatown Fights to Survive amid Building Boom," *Washington Post,* 3 January 1988.

SUGGESTED READING

Chinese American Conference Committee. *The Chinese American Experience: Papers for the Second National Conference on Chinese American Studies.* San Francisco: Chinese Historical Society of America and Chinese Culture Foundation of San Francisco, 1984.

"City Views Questions in the Chinese Community." *Washington Post,* 2 March 1978.

Cline, Marjorie. "Goodbye Snake, Hello Horse: Washington's Chinese Community Greets the New Year." *Washingtonian Magazine* (January 1966): 22–26, 48–50.

Fisher, Marc. "The Last Days of Chinatown." *Washington Post Magazine* (29 January 1995): 8–16, 19–22.

Lee, David J. "Social Transition of Chinese Americans in the Twentieth Century," Drexel University, 1979.

Smith, Schneider Kathryn, ed. *Washington at Home: An Illustrated History of Neighborhoods in the Nation's Capital.* Northridge, Calif.: Windsor Publications, 1988.

Sung, Betty Lee. *Mountain of Gold: The Story of the Chinese in America.* New York: Macmillan, 1967.

Takaki, Ronald. *Strangers from a Different Shore: A History of Asian Americans.* Boston: Little Brown, 1989.

Tung, William L. *The Chinese in America, 1820–1973: A Chronology and Fact Book.* Dobbs Ferry, N.Y.: Oceana Publications, 1974.

12.

Melding the Old and the New
The Modern African American Community, 1930–1960

Spencer R. Crew

In February 1932 the *Washington Tribune*, an African American newspaper, described a mass meeting organized by the local branch of the National Association for the Advancement of Colored People (NAACP). The group had gathered to protest the unequal funding of District schools and to call attention to an unjust system that forced black students to accept an education inferior to that provided for white students. Children attending three of the black schools—Garrison, Harrison, and Cleveland—endured enormous overcrowding and a shortened school day because the system of separate education did not provide enough money for the black schools to pay for sufficient numbers of teachers and classroom space. According to the protesters, these problems resulted from a school-board appropriations policy that deliberately funneled only 20 percent of its available monies into educating African American students, who represented 33 percent of the District's student population. Students such as Emma Louise Peters, who had moved to Washington with her parents and other relatives from Pearlington, Mississippi—specifically in search of better educational opportunities—had relocated in vain.

Not explicitly mentioned by the protesters was the role that the rapid growth of the city's African American population during the early twentieth century had played in the educational crisis. By 1920 more than 110,000 African Americans lived in Washington, giving the District a black population larger than that of any other city in the country. Ten years later the District's black population had grown by 20 percent to 132,000. Most of this growth resulted from the in-migration of African Americans in search of better economic opportunities. The children of these migrants placed an added burden on the racially segregated school system. The board of education's failure to respond to the influx of new students undermined the quality of education received by all black students during much of the twentieth century. This educational crisis also highlighted the challenges facing Washington's established black residents as newcomers moved in.

The newcomers came from all parts of the nation, some from as far away as California and Texas. While some migrants relocated from such northern locations as New York and Michigan, the majority came from southern states. As the South's agricultural system deteriorated after World War I, and share-croppers and other small farmers found it increasingly difficult to earn a living, they turned their hopes toward northern cities, including Washington. For many, the dream of owning land (and thereby controlling their own labor), which had evolved during the Civil War and Reconstruction, had proven elusive. In addition, increasingly severe restrictions placed on African Americans' civil rights and the threats of violence against their lives—including actual lynchings—pushed unprecedented numbers of rural blacks out of the South.

A 1935 census of African American migrants in the District indicates that the largest proportion came from Virginia, followed by North Carolina and South Carolina. Together these three states provided more than half of all African Americans who moved to the city in the 1930s.[1] Many sought to duplicate the success of W. H. Phillips, an independent contractor from Charlotte, North Carolina, who had won the bid to do the masonry work for a new building under construction at St. Elizabeths Hospital in Anacostia. Phillips's plan to hire twenty-five brick masons and their helpers, possibly fellow Carolinians, undoubtedly raised the hopes of many.

Transportation from the South to Washington was relatively easy to obtain. African American migrants often traveled by train, ship, or a combination of the two. They crowded the ubiquitous Jim Crow cars, taking advantage of reduced summer-excursion fares. Often migrants pooled their resources for the journey north. The Seaboard Airline Railway and the Southern Railway linked the interiors of Virginia, the Carolinas, and other southern states with the coast, and the Atlantic Coast Line Railroad, the Old Bay Line, and Old Dominion Steamship Company. The trip from the farthest points in southern Florida took no more than two days via the Atlantic Coast Line Railroad. Those living in port cities such as Savannah, Georgia, Charleston, South Carolina, and Newport News, Virginia, took advantage of the regular sailings between those cities and Washington. Fares were reasonable, and for longer trips passengers received separate overnight accommodations as part of the price.

Moving to the District proved far easier than finding a place to live and earning a decent wage. Segregation in housing allowed African Americans only a limited range of housing options. According to the 1930 census approximately 25 percent of the African Americans lived in those areas of southwest and southeast Washington that surrounded East Capitol Street, South Capitol Street, and the Mall. A somewhat larger number, approximately 33 percent, lived in the northwest Washington region bordered by Euclid Street and Michigan Avenue on the north, Rock Creek Park on the west, North Capitol Street on the east, and K Street on the south. Racial homogeneity tended to exist by blocks or clusters of blocks rather than by entire neighborhoods.

Another sizable concentration of African Americans lived across the Anacostia River, primarily in the Barry's Farm community, which had been established during Reconstruction. The Freedmen's Bureau had purchased this land from James Barry and then sold one-acre lots to freedpeople. Eventually, more than 500 families bought land and settled there. In the process they also built the Macedonia Baptist Church and a school, Mt. Zion Hill. By 1930 inmigration had increased Washington's African American population by nearly 12,000.

By the 1930s, however, northwest Washington, particularly the neighborhoods now known as Shaw and LeDroit Park, had emerged as the principal center of the city's African American community. Northwest Washington contained Howard University, one of the nation's oldest and best-known black colleges, and Freedmen's Hospital, both of which, like Barry's Farm, were created to assist freedpeople after the Civil War. The quadrant also boasted the Whitelaw Hotel (the only hotel in the city built for African Americans), the Industrial Savings Bank, the Thomas Frazier and Sons Funeral Home, and a host of small businesses providing a range of goods and services specifically to African Americans. These enterprises built on a strong tradition of black self-help and met the needs of those who were denied services and respectful treatment in establishments catering primarily or only to white Washingtonians.

The owners of these northwest Washington businesses, like their counterparts in other areas, believed that black-owned and black-patronized enterprises offered African Americans a crucial avenue for economic development. The businesses generated jobs, investment opportunities, and a chance to improve families' economic standing. The Industrial Savings Bank, for example, invested money in black-owned businesses and offered loans to home buyers who could not obtain favorable rates at other banks. For John W. Lewis, the founder of Industrial Savings Bank, and other black businesspeople, segregation offered opportunities as well as difficulties.[2]

To a certain degree this paradox also pertained to Washington's segregated schools. In the late nineteenth and early twentieth centuries—before they were overwhelmed with more children than they could comfortably educate in an era of diminishing resources—northwest Washington's M Street (succeeded in 1916 by Dunbar) and Armstrong in northwest Washington, among the nation's better African American high schools, produced such distinguished graduates as attorneys Charles Hamilton Houston and William Hastie, scientist Charles Drew, and Howard University professor and poet Sterling Brown. The separate schools benefited from the racial segregation that prevented many African Americans with advanced degrees from finding professional work. In 1921 three of Dunbar High School's female teachers held doctorate degrees. Indeed, Dunbar was so well known nationally that it became a reason in itself for migration to the capital. Foster R. Petty, an attorney residing in Savannah, Georgia, relocated his wife and four of their children to Washington so that the children could attend Dunbar. The Pettys believed that Savannah schools did not offer an education comparable to that of District schools, and they accepted the hardships of separating the family for the chance to improve their children's lives.

Northwest Washington was also home to some of the city's largest and oldest African American churches. For newcomers, churches constituted important reference points, providing them with familiar rituals and activities. In the 1930s churches in northwest Washington included the First Rising Mount Zion Baptist Church, Asbury United Methodist Church, the Nineteenth Street Baptist Church, John Wesley AME Church, and the newly established Temple of Freedom under God, Church of God, led by Elder Lightfoot Solomon Michaux.

Although many of these churches sought to help newcomers, Elder Michaux's was probably the best known and most appealing to new arrivals. Starting as one of the many area storefront churches, the Church of God grew rapidly in size and influence. Under Michaux's direction, it established programs to feed the hungry, to find desperately needed housing, and to locate employment opportunities. Michaux also maintained popular southern traditions, including river baptism. For his much-publicized baptism rituals, he would take congregants down the Potomac by excursion boat and baptize them in the river's waters.

Northwest Washington's less-advantaged African Americans shared the quadrant with wealthier blacks such as Congressman Oscar DePriest of Illinois and Dr. Ionia R. Whipper, founder of the Whipper Home for Unwed Mothers. Many southern migrants, however, had to settle into the only housing available to them: alley dwellings and low-cost apartments and homes. Out of view

Church of God congregants in 1938 at the Potomac River for baptism. (Courtesy D.C. Public Library, Martin Luther King Jr. Library, Washingtoniana Room, Washington Star *photo files)*

of white Washingtonians, alley communities such as Fenton Place and Snow's Court provided shelter for families unable to afford better housing.

Blagden Alley and Naylor Court, bordered by Ninth, Tenth, M, and O Streets, NW, in the Shaw neighborhood, still exist today; they constitute perhaps the best surviving architectural examples of an intimate street network that was once common to Washington, and that was provided for in Pierre Charles L'Enfant's drafts of the early capital city even before the city was built. By the end of the nineteenth century the area housed mostly freed slaves and some working-class whites, as well as artisan and service shops, metalworking shops, and alley stables. Middle-class whites generally occupied the residences facing the street, and working-class blacks were relegated to the alley dwellings behind them.[3]

Alley communities were not unique to northwest Washington. In southwest and southeast Washington, near the Mall and around the Capitol, similar living conditions prevailed. Southwest Washington had been home to the largest concentration of African Americans since the migrations spurred by the Civil War and Reconstruction, and by 1897 nearly half of its population was black. (In the city as a whole at this time, African Americans represented one-third of the total population.[4]) The need for low-cost housing drew residents in large numbers to the alley dwellings. As more migrants came to Washington following World War I, however, housing in these areas deteriorated. Southwest and southeast Washington soon contained some of the most over-crowded and poorly serviced alleys in the District, including Willow Tree Court near Fourth Street, SW, and Navy Place Alley near Sixth and G Streets, SE. In 1927 city officials rated Navy Place the worst alley in the city. The *Washington Tribune* called it a landmark to poor housing, unsanitary conditions, vice, crime, prostitution, and juvenile delinquency. A 6 June 1930 *Evening Star* article described Navy Place as a "squalid two rows of tiny brick houses separated by a narrow paved street with an unusual number of loafers before the doors."

While living conditions were indeed difficult, not all alley neighborhoods suffered as many problems as the media attributed to Navy Place. Nor did outside observers of those communities understand the support systems their residents had created to make alley life tolerable. Bonded by a common plight, dwellers within the same alley shared food with hungry neighbors; provided family members and friends—particularly newcomers—with temporary lodgings; and offered money or other assistance to unemployed neighbors. When Lucy Fletcher, a sixty-year-old resident of St. Mathews Court, was evicted from her home, neighbors collected money to sustain her as she searched for a new place to live. Such acts of mutual support paralleled the southern tradition of banding together in times of adversity and, especially important in a hostile racial environment, forged extended extrafamilial kinship networks that aided both new and established residents. While the lives led by alley residents struggling for subsistence and for better-paying jobs and decent housing may not have appealed to social reformers, their communities provided important mechanisms for survival.

Alley communities and overcrowded housing conditions were a direct consequence of Washington's housing market, in which active measures were enacted to restrict where African Americans could live. The passage of the Alley Dwelling Act in 1934 authorized New Deal reformers to tear down alley dwellings and to relocate residents to new or remodeled buildings, generally in other neighborhoods. Opposition to this project was so strong, however, that the Alley Dwelling Authority spent nearly two years fighting legal challenges to these relocations, most of which would have moved African Americans. Those cases in part attest to the attachment African Americans had formed to their communities, no matter how poor in material comfort.[5]

Attempts to replace alley dwellings or poor housing with upgraded structures, even when successful, frequently harmed or destroyed black communities. In 1939 the federal government replaced the homes destroyed in Navy Place with the white-only Ellen Wilson Dwellings, forcing many black residents to move elsewhere. Instead of helping the housing situation, the New Deal "urban-renewal" effort only aggravated overcrowding in other parts of southeast and southwest Washington, as would urban renewal "reforms" that would take place in southwest Washington in the 1950s.

The lack of adequate housing and the subsequent problems of overcrowding did not improve over time. In-migration continued to accelerate throughout the 1930s. The 1940 census shows that Washington's African Americans had increased to 187,000, a growth of 41 percent in ten years. By 1950, in the wake of World War II, the number of black residents had increased nearly another 50 percent to 281,000; and by 1960, 412,000 African Americans lived in the District. At the same time, African Americans represented a rising percentage of the District's total population. In 1930 they had represented 27 percent of the city's population—a higher percentage than that of African Americans in New York, Detroit, Pittsburgh, or Philadelphia, cities that had also experienced rapid growth in their African American populations. By 1960 African Americans, at 71 percent of the District's population, were the majority. Most of them were recent migrants—primarily from Maryland, Virginia, the Carolinas, Georgia, and Florida—who hoped to take advantage of increased job opportunities with the federal and District governments.

This burgeoning population, coupled with the city's inability to increase living facilities for low-income residents, worsened the housing crisis. The building boom that had occurred during the 1930s and World War II did not add significantly to the housing stock available to black migrants, who continued to contend with low incomes and racially restrictive covenants. As President Franklin D. Roosevelt established new agencies to organize the war effort, and as the responsibilities of the War Department increased, government offices launched nationwide efforts to bring additional workers of all races to Washington. The Pentagon's completion in 1943 meant the creation of office space for 40,000, in addition to the large staff employed by the War Department in other parts of the city. Those workers obviously needed places to live.

Although the District government issued more than one thousand building permits per month prior to and during World War II, demand far outstripped available housing. Many newly arrived government workers—both black and white—were forced to share apartments or single rooms with several fellow employees. This increased demand for living quarters placed even greater pressure on the meager housing available to African Americans, and while the boundaries of some black neighborhoods spread into adjoining areas, overall residential segregation increased around the city. None of the city agencies chartered to provide improved and increased housing for low-income residents significantly aided African Americans. Although the federal government did build a few new housing units specifically for African Americans, newcomers and established residents generally had to make do with existing units.[6]

Southwest Washington in particular became home to many of the city's poorer newcomers. Consequently, by the late 1940s and early 1950s it became one of the city's most depressed areas. Much of its housing, dating from the previous century, contained no electricity or running water. To many, the southwest area came to embody the housing crisis. Several projects that promised to replace dilapidated housing with new structures did not prove helpful to those residents most in need.

Problems of overcrowding, however, were not confined to southwest Washington. Poor living conditions existed in downtown northwest Washington, parts of northeast Washington, Foggy Bottom near Georgetown, and near the Capitol in southeast Washington. One report on poor housing conditions in the northwest described a house on Ninth Street in which forty-three people lived in nine rooms.

In addition to substandard housing, many migrants also faced unemployment. Unlike Chicago, Pittsburgh, Detroit, New York, and other cities to which post–World War I migrants had flocked, Washington lacked the industrial base that would have absorbed numerous low- and unskilled workers. Automobile manufacturing, steel production, the garment trades, stockyards, and similar industries were absent from Washington's economy.

By the Great Depression, when African American migration into Washington began to skyrocket, the employment situation had already worsened. Southern blacks, recruited to construct buildings for the U.S. Department of Commerce, for example, lost their jobs when the project was completed. They subsequently found it difficult, with government projects curtailed during the depression, to locate alternative work. In service occupations, where African Americans had traditionally found employment, whites, feeling the pinch of the depression, lobbied to replace them. The Hotel and Restaurant Employees' Alliance Local 731 sent a letter to the Democratic members of the House of Representatives demanding that they dismiss African American waiters who worked in the House restaurant and replace them with members of Local 731. The union offered no reason other than that it believed whites who were Democrats should receive preference over African Americans who, coming from the South, probably were Republicans.

Women, whose incomes, however meager, were crucial to their families' survival, suffered even greater difficulties, as the region's economic troubles mounted. A congressionally mandated 15 percent salary cut for government workers, as well as other cost-cutting measures taken during the Hoover administration, severely affected African American working women. For the nearly 65 percent of black women who worked as domestics or personal servants, the depression spelled disaster; families no longer able to afford their services either fired them or reduced their already low wages.

The general economic picture in Washington did improve slowly during the Roosevelt Administration, as New Deal programs gradually created more employment opportunities. African Americans' overall occupational status, however, did not improve significantly. By 1940 the three largest job categories for black men were the relatively low-paying occupations of nondomestic service workers (29 percent of all workers), general laborers in construction or nonmanufacturing companies, and "operatives," who were primarily chauffeurs, truck drivers, and delivery people. The top occupation for women continued to be domestic service (61 percent of all workers), followed by general service work as charwomen or janitors, and laundry operatives or seamstresses.

The immediate postwar decades brought some improvement. The federal government's growth during and after the war opened new, though still limited, opportunities for African American workers. By 1950 the federal government had become the city's largest employer of black men. The construction trades and the wholesale and retail trades followed government service as significant new sources of work. Although the largest job category for women remained domestic household work, they too began to gain greater access to federal government jobs, the second largest occupational category among African American women in the 1950s. These employment patterns continued for at least a decade.

Despite the bleak employment and housing situation during the 1930s and 1940s, the majority of the city's African American newcomers managed to create new support networks and organizations that paralleled those of native black Washingtonians. They maintained their ties to the South and kept track of recent births, weddings, and deaths through letters and regular return trips to their birthplaces. The stream of people traveling back and forth between Washington and points south—often aided by hometown clubs organized in churches—was constant, as evidenced in the activities reported in such black-owned newspapers as the *Washington Tribune* and the *Afro-American*.

The resulting networks eased the transition to life in Washington. They also encouraged "chain migration," in which newcomers moved in with or in proximity to home-based family or friends who had preceded them to Washington. When Silas Prioleau moved to Washington from South Carolina, he and his family lived with his brother until Silas saved enough money to purchase his own home. The cooperation between the brothers and the pooling of family resources made it easier for them both to get established and, eventually, to become property owners.

By talking with kin and friends visiting from Washington, potential migrants also learned that a vibrant and strong African American community prevailed in Washington despite the oppressive segregation. The segregated school system, whose underfunding distressed all residents, also remained a source of pride for African Americans. Commencement activities and other school-related programs at all levels were important occasions. The annual Armstrong-Dunbar Competitive Military Drill was a major event in the black community. So too were the various concerts, receptions, and plays in which students participated. In addition, African American schools housed lectures, demonstrations, and other activities sponsored by community groups and civic associations. At these meetings parents and other guests could learn about the latest in children's medical care, listen to a lecture by a Howard University professor, plan Parent-Teacher Association events, or just gather socially. These meetings also provided settings in which newcomers met older residents and developed new relationships, a process that strengthened the entire community.

The African American churches, especially the flourishing storefront churches occasionally located in alley dwellings, attracted people of similar religious traditions from the same areas of the South. In addition to offering religious uplift, they functioned as political and social forums and labor-organizing centers. During the 1930s and 1940s the Bible Way Church of Our Lord Jesus Christ World Wide, led by the Reverend Smallwood E. Williams, was so popular that it held services for overflowing crowds under a giant tent until a permanent structure was built on New Jersey Avenue, NW. Other institutions, such as the United House of Prayer for All People, under Charles "Daddy" Grace, and Elder Michaux's Church of God, also nurtured large congregations and successfully addressed the spiritual and practical needs of Washington's many newcomers. Church-sponsored food drives, sporting events, picnics, and

Classroom at Dunbar High School in 1949. Education remained a major goal of both new-comers and established residents. (Courtesy Library of Congress, Prints and Photographs Division)

theatrical performances all strengthened the sense of cooperation and inter-dependency within an increasingly diverse African American community.

Also easing the struggle to build a new life in Washington were the Phyl-liss Wheatley YWCA and the Anthony Bowen Colored YMCA. The Wheat-ley YWCA (named for a Revolutionary War–era emancipated slave and poet) sponsored summer camps that gave mothers and their children respite from the city's heat and frustrations. The camp also furnished training and information regarding child care and nutrition. At the same time, the "colored YMCA," which had been founded in 1853 by Anthony J. Bowen (a former slave in Maryland who had purchased his own freedom and moved to the District), continued to provide a host of programs for young African American men.

Sporting events were another important form of entertainment and tra-dition building for African American Washingtonians, as natives and new-comers united in support for local teams. Intercity high school athletic con-tests, as well as Howard University games, regularly drew large crowds. The

Howard University football games at Griffith Stadium drew the community together. (Courtesy Moorland Spingarn Research Center, Howard University)

Howard University versus Lincoln University Thanksgiving Day football game drew thousands of enthusiastic spectators to LeDroit Park's Griffith Stadium each year. The Washington Senators baseball team, with its large African American following, also played at Griffith Stadium. Even more important to these fans, however, were their own "colored" baseball teams: the Washington Elite Giants, the LeDroit Tigers, and the Washington Pilots, who all played before sizable crowds at Griffith Stadium.

The existence of the LeDroit Tigers, which took its name from the Griffith Stadium's neighborhood, exemplifies the changes within the African American community in the postwar era. LeDroit Park had been built on land purchased in 1873 from Howard University, which had sold it to raise money. When the development of grand Victorian houses had opened in the late 1870s, black Washingtonians had been barred from purchasing homes there, but by the 1890s they began to move into this formerly exclusive residential enclave. With the ensuing exodus of white residents, LeDroit Park became one of the most desirable neighborhoods for middle-class African Americans. After World War I, the economic mix of LeDroit Park changed as developers built low-rent apartments near the stadium and in other parts of the neighborhood. Thus, when the LeDroit Tigers played at Griffith, they were literally playing on their home field and drawing together the members of a community in transition.

Established and more recently arrived African American residents also congregated at neighborhood entertainment establishments. A variety of black-owned and operated theaters offered movies or live entertainment at modest fees. The most important of these was the Howard Theater at Seventh and T Streets, NW, in the commercially lively Shaw neighborhood. The Howard Theater primarily offered live entertainment and was the most popular entertainment center in Washington. For nearly forty years after it reopened under new management in 1931, the Howard attracted some of the best-known names in African American entertainment, including Duke Ellington, Ella Fitzgerald, Pearl Bailey, Bill "Bojangles" Robinson, Sarah Vaughan, Johnny Mathis, and Gladys Knight and the Pips—all of whom regularly played before packed houses. Other theaters, including the Foraker and the Alamo, offered live, vaudeville-style entertainment, but always in the shadow of the Howard.[7]

Movie houses offered even greater choices. The Lincoln Theater on U Street, between Twelfth and Thirteenth Streets, NW, the largest of the movie houses, featured first-run films, although sometimes to mixed responses. In 1939 its showing of Gone with the Wind was picketed by Howard University students and faculty to protest the film's sentimental depiction of plantation life. The Lincoln also showcased all-black movies such as Hallelujah; this film, however, also generated controversy in 1930 for its idealization of black life in the South. Other important, though smaller, theaters included the Booker T. Theater and the Republic Theater, both on U Street, and the Dunbar Theater on Seventh and T Streets.

The Lincoln Colonnade, located in the basement of the Lincoln Theater building, expanded the theater's role as a community center. College groups and other organizations rented the hall for charitable dances and social events. The Convention Hall, Odd Fellows Hall, and the Pythian Temple in northwest Washington, as well as Fishermen's Temple on F Street, SW, also regularly hosted similar events.

In addition to those organized activities, other smaller, more informal gatherings took place in the city's flowering African American community. Groups assembled in homes or other private locations throughout the city to play bridge, whist, or craps; to celebrate a college graduation, the completion of the Lillian Walker Haircare Course, or a birthday or anniversary; or to argue about sports, movies, politics, or the injustice of discrimination. Such gath-

Howard Theater, the center of African American cultural life for generations, stands today, awaiting restoration. (Courtesy Library of Congress)

erings played an unheralded but vital role in the emergence of enhanced self-awareness in the African American community. They served to soften the sting of segregation in Washington—especially where children were concerned. They served also to initiate newcomers to Washington life-styles, to broaden networks across class lines, and ultimately to create the climate for change that led to the end of official segregation in housing, employment, and education.

The difficulties that confronted African Americans in Washington (poor housing, economic discrimination, and inadequately funded schools) were the burning topics at gatherings during this period. Different segments of the African American community, forging alliances and acting for social change, found common cause in working for civil rights. For example, the New Negro Alliance was formed in 1933, when a coalition of professional and working-class residents began discussing concrete ways to open more jobs to African Americans. The alliance grew out of a "don't buy where you can't work" campaign that began on U Street after the white owners of a hamburger stand fired three black employees, replacing them with whites. A boycott was quickly

Lester Taylor was hired as a drug clerk at Feldman Drugstore as a result of the New Negro Alliance Campaign. (Photographed by Robert McNeill, courtesy Moorland Spingarn Research Center, Howard University)

organized, and two customer-less days later, the owners rehired the three black employees. Two years of such focused action against other businesses with primarily black clienteles—including the powerful Peoples Drugstore and Safeway chains—culminated in the opening up of nearly 300 additional jobs for blacks. The goal in picketing and staging sit-ins at Peoples was not only to get African Americans hired, but also to ensure that they would be served at Peoples' lunch counters. Although the alliance had only limited success in these campaigns, its pioneering actions represented some of the earliest direct efforts by African Americans to confront and end discrimination.

The New Negro Alliance's work was important also because it would later serve as a model for similar activities. In 1949 an integrated group of civil rights activists formed the Coordinating Committee for the Enforcement of the D.C. Anti-Discrimination Laws with the legal assistance of the interracial Ameri-

Civil rights pioneers picket a Peoples Drugstore circa 1933. (Courtesy Moorland Spingarn Research Center, Howard University)

can Veterans Committee. With Mary Church Terrell as its most renowned member, the Coordinating Committee launched a fight to integrate the city's public accommodations based on guarantees found in civil rights legislation of the 1870s. Those laws, once enforced throughout the city, had gradually come to be ignored and had been omitted from the District of Columbia Code published in 1901. The Coordinating Committee, however, was determined to force the courts to rule on whether the "lost laws" still governed the city. If so, segregated restaurants, theaters, recreation facilities, and perhaps even schools would be illegal.

Terrell led a group of three blacks and one white in asking for service at Thompson's Restaurant in the 700 block of Fourteenth Street, NW. When the restaurant refused to serve them, the case began its journey through the courts. At the same time, the Coordinating Committee launched a series of sit-ins in other downtown establishments. Soon the Hecht Company and other stores along Seventh Street opened their lunch counters to all customers. The Coordinating Committee won its fight in 1953, when the Supreme Court reached a ruling in the Thompson Restaurant case that ended segregation in most District eating places, theaters, and other public facilities.[8]

Although access to and service at public accommodations improved,

Washington's African Americans had to wait for nearly another decade for better-paying jobs in downtown stores. The NAACP's campaign against downtown stores that refused to hire African Americans had some success, but the campaign directed by the Congress of Racial Equality (CORE) in 1960 was even more successful. Under the leadership of Julius Hobson, a southerner who had migrated to Washington in the 1940s, CORE picketed those stores that still refused to hire African Americans as salesclerks. The campaign lasted for four years but, according to Hobson, resulted in the employment of more than 5,000 African Americans.

A series of meetings initiated by the NAACP nearly thirty years earlier had focused attention on entrenched segregation in the District's school system. As a result of public meetings held by the NAACP in 1932, the school board finally transferred $315,000 for use in educating African American students. Those funds, however, were not nearly enough to remedy the severe inequalities of the segregated school system. Even after the infusion of additional funds, complaints from various civil rights groups continued to flood Congress and the school board. Finally, in 1947, parents' concerns reached the boiling point; in December they launched a strike against the school system with the NAACP's full support. Parents and students boycotted the schools to protest the board's policy of transferring older white schools to black students—rather than building new facilities for them—and the long distances black children had to travel to reach those schools when newer, white schools were sometimes closer.

The boycott had two results: Congress appropriated additional funds for the construction of eight new school buildings, and it commissioned George Strayer of Columbia University to study the District's "colored" school system. Strayer's 1948 report argued that the system suffered from too few buildings for a growing population, too few teachers, and too little funding. He also found that bringing the black schools up to par with the white schools would require the school board to allocate 75 percent of its budget to black schools. Implied but not stated in Strayer's findings was that integrating the system offered a more cost-effective solution.

Segregation did not come to an easy end in the District schools, however. Only by taking additional actions were African American parents able to force the board to integrate the system. In 1950, for example, parents of black hearing-impaired students sued the school board to gain admission for their children to Kendall Green, the local school for the deaf, rather than to continue sending them to comparable schools in other states. Again, the American Veterans Committee provided legal and strategic help in the fight. Although the

U.S. District Court ruled in the parents' favor in 1952 and the children gained admission to Kendall Green, they were kept in segregated classes there until the 1954 Supreme Court decision in *Brown v. Board of Education*.

In September 1951, when John Philip Sousa Junior High School—an underused white school in southeast Washington—denied entrance to eleven African American students, parents mounted a direct challenge to the idea of segregated schools. The parents quickly brought suit against the school board, charging that there was no sound educational basis for restricting access to District schools because of race. Soon thereafter African American pupils at the Daniel A. Payne school in southeast Washington staged a four-day walkout to call attention to their inadequate educational facilities. The courts were initially unreceptive to African Americans' attempts to improve their educational circumstances, and the Sousa case (*Bolling v. Sharpe*) lost on appeal before the U.S. District Court. Subsequently, however, the case became part of the *Brown v. Board of Education* arguments, and in that landmark decision the U.S. Supreme Court ruled that "separate educational facilities are inherently unequal."[9]

These milestones did not, of course, bring an end to the challenges facing black Washingtonians. Overcrowded housing conditions did not disappear, access to better-paying jobs remained limited, and the school system remained underfunded. Achievements in civil rights, however, demonstrated that a network of institutions, organizations, and individuals had been forged among African Americans and that it could coalesce for the further improvement of the black community's opportunities.

African American migration both exacerbated the problems of and enriched the resources of Washington's African American community between 1930 and 1960. Those who had made the odyssey to the District broadened the base of leaders available to provide guidance in times of trouble and inspiration in times of celebration. Newcomers swelled the ranks of picketers, boycotters, church members, and customers who constituted the grass-roots support for many community reform endeavors. They made a significant impact upon the evolution of the city, as it stood poised for a new stage in the struggle for civil rights and home rule.

NOTES

1. Population figures for the District come from the *Fifteenth Census of the United States, 1930* (Washington, D.C.: Bureau of the Census, 1932), *Population*: III; *Six-*

teenth Census of the United States, 1940 (Washington, D.C.: Bureau of the Census, 1943), *Population*: II; *Seventeenth Census of the United States, 1952* (Washington, D.C.: Bureau of the Census, 1952), *Population*: II, part 9; and *Eighteenth Census of the United States, 1960* (Washington, D.C.: Bureau of the Census, 1963), *Population*: I, part 10.

2. See Michael Andrew Fitzpatrick, "'A Great Agitation for Business': Black Economic Development in Shaw," *Washington History* 2, no. 2 (fall/winter 1990–91): 49–73.

3. A *Washington Post* article reviewing the current renovation and planned reuse of Blagden Alley reminds us of its near demise: "In the early 1930s, Blagden Alley became the target of zealous New Deal reformers led by Eleanor Roosevelt, who wanted to eradicate deplorable living conditions in alleys citywide and used Blagden Alley as their model." See "'Common' Shaw Neighborhood Preserved," *Washington Post*, 11 October 1990.

4. Paul A. Groves, "The Development of a Black Residential Community in Southwest Washington: 1860–1897," *Records of the Columbia Historical Society* 49 (1973–1974): 264.

5. The most useful work on alley dwellings is James Borchert, *Alley Life in Washington, D.C.: Family, Community, Religion, and Folklife in the City, 1850–1970* (Urbana: University of Illinois Press, 1980). On housing in general, see William Henry Jones, *The Housing of Negroes in Washington, D.C.: A Study in Human Ecology* (Washington, D.C.: Howard University Press, 1929); Leonor Enriquez Pablo, "The Housing Needs and Social Problems of Residents in a Deteriorated Area" (master's thesis, Catholic University, 1953); Gladys Sellew, "A Deviant Social Situation: A Court" (Ph.D. diss., Catholic University, 1938); and Daniel D. Swinney, "Alley Dwellings and Housing Reforms in the District of Columbia," (master's thesis, University of Chicago, 1938).

6. See David Brinkley, *Washington Goes to War* (New York: Alfred A. Knopf, 1988).

7. See Bettye Gardner and Bettye Thomas, "The Cultural Impact of the Howard Theater on the Black Community," *Journal of Negro History* LV, no. 4 (October 1970): 253–65.

8. Marvin Caplan, "Eat Anywhere!" *Washington History* 1, no. 1 (spring 1989): 25–40.

9. See Keith Melder, Kathryn Schneider Smith, et al., eds., *City of Magnificent Intentions: A History of the District of Columbia* (Washington, D.C.: D.C. History Curriculum Project of Associates for Renewal in Education, 1985), 477.

ADDITIONAL READING

Fitzpatrick, Sandra, and Maria R. Goodwin. *The Guide to Black Washington: Places and Events of Historical and Cultural Significance in the Nation's Capital*. New York: Hippocrene Books, 1990.

Green, Constance McLaughlin. *The Secret City: A History of Race Relations in the Nation's Capital*. Princeton, N.J.: Princeton University Press, 1967.

Jones, William Henry. *Recreation and Amusement among Negroes in Washington, D.C.: A Sociological Analysis of the Negro in an Urban Environment.* 1927. Reprint, Westport, Conn.: Negro Universities Press, 1970.

Miller, Charles A. *Citizens Advisory Groups in the District of Columbia Government.* Washington, D.C.: Center for Metropolitan Studies, 1961.

National Committee on Segregation in the Nation's Capital. *Segregation in the Nation's Capital.* Washington, D.C.: National Committee on Segregation in the Nation's Capital, 1948.

Strayer, George D. *Report of a Survey of the Public Schools of the District of Columbia.* Washington, D.C.: Government Printing Office, 1949.

PART THREE

Multicultural
Washington

13.

The Latino Community
Creating an Identity in the Nation's Capital

Olivia Cadaval

In the late twentieth century immigrants are repopulating the major U.S. cities—including Washington, which during the 1970s and 1980s became a magnet for such ethnic groups as Latin Americans, Caribbeans, Southeast Asians, and Africans. Representing a new wave in Washington's urban odyssey, these immigrants are establishing communities and shaping new cultural landscapes in the nation's capital. Neighborhoods previously populated primarily by migrants from the Carolinas and Virginia, as well as transient federal employees, have become sites for the emergence of multicultural and multinational communities.

Many of these groups have settled in the adjacent neighborhoods of Adams Morgan and Mount Pleasant in northwest Washington, and have transformed this compact geographic area into a growing commercial and cultural hub. A walk along Eighteenth Street from Florida Avenue (the original northern boundary of the city) to Columbia Road, and then east to Mount Pleasant Street (once the end of the trolley line), offers a glimpse of the delicate coexistence of diverse immigrants, who are carving out physical and cultural space while creating new identities for themselves in Washington.

The proliferating restaurants and small stores reflect not only area residents' varying nationalities, but also the regional distinctiveness within national groups: Salvadoran restaurants tend to feature specialties from Oriente, the eastern region of that country, while Ethiopian restaurants prepare foods in Asmaran and Oromo styles.

Thirty years ago a handful of Latin American embassy domestic workers discovered an Italian grocery store in Adams Morgan that offered familiar tropical fruits and vegetables. Today mom-and-pop grocery stores, ethnic specialty

The Adams Morgan–Mount Pleasant barrio is one mile directly north of the White House. (Map by and courtesy Olivia Cadaval)

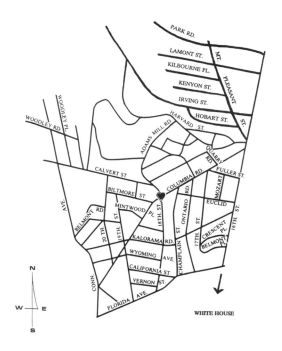

shops, and street-vending stalls, established by earlier immigrants and now run by more recent arrivals, provide a range of goods and services. A Cuban-owned store butchers specialty meats and offers regional products for its Latin American, African, and West Indian clientele. Additionally, social-service centers established to meet newcomers' needs reflect the new communities' vitality and organization.

The Latino presence predominates within the highly textured and complex landscape created by Washington's most recent arrivals.[1] In the 1980s more than 200,000 Latinos celebrated their claim to Adams Morgan–Mount Pleasant as the heart of their community in their annual street festival. The Latino Festival has recently moved to the Mall and Pennsylvania Avenue, and the Latino community itself has geographically spread to other parts of the District and beyond its borders to Maryland and Virginia. The Adams Morgan–Mount Pleasant area, however, remains at the heart of the barrio.[2] These neighborhoods have experienced both the beginnings of the Latino community and the transformation of the city that resulted from such major national and international events as World War II, the civil rights movement, the riots

Señora Diloné, originally from Puerto Rico, continues to run the grocery store Casa Diloné, which she had started with her Dominican husband in 1962. Like many store owners at that time, the family lived above the store. (Photograph by and reprinted with permission of Luis Salvatierra C.)

following the assassination of Martin Luther King Jr., the Vietnam War, and various Third World political and economic crises combined with emancipation from European colonial rule. The Adams Morgan–Mount Pleasant neighborhood, once a stepping-stone in the city's initial expansion in the late nineteenth century, is now, at the close of the twentieth century, the setting for the development of new cultural identities.

Washington's multiethnic, Spanish-speaking population began to develop after World War II, when Latin American embassies and international organizations became established in the nation's capital. Professional staff members of the Spanish-speaking embassies and international organizations, along with their domestic personnel, took up residence in Adams Morgan, Mount Pleasant, and Dupont Circle, neighborhoods that were convenient to the embassies situated around Sixteenth Street and Massachusetts Avenue.

Many of the domestic workers stayed after their employers' diplomatic tours of duty had ended or their host families had left the city. They settled in the affordable Adams Morgan–Mount Pleasant area and persuaded family and friends from home to join them. Latin American students in area universities were another significant segment of the growing Spanish-speaking population.

Puerto Rican and Mexican American white-collar workers, seeking the increasing numbers of federal jobs that had become available as a result of the New Deal and World War II, had come to the area in great numbers even earlier than the Latin Americans. For the most part, however, the students and professional Mexican Americans separated themselves from the nascent Latino community.

In the 1960s the Spanish-speaking population began to grow more rapidly. The economic hardships and political turmoil back home, combined with the attraction of an alluring image of the United States as a country "where the streets are paved with gold" spurred a flow of both legal and illegal immigrants. Luis Rumbaut, a Cuban-born lawyer and pioneering community member, described the typical process:

> The first person to arrive here from a given village sends his address back home, and he's the first stop when the next person arrives. One shabby apartment building just north of Ontario and Columbia roads is a de facto re-creation of a small village in the Zacapá province of Guatemala.

Another apartment building houses many people from Intipucá, El Salvador. Intipucá has become a prosperous village as a result of the money its emigrants have sent back home.

Cubans and Dominicans, seeking better economic opportunities, began arriving in the 1950s. Cubans came in the greatest numbers in the late 1950s and early 1960s, during and after the Cuban Revolution. This group generally included members of the educated upper or middle class. A later wave, known as the Marielitos, came in 1980 through the Mariel boat lift. In the 1980s a sizable flow of immigrants also arrived from Central America, particularly El Salvador.

In 1970 a group of individuals, mostly from Cuba, the Dominican Republic, Ecuador, Panama, Peru, and Puerto Rico, organized a festival that would demonstrate their presence to the District government. They met at the Wilson Center, on Irving Street, NW, which came to play a major role as a Latino cultural center and focal point for social and educational activities. The center, owned by the National Capital Union Presbytery, had once housed a large Presbyterian Church that had counted President Woodrow Wilson among its members. Many of its congregants, however, had begun to leave in the 1950s, when the neighborhood started to change as a result of white flight. The 1968 riots following King's assassination accelerated this out-migration, and the Wilson Center thus became a gathering place for the newly emerging Latino community. Leaders from this early period agree that the Latino community basically grew around three focal points: an Italian-owned store on Columbia Road; Saturday night dances in individual homes and church basements; and Spanish-language films at the Colony Theater on Georgia Avenue.

Casilda Luna, an early pioneer from the Dominican Republic who had come to the city in 1961, recalls today that there was no recognition of an organized Latino neighborhood at the time she arrived. In the 1960s, most of the Latin Americans were embassy employees, and most were women. Luna began to meet these women in the Italian store on Columbia Road, where they could purchase plantains and other familiar produce. The women were greatly relieved to be able to chat in Spanish, and they would often find that they shared similar problems with language, housing, and employment. According to Luna, "We would get together and speak the same language. We were from different countries but we felt so happy because we could speak Spanish." Later, they began meeting at the Church of the Sacred Heart of Jesus, where a Spanish-speaking priest helped them with English.

These activities provided the first opportunities for Washington Latinos to interact and, most important, to network in order to solve their problems. The late Carlos Rosario, one of the leaders who had became known as *El Viejo* (the old man, or the godfather), once recalled organizing Spanish-language film programs at the Colony Theater:

> In 1962 the first Latino theater was established. I remember that in the monthly theater program I always announced that any person who was looking for a job should call me, and I would help them. I would start calling restaurants and family residences. And there were people who wanted to bring others into the country, but they had to have an assured place here, and I'd help them. And this is how the community began to grow overnight. This has been the fastest-growing community in Washington, and the base for similar communities in Virginia and Maryland.

Foremost among the early leaders were Puerto Ricans and Cubans, who had had several advantages in making their adjustment to Washington. They had immigrated legally, spoke English, and—in the case of many Puerto Ricans—had stable federal jobs. Puerto Ricans were already U.S. citizens, and the Cubans who had immigrated after Fidel Castro's takeover in 1959 had received favored-immigrant status. Other immigrants, who would form the bulk of the emerging Latino community, most often came from rural or small-town backgrounds, although some had been schoolteachers or were skilled artisans. The majority, whatever their social or economic background, found work in homes, apartment-building maintenance, hotel services, and other work with low pay and few benefits. These jobs, most recently held by African Americans, were also sought by the growing English- and French-speaking Caribbean immigrants.

Rosario worked with other leaders to coalesce the community from within. They resorted to the familiar Latin American *compadrazgo* system, based on ritual kinship among families, which then served as the basis for social and political organization. According to Rosario, this system began to develop in Washington through the dances he organized:

> People got to meet each other there. They got married—Ecuadoran girls to Peruvians, Salvadoran girls to Hondurans. And I was godfather to their first child. People from these countries didn't usually speak to each other. Now each group has its own parties.

While individuals from this small Spanish-speaking population assumed leadership roles and began to organize as a community, they also collaborated with African American leaders and other neighborhood activists. Living side by side in a city that, like other major U.S. cities, was undergoing a period of economic and physical decline, residents sought to organize neighborhood-based advisory commissions and service agencies. Ruth Webster, an African American neighborhood activist, recalled that Rosario was an outspoken representative of Latinos during the meetings in which the Advisory Neighborhood Commissions were being formed in the 1960s. President Lyndon B. Johnson's Great Society poverty programs had created new sources of funds for community social services. Latino leaders initially worked with African American agencies to funnel these funds into programs for the city's Spanish-speaking population.

The 1960s and 1970s civil rights movement set the period's political mood. King's assassination and the ensuing race riots in Newark, Washington, and Chicago were traumatic events in the tense political atmosphere, underlining the nation's social and economic inequities. In Washington civil disturbances razed Fourteenth Street, at the margins of Adams Morgan and Mount Pleasant. Although these events accelerated white out-migration, they also spurred more positive reactions in those residents who remained. A black Panamanian Latino, for example, remembered a feeling of "owning the streets."

The consciousness that spurred African Americans to challenge discrimination inspired other minorities to organize politically. According to Casilda Luna, Latinos in Washington appropriated the objectives of the civil rights movement:

> The Cubans shouted for their rights as refugees. The Mexicans can fight because their land has been taken away, but then the Colombians and Dominicans are left without any rights. It was then that the Reverend Welty, a Colombian, organized the 8 A.M. breakfasts at the Wilson Center so people could come with their problems, their values. We had to 'think Latino' since we spoke the same language.

The struggle for civil rights became an intense self-coding process. Among African Americans a new style and political consciousness had developed around the motto "black is beautiful." Similarly, Mexican Americans identified with *La Raza* (the concept of mestizo roots) in homage to their often suppressed or denied Indian heritage. The more recent Latin American immigrants did not necessarily have either a black or Indian consciousness but understood the need to establish a new self-definition in a new land.

Although they came from different nations and experiences, Washington's Spanish-speaking immigrants began to forge a shared identity around a common language, shared cultural values, and similar legal, housing, and employment issues.[3] Without losing their individual national identities, they became "Latinos," a term unfamiliar in Latin America. Indeed, the increasing use of the term and the idea of Latino identity indicated that community formation was taking place, with diverse groups coalescing around common experiences and a shared language.

Thus a Latino aesthetic and culture emerged in the Adams Morgan–Mount Pleasant neighborhood, prompting continuing organization through community self-definition. A sense of home began to reshape the neighborhood and to transform it into the barrio. When shopping at Los Primos grocery store in Mount Pleasant, one would often be greeted with, "Hola, prima" ("Hello, cousin"). This Dominican-owned grocery, which had first been opened in the 1970s, has since changed ownership several times, but its employees have always welcomed Spanish-speaking clients with the familial term. This simple gesture, which recognizes a kinship broader than ethnicity or national origin, has become essential to building a new community.

Latino family grocery stores, providing both a hub for social interaction and an economic base for community development, have played a major role in establishing the barrio. Cubans and Dominicans owned the neighborhood's

A small restaurant on Columbia Road boldly advertises familiar Salvadoran fast foods. (Photograph by and reprinted with permission of Luis Salvatierra C.)

earliest Latino stores. Initially, produce was purchased in New York and New Jersey, probably from the same warehouses that supplied the Italian grocer on Columbia Road. Gilberto González, owner of La Americana, would make trips to these suppliers and purchase merchandise for all the stores; he eventually opened his own warehouse in Washington.

In the early days the stores, fulfilling the community's needs and appetites, offered mostly Caribbean produce and some Spanish and South American specialties. In the late 1970s and early 1980s most of them sold *empanadas* (filled pastries similar to turnovers) at the counter. Latino women baked them in their homes and sold them to supplement their meager earnings as housemaids and babysitters, or to sustain themselves during periods of unemployment. *Empanadas* are to Latin Americans and Caribbean islanders what hamburgers are to North Americans. In Washington's Adams Morgan–Mount Pleasant, they became a specialty and an affordable snack. Each national group lauded its par-

A few skilled immigrants have been able to establish small shops. Emberto Rojas, cabinet and music-instrument maker from Bolivia, first opened his shop on Eighteenth Street, NW, where he primarily repaired furniture for embassies. Although he no longer makes musical instruments, he incorporates into his furniture the inlay motifs that he had used to decorate stringed instruments. (Photograph by and reprinted with permission of Luis Salvatierra C.)

ticular version: the fried Dominican *pastelito*, the pleated Bolivian *salteña*, and the flaky Mexican *empanada*. These reflected a shared tradition with as many variants as there were nationalities and regions, and therefore encouraged solidarity among Latinos without homogenizing and leveling differences.

Other businesses followed in the wake of the early grocery stores. A Latino record-shop owner, who had begun selling records from his car trunk, now has outlets in the Maryland and Virginia suburbs and owns a national music production company. Some Latinos who had started out as waiters in non-Latino–owned restaurants opened their own cafes and cantinas. A shoe-repair shop began offering tailoring services, and several barbershops opened. This entrepreneurial sector developed independent of but parallel to the more politicized movement that established and maintained Latino social-service agencies. Washington's Latino leadership has emerged primarily out of these two groups: the business enterprises and the social-service agencies.

By the end of the 1960s, several social-service organizations for Latinos were established, and Latino leaders were ready to claim official recognition from the District government. Rosario described how in 1969 the office of the Spanish Community Advisory Committee was established under the D.C. Department of Human Relations with funds allocated by Congress. Rosario and a group of other residents began to "make noise" to let the city government become aware of the Latino community's needs and frustrations. They had already decided to request the establishment of an Office on Latino Affairs. In 1967 Rosario wrote to newly appointed Mayor Walter Washington to request a meeting. As he recalled, "the only thing that came out of that meeting was that the mayor named me to the board of the Office of Human Rights." The group continued to press the newly appointed city council. A meeting with Senators Robert Kennedy and Joseph Tydings and Maryland Governor Marvin Mandel was pivotal. "Tremendous luck," Rosario said. "They asked us did we want them to write to the mayor!" The mayor then agreed to talk with the city council, and stated, "If that is what you want, you get it." After the Spanish Community Advisory Committee was established, Mayor Washington attempted to move it from the Department of Human Relations to the Office of Human Rights, restricting the office to symbolic rather than actual power. Rosario mobilized his people, who laid down in front of the door to the mayor's office and sang "We Shall Overcome." Rosario was then named director of the committee, and later became the first director of the new Office on Latino Affairs, officially established in 1976.

Demonstration strategies modeled after the civil rights sit-ins and the later Vietnam War protests spurred the creation of the Latino Festival, which had come into being in the wake of the 1968 riots. Marcelo Fernández, a festival founder who had been active in the civil rights movement, argued that the festival was, in effect, a "pressure group" during the early stages of community formation. The 1970 census had counted 17,561 Latinos in Washington, but the leaders in the community knew that the number was much higher. It was critical that more accurate figures be obtained and documented for the allocation of adequate government funds for Latino social-service programs. Since an additional study would have been expensive, Fernández decided, "We will just take to the streets. We'll form a festival."[4] He knew that the Latino community would be drawn to a street festival, which would then serve as a concrete demonstration of the community's presence, with the media acting as unofficial census takers providing a more accurate count of the area's Latino population.

Factionalism was also an issue when the founders decided to organize the festival. Fernández contended that "to do a festival, the Argentinian has to come to terms with the Panamanian, or with other groups, to agree upon the order of floats, or upon the members of the festival committee, thus creating a dynamic." Even when alliances are created between two groups to go against a third, a "co-penetration" between groups emerges. Thus, according to Fernández, the festival, which functioned much like Rosario's dances, provided a base for networking rather than for homogenizing.

From the Latinos' perspective, the stores, businesses, social-service agencies, and the festival collectively proclaimed, "We are here." The community dynamic during this formation period is depicted in murals painted in the mid-1970s by members of El Centro de Arte, a Latino cultural organization. El Centro's motto became "Art is culture, is education, is the conscience of a people." This philosophy is apparent in one of its earliest projects, in which community members painted a mural on a neighborhood building's back wall. The mural visually evokes the Latino community and the changes taking place around it. The muralists also had their own motto: "A people without murals is a demuralized people."

The murals highlighted foodways and dance as central motifs, while also emphasizing the importance of the street. The street became the central design element, symbolically dividing and conjoining disparate aspects of the community. The murals themselves also physically delineated the Latino neighborhood, the barrio.

Carlos Rosario, the community's revered El Viejo throughout the 1960s and 1970s, died in 1987. In accordance with his will, his body was carried in a funeral procession through the neighborhood. The Spanish-language newspaper, El Pregonero, wrote:

> The funeral of Don Carlos Rosario not only proved his stature as a leader but also served to reaffirm the Hispanic presence in the Washington area. Symbolically, the funeral procession of Don Carlos proceeded on foot, from the Sacred Heart Church to Kalorama Park, on the same streets where the Hispano-American Festival, which he helped to establish seventeen years ago, has been held.

Marcelo Fernández suggested that Rosario's death marked the end of an era in the community. It was certainly the end of an era of charismatic leadership, which had managed to carry Latinos through the rifts and tensions of a rapidly growing heterogeneous community. Even before Rosario's death new groups of immigrants had become part of the community and were beginning to exercise their own leadership styles. A shared language and the migration experience continued to provide a common ground. However, as the community became more established, succeeding groups of immigrants also made their own claims on it.

Rosario and his followers, the "old guard," had sought primarily to be recognized by and to be integrated into Washington's mainstream social and political leadership. In the late 1970s and early 1980s a new and younger faction began to challenge the old guard's liberal stance and the old "family" style of politics. Some individuals in this group were recent Puerto Rican and younger South American immigrants, who had come to the United States for political reasons.

Particularly threatening to the old guard was a group that formed around El Centro de Arte. This new wave of Latinos included artists who, unlike most of the other immigrants, came from upper- and middle-class families. Primarily from South America, these artists, some of whom had collaborated on the murals, espoused a historical consciousness that saw Washington's Latino community as part of the Third World.

The nation's capital, in fact, was becoming increasingly connected with the strife and the economic crises in the Third World. Although it continued to be the promised land for many Latin Americans, many more were now propelled to the District by political persecution and war—not only economic distress. Immigration from Southeast Asia, Ethiopia and other African countries, and the Caribbean also increased dramatically—often for similar reasons.

The devastating civil war in El Salvador in particular provoked increased Salvadoran migration to the Washington metropolitan area during the 1980s.[5] These newcomers joined already established activists in organizing agencies to assist the large number of undocumented immigrants and to protest regulations and policies that denied them legal status. The federal Immigration and Naturalization Service routinely raided places of employment to find undocumented workers. By 1983, as community leader Irvin Flores editorialized in a local newspaper, "things were going from bad to worse." He cited the "audacity" of the Advisory Neighborhood Commission's recommendation for the police to "investigate" undocumented immigrants in the streets. He also mentioned reports that a carry-out restaurant franchise had attempted to prohibit the speaking of Spanish by its Latino employees. Moreover, in contrast to Central American immigrants, the Cubans who had arrived with the Mariel boat lift in 1980 were being granted refugee status and given special economic assistance, causing resentment and friction within the Latino community.

The community in general had grown more complex. The dances that had helped establish an interethnic social structure continued to be held in church basements but were now organized by formally constituted soccer teams, civic and religious associations, social groups, and professional promoters. These groups, formed along ethnic and regional lines, proliferated throughout the community. They have sponsored events ranging from fundraisers for the Salvadoran Intipucá City soccer team and the Casa de Colombia festival float, to the Guatemalan Señor de Esquipulas Patron Day celebration, to concerts and dances featuring international celebrities.

In the early days, dances, soccer games, and the Latino Festival—now community institutions—had been catalysts for the formation of these more specialized groups, which provided the stability and the confidence for the forging of a Latino identity that transcended but did not obliterate regional and ethnic differences. The initial intergroup solidarity created by the dances facilitated a different level of interethnic relationships as distinct groups formed. While each group's core was identifiably Salvadoran, Colombian, or some other ethnicity, non-Latinos could also join. Such interaction not only educated other District communities about the meaning of the Latino identity but also validated it as a concept. This self-ascribed identity remains central to the ongoing process of community formation in a time of rapid social change.

In the more recent stages of the Latino community's expansion and transformation, links between the growth of service-oriented enterprises and the rise of ethnic business ventures also play a major role. Although their occupational status in general has not diversified much, some Latinos have shifted positions within the employment hierarchy. Many former waiters are now restauranteurs, several janitors now manage their own cleaning and maintenance companies, and a few construction workers have become contractors. As such individuals move up the social and economic ladder, they in turn hire the more recent newcomers. For example, the Cuban owner of La Plaza Lauriol, a restaurant on Eighteenth Street, NW, started as a waiter for El Caribe restaurant and now employs mostly Salvadorans.

As the community has grown and become more visible—thus attracting greater scrutiny by regulatory authorities—early economic strategies have faded away. For example, homemade *empanadas* are no longer found on grocery-store counters, and only a few itinerant Salvadoran vendors sell their *pupusas* and *tamales* on street corners or door to door.

Many Latinos, some seeking the "American dream" or pushed out by rent increases and neighborhood gentrification, have moved to the suburbs. New Latino communities, with their own social agencies, stores, restaurants, and festivals, are developing in Maryland and Virginia. Salvadoran bakeries, which have proliferated in the suburbs, now supply Salvadoran bread and pastries to Latino- and Korean-owned grocery stores in Adams Morgan–Mount Pleasant.

Teresa Martínez, known as Mamá Tere, squeezes the whey out of cheese as she had done in her native El Salvador. (Photograph by Jeff Tinsley, courtesy Smithsonian Institution)

As many Latinos move out of the District, many more move in. The new-comers, like those who preceded them, continue to seek the land of opportunity, first setting their bags down in the already overpopulated barrio—although fewer affordable rooming houses and apartments remain. The Salvadoran population continues to grow, and increasing numbers of immigrants have also arrived from Guatemala, Peru, Bolivia, and Mexico.

The Simpson-Rodino Bill, which resulted in the 1986 Immigration Reform and Control Act, imposed civil and criminal sanctions against employers who hired undocumented immigrants and intensified fear and frustration in a community where jobs were already at a premium. Many undocumented immigrants, apprehensive about having to return to their homelands, rushed to purchase suitcases, which were recently added to inventories of Columbia Road stores in large quantities. The majority, however, could not return home and were left to settle for moonlighting jobs and underemployment. Some have joined the growing ranks of the homeless seen on the barrio's commercial streets.

The immigrants' unstable status and immigration officers' activities continue to haunt many. Additionally, immigration policies create and reinforce tensions among Latinos from different backgrounds, as well as between Latinos and African Americans, Caribbeans, East Asians, and other minorities who attend the same schools or compete for the same jobs and neighborhood space. In many ways, however, these groups depend on each other economically. Salvadorans work in Ethiopian restaurant kitchens, or with African Americans and Caribbeans in the new, upscale restaurants on Eighteenth Street and Columbia Road. They seek legal and health services, which the District government is attempting to consolidate, from the same agencies. Over the past few years the Latino Festival, reflecting the community's diversity and complexity, has included an increasing number of food booths and parading troupes from the Caribbean, Southeast Asia, West Africa, and Korea.

In May 1991, after the shooting of a Latino man by a District police officer during an arrest, looters, attracted from neighborhoods throughout the city by television coverage, destroyed businesses and clashed with police in the Mount Pleasant–Adams Morgan neighborhood. The incident was fueled by long-smoldering resentment over the abuses of the police and the insensitivity of the larger society, and the city's unresponsiveness to the Latino community's needs. The civil disturbances not only jostled the city but also spurred old, and some new, Latino leaders to organize a Latino Civil Rights Task Force, a permanent organization with elected officers and a paid staff. The Latino community, now considered anything but invisible, has moved from an intro-

A Dominican grocery store-owner nicknamed "El Gavilán," or hawk, first opened the doors of El Gavilán on Columbia Road in the early 1970s. The store's merchandise has reflected the needs of the area's emergent Latino, African, and Caribbean communities. El Gavilán has since returned to the Dominican Republic. The store is now owned by a Salvadoran family. Besides offering groceries, El Gavilán has a special delivery service to El Salvador, which is mostly used to send money back home. (Photograph by and reprinted with permission of Luis Salvatierra C.)

spective phase of seeking commonalities and support from within (which was focused on survival strategies and transcending of differences) to an outward-looking phase, focused on establishing a Latino presence and place—a "voice"—within the larger polity.

Latinos in the Mount Pleasant–Adams Morgan area have established a social, economic, and political base from which to assert their presence and have built programs that benefit both their own and the larger community. Un-expectedly, their efforts have also stimulated increased gentrification. Latino needs, life-styles, and aesthetics have reshaped the neighborhood and made it increasingly attractive to developers, who are now seeking to reclaim parts of the area and to draw more white professionals back to the city.

Meanwhile, community institutions continue to struggle for scarce funds. Employment remains unstable, and the influx of immigrants eager to work continues. The Latino community's social and economic infrastructure, however,

On weekends the barrio is an especially social place. Juan Pablo Rubio, a Latino photographer, stops to chat with a passerby on Columbia Road. (Photograph by and reprinted with permission of Luis Salvatierra C.)

is firmly established. In the past, Latino pioneers latched on to neighborhood projects initiated by African Americans and used them for their own purposes. Latinos today initiate projects that incorporate African Americans and other minorities. For example, the LatiNegro Theater Youth Project grew out of a concern to address black-Latino tensions in the schools. Skits developed from oral interviews examine the images youths have of themselves and of each other. As the Latino community has matured, it has opened up, beginning to examine itself and its relationship to the larger society. Tensions and challenges remain, but a basis now exists for addressing them.

Although Washington's Latino community has expanded into the suburbs, the Adams Morgan–Mount Pleasant barrio remains its core. When Latinos move out and form other communities, they extend rather than sever the network. In the process, older and newer immigrants nourish an even stronger community, one that still has its heart where it started.

NOTES

I thank my colleague, Luis Salvatierra C., documentary photographer and longtime member of Washington's Latino community, for generously contributing many of the images that complement this chapter.

1. There is little scholarship on or documentation of Washington's Latino community. Its evolution has been recorded and critiqued primarily by its members through anecdotes, oral histories, interviews, and newspaper editorials. This essay is written in the spirit of a history created from within the community. The primary sources are community members' literature and interviews. I have translated direct quotes that were originally in Spanish. All quotations in the text are from interviews in my possession. Articles in the local press (the *City Paper, El Barrio, El Latino, La Prensa, Pregonero,* the *Washington Post,* the *Washington Star,* and *Washingtonian Magazine*), particularly Spanish-language newspapers, have been a valuable resource. Interpretations are based on my experience as a participant and observer of the community. Much of the quoted material in this essay also appears in Olivia Cadaval, "The Hispano American Festival and the Latino Community: Creating an Identity in the Nation's Capital" (Ph.D. diss., George Washington University, 1989).

2. Although Adams Morgan and Mount Pleasant are two distinct neighborhoods, District Latinos usually refer to the area as Adams Morgan–Mount Pleasant, without making the distinction. In this essay the two areas are referred to as one. See also Olivia Cadaval, "Adams Morgan and the Latino Community," in *Washington at Home: An Illustrated History of Neighborhoods in the Nation's Capital,* ed. Kathryn Schneider Smith (Northridge, Calif.: Windsor Publications, 1988); idem, "Latinos in Washington, D.C.," in *Cut Across* (Washington, D.C.: Washington Project for the Arts, 1988); and idem, "'The Taking of the Renwick': The Celebration of the Day of the Dead and the Latino Community in Washington, D.C.," *Journal of Folklore Research* 22, nos. 2 and 3 (1985): 179–93.

3. New immigrant communities are also growing rapidly in other parts of the nation, including Chicago, Los Angeles, and New York, where new identities are being forged. For recent studies on the growth and movement of U.S. Latino communities, see Alejandro Portes and Rubén G. Rumbaut, *Immigrant America: A Portrait* (Berkeley: University of California Press, 1990). For the emergence of a Latino identity in Chicago, see Félix M. Padilla, *Latino Ethnic Consciousness: The Case of Mexican Americans and Puerto Ricans in Chicago* (Notre Dame, Ind.: University of Notre Dame Press, 1985).

4. The phrase, "taking the festival to the streets," was also used by the *Washington Post* in 1983. See Cadaval, "Hispano American Festival."

5. Salvadorans' immigration to the area, spurred by intensifying political and economic difficulties at home, started as early as the 1960s. Early Salvadoran immigrants were mainly women who came from the less affluent eastern part of the country. The current Salvadoran immigrant population is dominated by young men.

ADDITIONAL READING

Cafferty, Pastora San Juan, and William C. McCready. *Hispanics in the United States: A New Social Agenda.* New Brunswick, N.J.: Transaction Publishers, 1985.

Cohen, Lucy M. *Culture, Disease, and Stress among Latino Immigrants.* Washington, D.C.: Smithsonian Institution Press, 1979.

———. "Latin American Women Lead Migration." In *Festival of American Folklife: 1988.* Festival catalog. Washington, D.C.: Smithsonian Institution and National Park Service, 1988

Development Associates. "A Survey of Adams Morgan/Mount Pleasant/Encuesta de la Comunidad, September to October 1979: Housing and Demographic Characteristics of Its Latino Community." Executive Summary. February 1980. Office on Latino Affairs and Department of Housing and Community Development of the District of Columbia. Archives of the Office of Latino Affairs. Washington, D.C.

Henig, Jeffrey. *Gentrification in Adams Morgan: Political and Commercial Consequences of Neighborhood Change.* Washington, D.C.: Center for Washington Area Studies, George Washington University, 1982.

May-Machunda, Phyllis. "Migration to Metropolitan Washington: Making a New Place Home." In *Festival of American Folklife: 1988.* Washington: Smithsonian Institution and National Park Service, 1988. 34–37.

Paredes, Americo. "Tributaries to the Mainstream: The Ethnic Group." In *Our Living Traditions,* edited by T. P. Coffin. New York: Basic Books, 1968.

14.

From "Down the Way Where the Nights Are Gay"
Caribbean Immigration and the Bridging of Cultures

Keith Q. Warner

Harry Belafonte has done much since the 1950s to popularize the Caribbean in his well-known versions of calypso music and folk songs. In the chorus to "Jamaica Farewell," he sings:

Sad to say, I'm on my way,
Won't be back for many a day . . .

He continues with the lament that he has to "leave [his] little girl in Kingston town." Virtually all immigrants from the Caribbean can identify with that couplet of Belafonte's chorus, which evokes sadness at having to leave the Caribbean—for whatever reason—and regret over the potentially lengthy stay away from the natural beauty of the West Indies:

Down the way where the nights are gay,
And the sun shines daily on the mountain top.

For all their emotional attachment to their homeland, Caribbean peoples, like those elsewhere, do migrate, and, increasingly, many of them settle in Washington.

Immigrants from the English-speaking Caribbean are also called West Indians because of their link with those territories loosely termed "the West Indies." They are thus seen as culturally different from other Caribbean immigrants. For example, the Washington area's Spanish-speaking Puerto Ricans, Cubans, and Dominicans are considered "Hispanic" or "Latino" and are not primarily identified as Caribbean. A similar situation exists among the French- or creole-speaking Haitian immigrants, though continued media attention to the social and political problems of present-day Haiti has generated more rapprochement between Haitians and other Caribbean immigrants.

"Caribbean" in this essay refers to English-speaking people of the former British colonies (or Commonwealth member countries) in the Caribbean basin: Belize, Jamaica, Trinidad and Tobago, Barbados, the Leeward Islands, the Windward Islands, and Guyana. It examines their reasons for emigrating, their lives in Washington, and their reasons for staying.

As social geographer Bonham C. Richardson points out, "Migration to the United States from the states of the Commonwealth Caribbean since 1965 has represented a recent surge to some Americans but continuity to many West Indians."[1] Indeed, Harold Cruse's pioneering book, *The Crisis of the Negro Intellectual*, devotes an entire chapter to West Indians' influence on African American intellectuals and aspiring politicians in the 1920s and 1930s.[2] It is well known that the Caribbean has produced such writers as Claude McKay, such activists as Marcus Garvey and Stokely Carmichael, and such politicians as Mervyn Dymally. There is plainly a long history of Caribbean migration to the United States. Nevertheless, this migration was greatly increased in 1965, when the United States abolished the quota system in favor of immigration based on the need for labor, with preference given to those with relatives already here.

Although the vast majority of Caribbean immigrants reside in the New York City area, more of them are moving away from that original pole of attraction in favor of other areas—especially that of metropolitan Washington. A principal attraction has been Howard University, whose renown as the world's leading predominantly black university has drawn to its campus many who eventually have become leaders in their Third World countries. Eric Williams, for example, taught at Howard before returning home to lead Trinidad and Tobago to independence in 1962.

The university's Caribbean students and professors set in motion a cycle of migration, encouraging compatriots—particularly through alumni associations—to come to the United States to study at Howard. Many Caribbean students remained in the city after graduation, ostensibly changing their status from transient international students to potentially more permanent immigrants. With the continued in-migration of students, these immigrants have become an important group within Washington's Caribbean community.

The students who came in the 1940s, mainly from Jamaica and Trinidad, found other Caribbean immigrants already in Washington, including women who were working as domestics for white families. Not all of these women had been domestics back home. According to Richardson, "some immigrant West Indians who had regarded themselves as middle class at home were often forced to accept menial, working-class positions in the United States."[3] Household workers were sometimes embarrassed if they were recognized in their new role by compatriots pursuing higher studies.

The 1950s and 1960s saw a continuing influx of students. This period coincided with Caribbean peoples' gradual awakening to the idea that they could control their own destinies. When Jamaica and, later, Trinidad and Tobago achieved political independence in 1962, many of their nationals, fully intending to return home afterwards to help build their countries, came to the District to study at Howard. Others came to work at the city's international organizations.

If international civil servants managed fairly well, such was not the case with students, many of whom had insufficient finances, and often little or no scholarship funds. Forced to work part-time to earn extra money, many of the male students drove taxicabs, while the female students clerked in department stores. Throughout their studies these students usually remained highly motivated and, as a group, performed far above the college average.

The prevailing attitude among the students—both before and after their graduation—was that they were only in Washington for a short time and would eventually return to the Caribbean to better their respective countries. However, it soon became clear that the infusion of too many qualified graduates into a static work force back home would pose more problems than it would solve. In fact, beginning in the 1970s, many would-be returnees became permanent immigrants, forced to await an opportune moment to return to their island homelands.

While Trinidad and Tobago, with an abundance of petroleum, enjoyed an economic boom in the late 1970s, most Caribbean Commonwealth nations (Guyana, for example) saw their prosperity dwindle to the point that their nationals began fleeing. The traditional lure of opportunity in the United States was reinforced by the growing need to escape economic decline—a cycle that would catch up with Trinidad and Tobago in the late 1980s and continue into the 1990s. The result was fairly heavy migration to the United States or Canada, since England had long since become inhospitable. The Caribbean immigrant population in Washington was thus increased by this latest wave. For the first time most Caribbean immigrants were neither students (current or former) nor professionals, but rather members of the working classes— including nurses, mechanics, tradespeople, and laborers.

This new group also believed initially that they were in Washington temporarily. Returning permanently to the Caribbean, however, has grown increasingly difficult for three main reasons. First, the immigrant who does not return home as an outstanding success is generally considered to have wasted his or her time "in the land of plenty," the stereotypical Caribbean view of the United States. Second, the economies of many Caribbean countries benefit from the constant transfer of cash and other commodities. According to Richardson,

> Money sent home by migrants helps sustain insular West Indian societies. Whereas a "brain drain" may siphon off many of the best educated of the region, a money flow heading back in the other direction helps cushion the loss.[4]

Third, and more important, these immigrants, like many other second- and third-generation immigrants, grow to appreciate living in the Washington area. They become "Americanized," accepting and enjoying life in a society that—even with its problems—offers more possibilities than the depressed economies of the Caribbean. While Americanization does not eradicate their "Caribbean-ness," and would even be criticized by those Caribbeans intent on preserving their own identity, it enables them to blend more easily into the fabric of the society around them.

Significantly, Caribbean immigrants do not generally consider themselves to be refugees. Although some Trinidad and Tobago nationals, claiming that the political situation in their country had become untenable, did seek political-refugee status in Canada in the late 1980s, the Canadian government turned them down.

One final group of Caribbean immigrants that must be considered are those who are in Washington illegally. Although the U.S. Immigration and Naturalization Service (INS) initiated an amnesty program in 1987, giving illegal immigrants with more than five years' residence several months to register without penalty, not all persons with irregular status took advantage of the government's attempt to regularize their situation. There was among the Caribbean immigrants, as among most undocumented newcomers, a feeling of skepticism and uneasiness about calling attention to their status. Since the end of that amnesty program, and with the downturn in several of the Caribbean nations' economies, many visitors on holiday visas (now increasingly difficult to obtain) have simply refused to return to the Caribbean when their visas expired.

The percentage of undocumented West Indian immigrants has risen in direct proportion to the increase in unemployment in the Caribbean countries.

Jamaican-born Percival Bryan (left) and Edward E. Scott, from Maryland's Eastern Shore, in October 1990. They are both longtime District cab drivers. (Photograph by Craig Herndon, © Washington Post)

Further, these immigrants cannot return to the Caribbean on holiday or business, for they would not be allowed reentry into the United States. They prefer instead to take various jobs in private homes, where laws requiring that their status be reported by employers have been difficult to enforce. Undocumented immigrants, however, are still immigrants, with the same needs as those who are here legally. They too must find housing and food, and adapt to the community in which they live; and they too experience the desire to forge links with the Caribbean they have left.

Most Caribbean immigrants in Washington are somewhat surprised to learn that the nation's capital is considered a part of the South, with all the connotations of lingering racism and Jim Crow practices; they generally experience a sense of comfort at being in a city with a predominantly black population. They also appreciate the city's livable and likable physical environment.

Their perspectives, however, are tempered by uneasiness at being in the South, a part of the nation whose history they like least. They thus instinctively tread carefully. However, their different cultures and traditions and their upbringing in colonized or newly independent countries give them a sense of naïveté vis-à-vis the history and struggles of African Americans.

Caribbean immigrants therefore follow the paths trodden by their compatriots who preceded them, particularly with regard to housing. Many of the early Caribbean immigrants have lived in clusters along the Sixteenth Street, Georgia Avenue, and Florida Avenue corridors, as well as in Mount Pleasant, Southeast Washington, and around Howard University. In later years, following the area's demographic trends, many have pushed into the Maryland suburbs of Silver Spring, Takoma Park, Langley Park, and Hyattsville. The thrust into Virginia, perhaps because of its more pronounced association with the Old South, has been much less developed.

Early Caribbean immigrants played a pivotal role in housing. In many instances newer arrivals moved in with relatives or friends, or found housing previously occupied by other Caribbean nationals. The problem of finding shelter was thus lessened or solved altogether.

After their initial adaptation to the Washington environment—for example, learning how to get around the city, where to shop, where to worship, and how to get to and from work or school—Caribbean immigrants began to seek those aspects of the community that would help them to maintain their Caribbean identity. One major link to home has been food. Caribbean immigrants literally travel with their food. (This fact is so well known to U.S. Customs officials that travelers from the West Indies are routinely examined carefully upon their arrival, lest they inadvertently bring in any unwelcome diseases in fruits or other food products.) It does not take long before Caribbean taste buds begin to yearn for Caribbean cuisine.

Apart from the relatively recent (and expensive) gourmet departments of the major grocery chains, supermarkets have not carried the full variety of foods and other West Indian products that Caribbean immigrants crave. This lack has given rise to the opening of many small, privately owned markets stocking Caribbean goods. In stores along Georgia Avenue, in Mount Pleasant, and, more recently, in Silver Spring and Takoma Park, Jamaicans can now find the ingredients for their patties; Trinidadians can purchase the curry for their rotis and the peas for their pelau; and Guyanese can obtain the casareep for their pepper pot. In recent years, some of these items have also become available in markets with predominantly Latino or Asian clienteles.

Customers can also find the same imported products they were accustomed to in the Caribbean: Canadian Healing Oil, Ferol Cough Syrup, Limacol, Eno's Fruit Salts. Although there is no hard evidence that these products are any better than equivalent (and probably less expensive) U.S.-manufactured merchandise, they serve an important function: they evoke the Caribbean in a tangible way.

Similarly, Caribbean immigrants have opened restaurants and bakeries, thus allowing other Washingtonians to partake of many West Indian delicacies and facilitating further interaction between Caribbean and American customers. They are also ideal meeting spots for community members, in addition to being convenient ticket outlets and poster-display centers for all the cultural events geared to Caribbeans. Thus, on a typical Saturday at Mike and Rita's on Georgia Avenue, one may see Caribbean immigrants as well as other Washingtonians dropping by to make a purchase, to enjoy a meal, to share information on the latest happenings in the Caribbean, or to discuss that evening's scheduled calypso or reggae show at Howard University.

Such talk of entertainment is fairly commonplace, for another major link among Caribbean immigrants, their homelands, and the Washington area results from the increasing number of cultural manifestations, such as calypso and steel-band performances, Carnival-costume presentations, and visiting theatrical players and comedians. There is thus no need for today's Caribbean immigrants to feel as homesick as their counterparts of some twenty years earlier, when such events were rarities. In addition, the totally mixed Caribbean and Washingtonian audiences at these events provide ample evidence of the interpenetration of both cultures.

Because Carnival plays a major role in the lives of many Caribbean people, it is difficult to explain why Washington's Caribbean immigrants have been unable to mount a Carnival parade to match the one that takes place on Labor Day in Brooklyn or during Toronto's Caribana. Trinidad's Geoffrey Holder, internationally known for his work in films and advertisements, adequately sums up this festival's significance: "This is our grand release. We sing, dance, laugh, and boogie. . . . We are purified and revitalized through Carnival."[5] While Washington does not have as many Caribbean residents as do Brooklyn and Toronto, cities with fewer Caribbeans (Baltimore and Atlanta, for example) have managed to organize a Carnival parade. They simply invite other cities to join in the festivities.

As early as 1976 the West Indian American Carnival Association organized a parade in Washington, but found that it could not do so after 1977. The Smithsonian Institution tried its hand for a while, as did Caribbean Festivals, Inc., and the Caribbeana Arts Festival. In the late 1980s the Smithsonian,

Costumed Caribbean Carnival performer in Washington in 1992. (Photograph by Harold Dorwin, courtesy Anacostia Museum, Smithsonian Institution)

which launched its 1989 Caribbean Festival Arts exhibition with a mini-Carnival, became involved once again through its sponsorship of Carnival on the Mall. This event, emblematic of the unifying nature of this festival, has thus far featured Carnivals from Trinidad and Tobago and the Virgin Islands.

The lack of a regular annual parade does not, however, totally deprive Washington of Caribbean Carnival. There are several local festivals that include participation by costumed Caribbean Carnival revelers or parading steel bands. The annual Georgia Avenue Day, for example, includes a sampling of Carnival costumes, and its one or more steel bands ensure some semblance of a Caribbean Carnival–like atmosphere, enjoyed by both Caribbeans and other Washingtonians. In 1993 D.C. Caribbean Carnival, Inc. made plans to annually celebrate D.C. Caribbean Carnival on the fourth Saturday in June with a parade along Georgia Avenue, NW.

Caribbean music, with its distinctive sound, has long been used to identify people from the West Indies in an almost stereotypical way. Chief among
these musical forms have been calypso, closely associated with Trinidad and
Tobago, and more recently, reggae, with its Jamaican roots. The annual appearance by artists such as the calypsonian Mighty Sparrow in the 1960s has
given way to almost weekly musical festivals.

All of the Caribbean community's musical entertainment, however, is not
imported from home. More than twenty-five years ago Howard University students were instrumental in starting a steel band that—despite many changes
in personnel—has survived up to the present, and has even spawned a rival or-
chestra. Prominent calypsonians from the Caribbean (Lord Melody, Lord Laro,
and Beckett) have lived in Washington, making it no coincidence that the city
has produced its own calypsonians (Blackbird, Seales, Baker, and Kwame,
among others) who have taken part in their own calypso monarch competitions.

Similarly, reggae and other bands comprising Caribbean immigrants (for
example, Carlos Malcolm and the Positive Vibrations, Image Band, and Roots
Vibration) regularly perform in a variety of settings. These entertainers have
played a key role in projecting a positive image of the Caribbean, and are in
continual demand by non-Caribbean organizations—from embassies to private
firms—to provide music for their many social functions. Invariably, however,
these bands perform at fund-raising events for the Caribbean community, working in association with many of the city's Caribbean deejays. They provide the
music for and attract well-wishers to many of the efforts initiated by groups
aiming to improve the social and economic conditions of either the Caribbean
immigrants here in Washington or their relatives back home.

There is close collaboration between these entertainers and the various
groupings of nationals, such as the Trinidad and Tobago Association, the Jamaica Nationals Association, and the Barbados Nationals Association. These
organizations were among the first to streamline the efforts of a particular
group. The Trinidad and Tobago Association, for example, has its own clubhouse, which serves not only as a venue for social functions and meetings but
also as a haven for homesick nationals. Such organizations reflect the concerns,
propensities, and sometimes even the prejudices and rivalries of the West Indian nations.

In addition, several special-interest groups have emerged: sports clubs that
continue the friendly rivalry of cricket and soccer (which, incidentally, all
Caribbean immigrants know as the *real* football), as well as the more insular
games, such as dominoes among the Jamaicans and Guyanese, and all fours

A Jamaican Cricket Club match in Washington in 1993. (Photograph by Harold Dorwin, courtesy Anacostia Museum, Smithsonian Institution)

among the Trinidadians. There are also associations of former students ("old boys" and "old girls") of prominent West Indian high schools such as Bishop's of Tobago, Queen's College of Guyana, and Bishop Anstey's of Trinidad; organizations of *mas* (popular Trinidad and Tobago designation for Carnival) designers who make Carnival costumes and travel from city to city to show them off; and East Indian merrymakers, who keep alive traditional Indian dances and songs. Finally, a variety of organizations, such as GuyAid and Love in Action, provide aid to Caribbean immigrants in Washington and the needy back home.

There is no umbrella group of national cultural organizations, although the Caribbean American Intercultural Organization's name clearly indicates such an intention, and the Council of Caribbean Organizations (COCO) and the Organization of Caribbean Businesspersons (OCB) bring together a broad spectrum of immigrant businesspeople. In addition to striving to improve opportunities for immigrant-owned businesses, these groups also monitor the general image of the Caribbean within the Washington media and the Washington community.

COCO, for example, met with District police officials to protest the ill-fated Operation Caribbean Cruise of 22 February 1986. According to the police, a number of suspected drug users or dealers were targeted for a surprise raid. The operation was a fiasco—due mostly to alleged leaks—and netted virtually no drugs. However, it was obvious that most of the people targeted were victims of the erroneous stereotyping that portrays all Caribbeans as Jamaicans, and all Jamaicans as drug users or pushers. The police eventually apologized for the operation.

Incidents such as Operation Caribbean Cruise highlight the importance of another group of Caribbean nationals: members of the diplomatic corps, who immediately take up, at the highest possible levels of government, the cause of nationals perceived to have been unjustly treated. In addition, diplomats provide vital services to Caribbean immigrants, as well as to the many Washingtonians seeking information about the West Indies—whether for travel purposes or for business ventures. Thus, Caribbean immigrants find a generally hospitable atmosphere in Washington, and, although the city itself has undergone radical changes during the period of increased Caribbean immigration, by and large both immigrants and the city have benefited from these rapidly changing circumstances. The Caribbean community's numerous cultural activities attract growing numbers of Washingtonians—not only as spectators but also as active participants. Similarly, Caribbean immigrants play ever-increasing roles in Washington's cultural activities. The Smithsonian Institution, the local Fondo del Sol art gallery, and several Washington churches all have significant numbers of Caribbeans involved in their projects and activities.

Despite desires to remain essentially and integrally Caribbean, immigrants cannot but be changed by their new environment and their new culture. Admittedly, change is not always easy. For example, few Caribbean immigrants enjoy Washington's winter weather. Additionally, Caribbean parents generally do not allow their children the freedom they see given by their American counterparts. This causes considerable disagreement and frustration between first-generation Caribbean parents and their children. Despite parents' fears, their children's attendance in area schools provides an opportunity for the bridging of cultures. On one hand, Caribbean children learn about American culture and in turn involve their parents in such activities as football or the celebrations of Halloween and Thanksgiving. On the other hand, the children's Americanization often means that they do not actively seek Caribbean mates, which is a source of considerable concern, particularly for first-generation Caribbean parents.

For many second- and third-generation West Indians, the Caribbean area has become merely "the islands" rather than "home," and the children have grown to consider themselves Americans with Caribbean roots, rather than so-

Von Martin, host of the popular Caribbeana *program on public radio station WPFW-FM. (Photograph by George de Vincent, courtesy Arena Stage)*

journers from the Caribbean. Because these second- and third-generation children often have never seen the Caribbean, Washington is the only geographical home they know and the only community to which they are attached.

Political involvement is the ultimate benchmark of a group's integration into a host community, and the Washington area has seen such Caribbean immigrants as Joslyn Williams become head of the D.C. Democratic Party, Patrick Hylton serve as a top aide to D.C. Councilmember Hilda Mason, and Acklyn Lynch run a local political campaign. Such participation indicates that the Caribbean "guests" are now ready to move beyond the role of sojourner and to assume full responsibility for ensuring that the voices of a growing segment of the Washington area population will be heard in the corridors of power.

The Caribbean community's interaction with each other and with outsiders has done much to unify the Caribbean immigrants as well as to integrate this group with other Washingtonians. Increased communication has also dispelled some of the stereotypes that groups have held about each other: life is not all sea and song in the West Indies, and other Washingtonians are not all rich.

Although there have been intermittent appearances of Caribbean newspapers (*Iere* and *Caribbean Sun*, for example) and magazines, the most important communication method is radio. Weekly programs, such as *Caribbeana* on WPFW-FM, hosted by Von Martin, and *The Caribbean Experience* on Howard University's WHUR-FM, hosted by John Blake, provide up-to-date Caribbean news. They also play the latest Caribbean music, interview community members, and generally act as the voice of the Caribbean community. During tense periods when most Washingtonians were focused on the Caribbean—for example, during the 1983 U.S. invasion of Grenada, and during the 1990 attempted coup in Trinidad and Tobago—they turned to these programs for accurate information as events unfolded. There is no Caribbean-oriented television station, although Howard University's WHMM-TV does feature an occasional program from the Caribbean. The station's popular *Evening Exchange*, a nightly look at a variety of the issues that concern the Washington community, is hosted by Guyana's Kojo Nnamdi.

Of these programs, only *The Caribbean Experience* has a commercial orientation. Its advertisers give a good indication of the breadth of the area's Caribbean-owned businesses and services: the restaurants, bakeries, small grocers, auto-body shops, gas stations, liquor stores, real estate agencies, nightclubs, and travel agencies, as well as doctors, lawyers, engineers, and other professionals. Their numbers suggest that their survival depends on both a Caribbean and a non-Caribbean clientele.

West Indian immigrants do not blend into the landscape but rather stand out proudly as Caribbean people. They retain their language, often deliberately using their island twangs to amuse and befuddle their fellow Washingtonians. They have also added new words to the Washington vocabulary: jerk pork, patty, soca, jump up, saga boy, pan, parang, and reggae. Many have become U.S. citizens, although they retain the cultural identities of their birthplaces. They eventually see themselves as having two homes, and are as eager to fly to the Caribbean as they are to return to Washington. Yes, they all want to go back for the one left behind in some Caribbean town, only now they will likely try to bring him or her back to Washington with them, back from "down the way where the nights are gay, and the sun shines daily on the mountain top."[6]

NOTES

1. Bonham C. Richardson, "Caribbean Migrations, 1838–1985," in *The Modern Caribbean*, ed. Franklin W. Knight and Colin A. Palmer (Chapel Hill: University of North Carolina Press, 1989), 221.

2. See Harold Cruse, *The Crisis of the Negro Intellectual* (New York: William Morrow, 1967).

3. Richardson, "Caribbean Migrations," 213.

4. Ibid., 224.

5. Quoted in John Nunley and Judith Bettelheim, eds. *Caribbean Festival Arts* (Seattle: University of Washington Press, 1988), 85.

6. Further information on the Caribbean can be obtained from the relevant embassies in Washington, or from organizations involved in educational, policy, or development work related to the Caribbean: for example, the Development Center for Alternative Policies, and Ecumenical Program on Central America and the Caribbean (EPICA).

ADDITIONAL READING

Caribbean Databook. Washington, D.C.: Caribbean Central American Action, 1983.

Laguerre, Michael S. *American Odyssey: Haitians in New York City.* Ithaca, N.Y.: Cornell University Press, 1984.

Mintz, Sidney W., and Sally Price, eds. *Caribbean Contours.* Baltimore: Johns Hopkins University Press, 1985.

Sunshine, Cathy A. *The Caribbean: Survival, Struggle, and Sovereignty.* Washington, D.C.: Ecumenical Program on Central America and the Caribbean, 1988.

Sutton, Constance R., and Elsa M. Chaney, eds. *Caribbean Life in New York City: Sociocultural Dimensions.* New York: Center for Migration Studies, 1987.

15.

Washington's New African Immigrants

Bereket H. Selassie

The African presence in Washington, D.C., is as old as the city itself. A few free African Americans of independent means graced the city from its infancy, and the free black community grew steadily up to the Civil War, as James Oliver Horton discusses in Chapter 2. For the most part, however, the African presence was a shadowy one, existing on the periphery of white consciousness and living precariously at its sufferance. That condition persisted even after the Emancipation Proclamation of 1863 abolished slavery in the Union-occupied South, and after the Civil War ended in 1865, bringing freedom to all slaves in the United States.

The establishment of Howard University in 1867 reflected African Americans' need for a center of learning and social interaction in the nation's capital. Howard soon emerged as the nation's premier higher-education institution for African Americans. By the mid-twentieth century Howard became a magnet as well for African students from a continent colonized by European powers. Although other American universities, such as Lincoln University in Pennsylvania, also attracted them, Howard became the principal mecca for Africans seeking learning.[1]

The African presence in Washington acquired even greater significance in the late 1950s and throughout the 1960s, with the appearance of new African embassies in the wake of Africa's emancipation from European colonial rule. As African nations gained political independence, an increasing number of students, scholars, embassy staff, and employees of such international organizations as the World Bank came to Washington, setting the stage for the arrival of more African-born immigrants who, in the 1970s and 1980s, built on established networks of compatriots to create new communities.

Decolonization coincided with the civil rights movement in the United States, and the two sets of historic events seemed mutually reinforcing. It was an exciting time, full of challenges and vigorous attempts to rectify centuries-old injustices. Still, the personnel of the new African embassies did not escape traditional discriminatory practices in America. Former Sen. Harris L. Wofford, while U.S. special assistant on civil rights to President John F. Kennedy, recorded that African diplomats traveling from Washington to New York were refused service in the hotels and restaurants along Route 95.[2] The political significance of the advent of diplomats representing newly independent African nations fell short of furthering the dream to create a more tolerant society. As a result, members of the nascent African diplomatic community, with rare exceptions, kept themselves aloof from the larger Washington social scene.

Today visitors arriving at Union Station or Washington National Airport may be struck by the number of taxi drivers from Somalia, Ethiopia, Nigeria, Ghana, Eritrea, and other African nations, who greet them in pronounced Afro-English accents. Throughout the city, visitors meet African parking-lot attendants, hotel staff, gas-station operators, cashiers, street vendors, and others engaged in a host of service-industry jobs. A closer look reveals the presence of African physicians, nurses, real estate agents, accountants, and business owners and merchants, whose numbers—though small by comparison with other immigrant groups—are significant given their fairly recent arrival.

Indeed, the contemporary voluntary immigration from Africa to the United States is more numerous and diverse than ever. Beginning in the 1970s and accelerating in the 1980s, Washington emerged as a major magnet for this new worldwide migration—an odyssey that reflects the political and economic circumstances and the cultural complexity of the changing African continent itself. While mindful of the need for further research into all African immigrant communities in light of their diversity, this essay focuses on Washington's emerging Ethiopian, Eritrean, and Nigerian communities.

The largest concentration of Africans living in the United States, estimated at more than 50,000, is in the Washington area. The majority have come from the Horn of Africa, more than 30,000 Ethiopians, Eritreans, and Somalis combined, with the largest numbers from Ethiopia and Eritrea. The next largest national group, at least 10,000 to 15,000, are those from Nigeria. Substantial numbers from Ghana, Sierra Leone, Senegal, Cameroon, and dozens of other African countries add to the mix of African cultures.[3] Altogether, these newcomers constitute a visible African presence in Washington's cultural landscape.

The most striking evidence of this presence is the number of restaurants,

The 1990 Eritrean wedding of Yemane Tewolde and Algetta Belay was celebrated in Washington. (Courtesy Abiyi Ford)

largely concentrated in the city's Adams Morgan neighborhood, that offer African cuisines—mostly Eritrean and Ethiopian but also Somali, Kenyan, and Ghanaian, among others. Several clubs that feature African bands, such as the Kilimanjaro (owned by a Kenyan) and the Kalabash (owned by a Ghanaian), are equally popular among Africans and other Washingtonians. A survey of more than a dozen of the restaurants' clientele indicates that about 65 percent are American, including former Peace Corps volunteers and U.S. government employees familiar with Africa. As for the African diners, many come from nations on the Horn of Africa, while others represent the more diverse diasporan community. Whatever their orientation, the restaurants—reflections of African entrepreneurship—have become gathering places not only for enjoying a meal reminiscent of home, but also for sharing news and social interaction among a variety of individuals and national groups. As a local Ethiopian leader suggested: "If you feel lonely, you go to one of the restaurants because you are likely to find someone you know."[4]

Although the more recent African immigrants came by choice, circumstances beyond their control usually influenced their decision to migrate. This "push" factor is certainly true for Eritreans, Ethiopians, and Nigerians, most of

Somalis gathered at the Mogadishu restaurant (named after the capital of Somalia) in Adams Morgan in December 1992. (Photograph by Nancy Andrews, © Washington Post)

whom have fled prolonged and devastating civil wars or military and political oppression in their homelands.

A war between Eritrea and Ethiopia from 1961 to 1991, for example, led to a steady, massive stream of refugees from Eritrea. More than 30,000 Eritreans fled to North America alone (about 80 percent of these between 1981 and 1988), with at least one third, or 10,000, settling in the Washington area. In Ethiopia unending war, drought, and famine, and an undemocratic political regime combined with militarization in the 1970s and 1980s, led many young Ethiopians to flee to Sudan, Kenya, Djibouiti, and then out of Africa altogether to Europe and North America. Today Ethiopian refugees, the largest African national group in the Washington area, make up the largest Ethiopian community in the United States.[5]

In the late 1960s the Nigerian civil war (the Biafra War) drove thousands of Nigerians out of their nation's Eastern or Ibo-speaking region. Many of them remained abroad after the war. Nigerians had long sought higher education abroad, mostly in Great Britain and the United States, and most had tradi-

Nigerian wedding celebration in the Washington area. (Photo by and courtesy of Joy Wigwe)

tionally returned home. Since the early 1980s, however, questionable economic policies, worsened by declining oil revenues and continuing political crises under an undemocratic military regime, have pushed additional thousands of Nigerians out of their nation and have discouraged the return of those living abroad. Nigerian Nobel Laureate Wole Soyinka spoke for many in lamenting the "atmosphere of fear . . . replacing what once was openness."[6] A growing number of Nigerians in the Washington area now say that they doubt they will ever return home—even if civilian rule is restored. A few say they will wait and see, "to make assurance doubly sure," as one Nigerian student put it.

A colleague from the Horn of Africa observed not long ago: "Every time I see a new restaurant in Adams Morgan with a Third World name, I think of a failed cause somewhere out there in Africa, Asia, or Latin America." While the comment refers to the context of exit that compelled migration, it also reflects the opportunities that America presents to newcomers, for whom social and economic mobility in their homelands remains an unfulfilled dream. Most African immigrants in Washington are not "the huddled masses" and "wretched refuse" of Emma Lazarus's poem inscribed on the Statue of Liberty. They are primarily young and comparatively well-educated men and women, many of whom have come to the United States with professional skills and entrepreneurial drive. The success of the many restaurants "with Third World names" attests to these traits. The "brain drain" from Africa is thus America's gain.

Africans choose the Washington area for a variety of reasons. The key factors include the city's majority African American population; the continuing draw of Howard University and, today, other Washington-area universities; the large international community; and, especially, the availability of entry-level jobs in the growing service industry. No less crucial is the fact that newcomers tend to gravitate to areas where compatriots already live and work. U.S. immigration policy, particularly regarding the settlement of political refugees, encourages this concentration, because existing social networks provide newcomers with support systems that reduce the burden on public funding. An additional benefit that ethnic concentration affords is the opportunity for parents to organize weekend language classes for their children, thus perpetuating the strong cultural ties that sustain Africans settling abroad. From an immigrant's viewpoint, such networks are lifelines in a new world.

Immigrants' legal status determines their U.S. residency and legal employment. Political refugees—a majority among Africans—are automatically eligible for employment in the United States under current immigration laws. Students and visitors, however, must adjust their status to that of permanent resident if they wish to work and to remain in the country legally. U.S. immigration policy does not usually grant Africans political-refugee status, and it has restricted immigration from Africa for economic reasons. The annual African quota thus falls disproportionately short of that set for other non-European nations. The fact that many Africans stay with expired visas or questionable legal status and work in Washington's "twilight" service economy largely accounts for the city's official underreporting of Africans.

Washington's African communities face problems similar to those of the city's other immigrant communities: limited access to good jobs, a shortage of affordable housing in safe neighborhoods, and inadequate health services and child-care programs, all of which affect their socioeconomic adjustment.[7] Since established residents need similar services, these problems are often exacerbated for newcomers. Their ability to develop support systems within their own national groups is therefore as critical as are the opportunities offered by the host country. In addition to ethnic grocery stores and restaurants, some Africans have established organizations such as the Ethiopian Community Center and the Organization of Nigerian Professionals to help compatriots get settled, find jobs, and deal with emergencies. Others have founded churches or

Martha Kadsla, a popular vocalist, at the 1992 Ethiopian New Year's celebration in Adams Morgan. (Photograph by Harold Dorwin, courtesy of the Anacostia Museum, Smithsonian Institution)

mosques, soccer teams, and newspapers to meet the need for fellowship and provide forums for social exchange and emotional support.[8]

A significant portion of African immigrants, particularly those who arrived in the 1960s and 1970s, came to Washington as sojourners, hoping to return eventually to their homelands. Consequently, many did not initially make a psychological or emotional commitment to establishing a life for themselves in this country. However, as conditions deteriorated or failed to improve in their homelands, or as immigrants began to adjust to their new environment and to establish a sense of community, their attitudes gradually changed. Today more Africans are getting married, buying homes, and starting families, and some are becoming U.S. citizens. While eager to contribute to their new home, they continue to maintain close ties to their countries of origin.

First-generation African immigrants, like their European predecessors and non-European immigrant contemporaries, struggle to maintain a balance between putting down roots in America and preserving their ethnic heritage and identity. The tension between these two considerations is especially visible in the daily interaction between parents and their children. The adults strive to instill African values in their children—especially a sense of community solidarity and respect for elders—while the latter, often more fluent in English, pull their parents toward a better understanding of the American culture. Ultimately, the practical necessity of having children succeed in the American milieu—at school and later in the workplace—takes precedence. To a certain degree, the children, living between two worlds, become their parents' guides.

In traditional African cultures the extended family has provided a framework of cradle-to-grave care for community members. A network of obligations based upon a common ancestor has benefited any person who could prove his or her ancestry. This kinship bond is today being broken even in African urban life, and is under tremendous pressure in new, immigrant environments. The nuclear family among immigrants is emerging as the center of daily concerns, eroding the traditional kinship-based identity. The pervasive power of television and the mass media, and the competitive and acquisitive blandishments of the marketplace, are also difficult to resist. Young African immigrants are increasingly self-identifying as Americans, despite their parents' efforts to the contrary.

The Washington area's African immigrants pursue a wide range of occupations, "from dishwasher to World Bank engineer."[9] Among Ethiopians in the labor force, for example, about 13 percent are employed at hotels and restaurants, and 3 percent are taxi drivers. In addition, 5 percent own businesses, 12 percent work as nurses or social workers, and 30 percent hold professional or managerial positions.

Such statistics do not reveal job satisfaction or quality of life; nor is there unanimity regarding the criteria for making such assessments. For recent immigrants, having job security and a regular paycheck may not be enough if their professional aspirations cannot be realized, they are underemployed, or they have experienced downward social mobility from the status they once had in their home countries. For many, the gap between expectations of "the good life" in America and stark reality adds to the stress of adjustment. Olaniyi Areke, a Nigerian filmmaker who came to Washington in the 1980s, claims that "the majority of Nigerian cab drivers have M.A. and Ph.D. degrees." Policy analysts studying the results of the 1990 U.S. census substantiate this claim. New immigrants, they report, work predominantly in low-wage service jobs, regardless of their educational backgrounds. The reports show that although immigrants compose 6 percent of the area's lawyers and 11 percent of its managers and professionals overall, the overwhelming majority of the region's household workers are immigrants, and 50 percent of the area's parking-lot attendants, taxicab drivers, and busboys are foreign-born.[10]

Compounding the search for job satisfaction and career opportunities—

The arts and culture of Ghana were celebrated in the Washington area in 1992. (Photograph by Harold Dorwin, courtesy of the Anacostia Museum, Smithsonian Institution)

which enable African immigrants to support family and community life, and thus figure prominently in any decision to stay—is the issue of race and ethnicity in the United States. Whether or not assimilation into the American mainstream, the traditional path of European immigrants' acculturation, is possible for African newcomers remains problematic, especially given the paramount importance they place on maintaining ethnic identities. The Africans in Washington Project found that although the African experience is similar to that of other immigrant groups, it is also different. The history of Africans in America and on the African continent has created discontinuity between the African American experience and the African heritage, a rupture reflected in the fact that until recently no Africans could enter this country on the basis of family reunification—one of the major categories for the entry of immigrants under current law. Like black immigrants from the Caribbean and Latin America, African immigrants are developing a new ethnic identity that is not necessarily "African American" as the racial/cultural designation is generally understood in the United States, where race is seen as an undifferentiated cat-

African Heritage Society dancers, directed by Melvin Deal, performed at Freedom Plaza in downtown Washington circa 1992. (Photograph by Harold Dorwin, courtesy of the Anacostia Museum, Smithsonian Institution)

egory.[11] Africans in Washington thus continually negotiate their evolving identities on the terrain of U.S. race relations while remaining conscious of their particular ethnic and national identities, their ties to African homelands, and their social relations to African Americans and to U.S. society as a whole.

In this context, the incorporation of new African immigrants into American culture depends as much on the host community's ability to support fluid multicultural relations as it does upon the business segment's willingness to tap into the African potential. It is also necessary for different African national groups to organize around common goals, an effort that some of the area's diverse Latino immigrants, for example, have begun to undertake. For African newcomers, this is easier said than done. Despite an underlying cultural commonality among Ethiopians and Eritreans, and among Nigerians and other West Africans, conditions that create division and acrimonious relationships in their homelands have inhibited "pan-African" community formation across cultures, national origins, and linguistic groups in the Washington area and elsewhere in the United States. Thus, African immigrants' cultural presence in Washington has not yet translated into a strong political presence. Perhaps as the emerging African-born community matures, it will consolidate its political presence in ways that bridge cultures and afford its members both economic security and opportunities to preserve their ethnic traditions and identities.

The lack of general knowledge about the complex histories and cultures of diverse African nations and of Africans in America complicates the adaptation process. Still, some progress is being made. The Africans' interaction with African Americans and their culture is considerable and promises increased understanding and communication. For example, the African American holiday of Kwanzaa, created by Maulana Ron Karenga in California in 1966, incorporates elements from many African harvest festivals. The annual celebration, now an important part of Washington's social scene during the last week of December, focuses on African art, music, dance, and food. The Smithsonian Institution's National Museum of African Art also plays a crucial role in increasing public awareness of the continent's cultural and artistic heritage through exhibits such as "Nine Centuries of African Art and Thought," which featured Yoruba art. Folklife festivals on the Mall, youth conventions (Howard University hosted the first International Youth Convention in 1990), and public-radio programs airing African music provide further opportunities for Washingtonians to learn about African cultural diversity.

Such efforts are dispelling myths about African culture and creating a framework for communication among African newcomers and between them and established residents. African immigrants will continue to contribute their talents and traditions to Washington's social and cultural life. The growing African presence in Washington holds much promise for the city's evolving multicultural identity.

NOTES

1. Little research has been done on Washington's new African immigrants. This study is based on published conference papers, recent studies of the African migration to the United States, and newspaper and journal articles. Particularly helpful were John Scanlan, "Who Is a Refugee? Procedures and Burden of Proof under the Refugee Act of 1980," in Lydio F. Tomasi, ed., *Defense of the Alien; Refugee and Territorial Asylum* (New York: Center for Immigration Studies, 1987); and "Ethiopian Refugees in the United States: Conference Proceedings" (Washington, D.C.: Ethiopian Community Development Council, in association with the District of Columbia Office of Refugee Resettlement, Department of Human Services, 1983). My research on

refugees from Africa—including surveys of ethnic businesses, interviews with more than 100 people, and responses to 500 questionnaires—forms the basis for the observations and interpretations offered as preliminary findings in this essay.

2. Harris L. Wofford, *Of Kennedys and Kings: Making Sense of the Sixties* (New York: Farrar, Straus and Giroux, 1980).

3. Estimates have been provided by members of Washington's African communities, surveys by organizations of various national groups, and scholars engaged in research on the emerging communities. Precise numbers for each national group are difficult to obtain, in part because many Africans, like other immigrant newcomers, are reluctant to talk to government officials and census takers. It is thus generally acknowledged that the number of Africans is undercounted in official reports. Under the Refugee Act of 1980, immigrants fleeing nations that the U.S. government does not support—including those with communist governments—are eligible to enter the United States as "political refugees." Most but not all Africans in the Washington area are political refugees.

4. Lissane Negussie, director of the Ethiopian Community Center, quoted in Carole Sugarman, "Cultural Stew: Ethiopians Turn to Their Cuisine to Stay in Touch with Home," *Washington Post*, 12 June 1991, E1. For Somali immigrants who gather at the Mogadishu restaurant (named after Somalia's capital) in Adams Morgan to share news of their war-torn homeland, see Stephanie Griffith, "As Fears of Famine and War Ease, Local Somalis Dare to Hope," *Washington Post*, 10 December 1992, A34. Griffith wrote that the Somalis who meet at the Mogadishu "are among more than 3,000 who live in the Washington area." See also Laura Bigman, ed., *Africans in Washington* (Washington, D.C.: Africans in Washington Project, 1989).

5. See Peter Koehn and Girma Negash, *Resettled Refugees and Asylum Applicants: Implications of the Case of Migrants from Ethiopia for United States Policy*, Monograph no. 2 (Arlington, Va.: Center for Ethiopian Studies, 1987).

6. Quoted in Paul Lubock and Michael Watts, "Structural Adjustment, Academic Freedom, and Human Rights in Nigeria," *The Association of Concerned African Scholars Bulletin* no. 20 (1989): 21 and passim.

7. Bereket H. Selassie, "Refugees of the Horn of Africa: A Case Study in Human Displacement, Its Causes and Consequences" (forthcoming).

8. See Bigman, ed., *Africans in Washington*, 7–9 and passim.

9. Koehn and Negash, *Resettled Refugees*, passim.

10. Liz Spayd, "A Daunting Economic Divide: Nature of Area Work Force Puts Immigrants at Bottom," *Washington Post*, 5 July 1993, A1, A10.

11. See Bigman, ed., *Africans in Washington*; Ellen K. Coughlin, "Sociologists Examine the Complexities of Racial and Ethnic Identity in America," *The Chronicle of Higher Education*, 24 March 1993, A7, A8; Scott Heller, "Worldwide 'Diaspora' of Peoples Poses New Challenges for Scholars," *The Chronicle of Higher Education*, 3 June 1992, A7, A8; Chris Raymond, "Global Migration Will Have Widespread Impact on Society," *The Chronicle of Higher Education*, 12 September 1990, A1, A6; Mary C. Waters, *Ethnic Options: Choosing Identities in America* (University of California Press, 1990); and Michael Omi and Howard Winant, *Racial Formation in the United States: From the 1960s to the 1980s* (New York: Routledge, 1986).

16.

"We Must Become Part of the Larger American Family"
Washington's Vietnamese, Cambodians, and Laotians

Beatrice Nied Hackett

There are more Vietnamese, Cambodians, and Laotians in the Washington metropolitan area than there are residents in Kokomo, Indiana, or Asheville, North Carolina. With roughly 55,000 Vietnamese, Cambodians, and Laotians, the Washington area is the nation's sixth-ranking population center of Southeast Asians. Why did they come to this federal district on the Potomac River; what makes them stay; and how did they build their community?[1]

Washington's Southeast Asian community began when Vietnamese, Laotians, and Cambodians arrived as refugees and stayed to make new lives. Like that of other immigrant groups, their community is both rooted in cultural tradition and undergoing dynamic change, and is built on shared goals—economic security, freedom, and opportunity—and shared memories. Their memories, however, are recent, tragic, and violent, and the chance that they can return to their homes seems remote.

The French initiated the term "Indo-China," which implies relationships with the great cultures of China and India, to designate their former colony of Vietnam and the protectorates of Cambodia and Laos on mainland Asia's southeastern peninsula. Though the term "Indo-Chinese" has colonial overtones, Vietnamese, Cambodians, and Laotians in the United States have redefined the term. They use it to signify a new coming together in a new place in which they seek to act as a single unit, usually for political or social-service reasons.

However, Vietnam, Cambodia, and Laos—as ancient kingdoms, as French colonies, and as modern independent nations—have different peoples, histories, languages, religions, and cultural traditions. After gaining independence from France in the 1950s, each nation followed its political paths colored by its particular historical experiences and traditions. Soon, however, each nation, caught between global politics and internal political upheaval, was drawn relentlessly into wars that caused enormous and lasting physical, political, and psychological damage.

The Washington-area Southeast Asian community is a legacy of the Vietnam War, linked to its historical and social processes and to the American presence in Vietnam. The 1975 victory of indigenous Communist forces triggered an exodus of hundreds of thousands of refugees, who chose to flee rather than to live under political systems they feared and could not support.

A historical background of Vietnam, Cambodia, and Laos is necessary to understand Washington's Southeast Asian community. Archeological records show that centuries before the Christian era, the peoples of Vietnam, Cambodia, and Laos were skilled farmers, hunters, boat builders, and traveling merchants. They cultivated irrigated rice fields and domesticated buffalo and oxen. In the sixth century A.D., Khmer peoples from the middle Mekong Valley overthrew an ancient state called Funan in the Mekong River delta. By the twelfth century, when Europeans were building great cathedrals, the Khmer had completed their magnificent temple complex at Angkor (Angkor Wat) and had made it the centerpiece of their ancient kingdom. At the time Angkor controlled all of modern Cambodia and much of southern Vietnam and southern Laos. The Khmer abandoned Angkor in the fifteenth century and established a new capital where the city of Phnom Penh now stands.

What we now identify as Vietnam was an area in the Red River delta, near Hanoi and Haiphong, that had been conquered by the Chinese in the first and second centuries. After rebelling against the Chinese in the tenth century, the Vietnamese expanded outward down the east coast, taking with them much of the Chinese cultural influence and administrative policies they had absorbed in 900 years of association.

Laotian peoples from China's Yunnan area migrated to the north of modern Laos in the seventh century but did not establish the Lao kingdom of Lan Xang, encompassing all of present-day Laos and part of Thailand, until the mid-fourteenth century. However, two centuries of almost constant fighting—both inside and outside the kingdom—weakened it and made it little more than a series of vassal states under Siam (Thailand).

Most areas in the central and southern parts of the "Indochinese" peninsula in the ninth century were governed by followers of Hinduism and Buddhism. These imported religions were integral to a process that had begun in the second century with the expansion of Indian culture into the entire Southeast Asian region. The Indian influence did not force ready-made administrations upon local rulers; instead it provided a technique of civil administration linked to religion. The successful spread of Indian culture owed a great deal to its easy fit with existing cultural patterns and religious beliefs. However, India's cultural gifts—religion, art, and theories of government, for example—were altered, becoming instead Cambodian or Laotian. In some cases, fundamental characteristics of Indian culture—India's caste system, for example—were simply not adopted.

The source, intensity, and character of cultural influences on Vietnam differ from those of the Indian-influenced areas. Chinese culture had been introduced to Vietnam for political reasons centuries earlier, when China had administered the area as one of its remote provinces. There is thus no denying the influence of Chinese religion, art, and civil administration on Vietnam's development. Vietnam adopted Chinese traditions of Confucianism and Taoism, medicines and herbal remedies, and even used Chinese characters to write its language. Yet, indigenous forms adapted and survived. Vietnamese mythical traditions outlived Chinese domination to emerge transformed, and the Vietnamese language, though borrowing vocabulary from Chinese, still remained overwhelmingly Vietnamese.

For more than four thousand years, China, India, and even Polynesia contributed to the cultures of Indochina. When the Portuguese, French, and Americans came—whether as missionaries, administrators, entrepreneurs, or soldiers—they added their Euro-Christian influence. Still, Vietnam, Cambodia, and Laos retained their individual cultures, though adapted and transformed.[2]

When European nations were competing to secure colonies in Asia, the French proclaimed the Union of Indochina in 1893, establishing French protectorates in Cambodia, Laos, Tonkin, and Annan (northern and central Vietnam), and the colony of Cochin China (southern Vietnam). Independence movements in each region began before World War II, but the area remained under French control—except for the Japanese occupation during World War II—until the 1950s. In 1950 France signed separate treaties recognizing Vietnam, Cambodia, and Laos as independent states within a loose French union. In 1954, however, after Ho Chi Minh's defeat of French forces at Dien Bien Phu, the Geneva accords were signed to dissolve the French union, and Vietnam, Cambodia, and Laos were recognized as independent nations, with Vietnam divided into northern and southern parts at the seventeenth parallel.

As the four new nations struggled with independent statehood, leftist movements that had been active in the fight for independence from France stepped up their fight for political control. French and then American military forces intervened to help stem the leftist tide, but ultimately the capitals of Phnom Pehn in Cambodia and Saigon in Vietnam fell in April 1975. In December 1975 Vientiane in Laos followed. The refugee flight soon was under way.

Before 1975 there had been only a few Vietnamese, Cambodians, and Laotians in the Washington area. Most were students, U.S. government employees at the Voice of America or the Foreign Service Institute, or associates of the various embassies and military missions. The mass influx of refugees began when the Vietnam War ended.

The first Southeast Asian refugees to arrive in the Washington area, as elsewhere in the United States, were Vietnamese. They came in three phases: the first arrived after the fall of Saigon in April 1975, when those in the military and civil governments and those who had worked for Americans fled in fear of reprisals. A second wave ensued when registration for reeducation camps began and nationalization of the private sector increased. In 1978 a third wave included, among others, peoples from the coastal areas and most of Vietnam's ethnic Chinese and Sino-Vietnamese populations, who had been forcibly expelled.

The exodus from Laos also began in 1975, and those who came to Washington first were urbanites who had worked for the Laotian government or U.S. missions in Laos. A later group included rural peoples and a few highland Hmong. Some Cambodians escaped in 1975, but the large Cambodian exodus began after 1979, when Vietnam invaded Cambodia and the Khmer Rouge regime of Pol Pot fell. Only then did the world learn of the "killing fields" where millions of Cambodians—Khmer, Sino-Khmer, and Chinese—had lost their lives between 1975 and 1979 in Pol Pot's bloody social experiment. (Khmer designates both Cambodia's major ethnic group and language, although Khmer, Sino-Khmer, and Chinese from Cambodia in the United States all refer to themselves as Cambodians.)

Unlike earlier immigrants, Vietnamese, Cambodian, and Laotian refugees did not choose to come to Washington or the Washington area. Instead, they were dispersed across the country by U.S. policy according to the general availability of housing, employment opportunities, and social services. When they arrived in the United States, many refugees were still suffering from the trauma of death and loss and the physical and psychological effects of war, refugee flight, camp life, and cultural displacement. Although there was not yet a Southeast Asian immigrant community and support system, the refugees did find in the nation's capital a generally sympathetic reception from a multiracial, multicultural host community, a relatively stable job market with entrepreneurial advantages, and social services to help them rebuild their lives.

Estimates of the numbers of Vietnamese, Cambodian, and Laotian refugees now living in Washington and the metropolitan area are difficult to make and harder to verify because the communities are changing. The location of the sponsoring agency is the first recorded residence for refugees admitted to the United States. Since many voluntary resettlement agencies are located in Washington, the District is counted as the place of initial resettlement for many—most of whom have not remained. After a period of adjustment, a secondary migration began (and still continues), as refugees moved throughout the country to join relatives or to find more favorable employment, housing, and educational opportunities. Today those who work most closely with the Washington area's refugee population estimate its size at 35,000 to 45,000 Vietnamese, 8,000 to 9,000 Cambodians, and 8,000 to 9,000 Laotians. Of these, approximately 4,500 to 5,500 live in the District, principally in the Mount Pleasant area where they were first resettled. There are nearby concentrations of Indochinese in suburban Chillum Heights, Cheverly, Riverdale, and Hyattsville in Prince Georges County, Maryland; in Silver Spring, Takoma Park, and Rockville in Montgomery County, Maryland; and throughout Alexandria, and Arlington and Fairfax Counties in Virginia. Like other area residents, these refugees consider the metropolitan area a single unit in terms of employment and shopping, for example, and there is considerable movement back and forth across the area's political boundaries. Southeast Asians have also learned to make distinctions between the housing (and its costs), schools, and social services available in each jurisdiction.[3]

In the Washington area the several communities of Vietnamese, Cambodians, and Laotians often unite as "Indochinese," but more usually remain separate communities in and of themselves. Each community centers on the family and is made up not so much of individuals as of family units. As the individual families change, so do the communities.

In Vietnam, Cambodia, and Laos, as in all of Asia, the family is the principal social unit and determines the fundamental organizational and economic structure. Individuals are irrevocably linked to their ancestors and to those who will follow in an unbroken family line. The head of a family is responsible for its welfare and for seeing that traditional values and behavior are nurtured. Emphasis is placed on an entire family's welfare rather than on individuals, and the resources of one family member are the resources of all. Family in the Vietnamese, Cambodian, and Laotian sense can thus mean a nuclear family (parents and children), a three-generation family, or a large and complex unit with distantly related and allied kin on several continents.

Vietnamese, Cambodian, and Laotian families in the Washington area tend to be smaller than those in Vietnam, Cambodia, and Laos because some members were unable or unwilling to flee, and because so many people died in the war, its aftermath, and in refugee flight. Gradually, however, complex family units are being rebuilt and transformed through marriages, births, the reuniting of relatives who had been dispersed, the joining of more distantly related kin, and alliances with other families. These circumstances tend to foster communities in which large segments know or are related to each other.

Vietnamese, Cambodian, and Laotian family welfare is based on economic security, particularly steady, growing, and controllable income and savings. Most refugees arrived in America with little or no English-language training and therefore took low-paying, unskilled, or semiskilled jobs where English was not essential: for example, in hotel housekeeping and kitchen work; janitorial, maintenance, and garage work; seamstress piecework; and poultry processing. On the other hand, some Vietnamese, who had had sustained contacts with Americans in Vietnam and had become proficient in English, and those who had been able to bring capital with them, found a quick foothold in entrepreneurial ventures.

Newly arrived refugees often held two full-time jobs, juggling child care and a spouse's job schedule with English classes and social obligations. Over the years many have moved on to become assemblers in electronics plants, clerks for local and federal government agencies, bank tellers, securities and insurance representatives, Metrorail technicians, and warehouse supervisors. Some have become cooks, postal clerks, waiters or waitresses, landscapers, library aides, sales clerks, teachers' aides, or construction workers; and others work for the Red Cross and other relief organizations, or with and for the refugees themselves as social workers, teachers, health aides, and clerical staff at mutual-assistance associations. Along with the District and the state and county governments of neighboring jurisdictions, the federal government employs ethnic minorities, including Southeast Asians, who perceive government jobs as prestigious and secure.

Most Vietnamese, Cambodians, and Laotians have not yet broken through the barrier to upper-level management jobs in either the government or the private sector. How long it will take for them to do so—or how many will even try—remains to be seen. Many have already chosen another traditional route to economic security by operating their own businesses. The federal government, as Washington's major industry, remains the area's principal contractor for the myriad public and private businesses that service, supply, support, and benefit from its vast undertakings. Many Southeast–Asian-owned enterprises do business with the federal government. The Vietnamese and

Sino-Vietnamese businesspeople predominate among Washington's Southeast Asians because of the size and resources of their communities.

One of the area's earliest concentrations of Vietnamese grew around the Clarendon neighborhood in Arlington County, Virginia (across the Potomac River from Washington), an area sometimes referred to as "Little Saigon." In the late 1970s this depressed section was poised for development with the opening of its own Metro subway station. Vietnamese entrepreneurs, whose families pooled talents, experience, and financial resources, leased and bought run-down stores and opened some of the region's first and most successful Southeast Asian food markets and restaurants. Other services soon appeared: furniture repair, package-shipping services, and seamstress and tailor work. These businesses, which primarily served the refugee community, were not capitalized by bank loans but by family funds—in some cases brought by earlier refugees from Vietnam, and in other cases saved from the pooled earnings of multiple jobs—a practice still adhered to but now enhanced by bank loans. Food-related businesses in particular provided places where people could meet, talk over the old days, and exchange information. Weekends in Clarendon became almost festivals in themselves.

Clarendon restaurants and food markets used the talents of entire families. Heads of families ran the day-to-day operations and spouses shared in the tasks of accounting, ordering, stocking, and serving. Grandparents or aunts and uncles, less fluent in English, contributed their culinary skills. Teenagers waited on customers after school, and younger children played—just as they would have done in Vietnam. Everyone in the family would be in the store or restaurant at some time every day, contributing to the family's welfare under watchful eyes. Thus, the businesses served both an economic and a cultural purpose.

Clarendon has a different character today. Earlier businesses have been torn down or have changed hands as the area's development has accelerated. Many Vietnamese who ran stores ten years ago have achieved their intermediate goals and have opened bigger restaurants or shops further into the Virginia suburbs. They have been followed in Clarendon by others who have taken longer to acquire enough capital and resources to open their own businesses. The large, multifaceted food-market ventures have been replaced by smaller ones, some looking run-down next to newly built office buildings. Yet there has been a slow but steady rise in income among the Vietnamese, as well as the Cambodians and Laotians. Their economic mobility is reflected in moves from apartments to rented houses in the suburbs and, for many, to homes bought with pooled savings.

Most Southeast Asian refugees in Washington live in the bustling multiracial, multicultural Mount Pleasant and Adams Morgan neighborhoods. In the late 1970s and early 1980s, when Asian refugees began resettling in Washington, these centrally located areas still offered affordable rental apartments and houses.

On arrival, the refugees were taken by their sponsors to assigned houses or apartments, given basic necessities, and introduced to the intricacies of using Washington's Metro subway system to visit doctors, to get children registered for school, to apply for social security cards and driver's licenses, to register for job-training and English classes, and to fill out job applications. The apartment houses in which most refugees lived had relatively low rents, were badly in need of repairs, and were not endangered by gentrification efforts—although this is less true today. Other new immigrants have also been attracted by the reasonable rents and the centrality of the area. It was thus in Mount Pleasant and Adams Morgan that Vietnamese, Cambodian, and Laotian refugees first encountered the culturally diverse environment that is part of the city's identity. New to such interaction, some refugees became more withdrawn into their families, while others immediately joined the community.

Some refugees were resettled in groups in large, single-family homes in Mount Pleasant. One house near Park Road housed ethnic Chinese from Cambodia—a young couple and their infant daughter; the husband's sister, her husband, and their child; an elderly couple; and a widow with her five-year-old child. These ten people lived together for nearly four years. They organized themselves as a family and shared child care, while each adult worked at one or two jobs. The group accepted the elderly man as symbolic but not economic head of their "family." They cooked and ate separately because of expenses and schedules, and managed their own economic affairs. Eventually the group dispersed, as members left to join kin elsewhere in the country; only one member remained in the area.

Apartment houses along Park Road in Mount Pleasant still provide low-cost rental housing for refugees. Some of the most recent Vietnamese refugees, Amerasian children of American GI fathers and Vietnamese mothers, have been resettled there with their mothers.

Refugees in the suburban areas were initially resettled in low-rent garden or high-rise apartment buildings and projects. An early organizational effort that united Vietnamese, Cambodian, Laotian enclaves into one Indochinese community was an effort to fight the planned conversion to condominiums of a rental-apartment complex in Chillum Heights, Maryland. By 1982, however, the conversion was completed, and 100 Southeast Asian refugee families and Central American immigrant families were forced to move. Although unsuccessful, the cooperative effort provided a political and organizational lesson for the refugees, enabling leaders to emerge and solidarity to form.

Several years after their arrival, Southeast Asian refugee families, following the example of other immigrant and migrant groups, were buying houses in the suburbs. Refugees usually believe that a home of their own amounts to increased financial control and security, a means to save money, and a better place to be together as a family. Affordable housing, economic concerns, and proximity to kin are most important in decisions to move or to buy a house.

One reason many Vietnamese, Cambodian, and Laotian refugees choose to remain in the Washington area is to be politically active on behalf of their homelands. They are involved in educational and political advocacy groups, such as the Southeast Asian Resource Action Center (formerly, the Indochina Resource Action Center), which seeks to shape U.S. public opinion and influence legislation concerning political or humanitarian conditions in their native countries. These groups, acting like other ethnic interest groups by making their interests known to elected representatives, hold conferences, invite congressional guests and speakers, testify at congressional hearings, publish newsletters, and hold rallies. While such organizations exist across the United States, refugee advocacy groups tend to cluster in Washington. Smaller political organizations (mostly Vietnamese) have recognized their potential voter impact on local politics and address problems affecting them, particularly in suburban areas.

Many area Southeast Asian refugees have become naturalized U.S. citizens. Older refugees, who may never pass or even attempt the citizenship examination, are content that someone in the family is a citizen. Most of these new citizens claim to be too busy for active political participation, while others have learned that they represent a significant voter bloc and can thus affect local politics. Although they act separately as Vietnamese, Cambodians, or Laotians when working in political groups for their homelands, they act as a single Indochinese unit when they face such local challenges as condominium conversions.

The Indochinese Community Center, one of Washington's oldest Southeast Asian mutual-assistance associations, exemplifies the three communities' capacity for unity. This nonprofit center was formed in 1978 by Southeast Asian refugees, aided by local churches and voluntary agencies, to provide a forum in which to assess and to articulate problems and needs, and to find ways to help each other. The center also provided a place to hold English-language, cultural orientation, and job-training classes. Although other area mutual-assistance associations serve the individual communities, the center's federal and

Southeast Asians learn English at the Indochinese Community Center. (Courtesy Indochinese Community Center)

state funding was specifically for programs aimed at all Indochinese refugees working to find common goals and the methods needed to achieve them.

Today, as federal and state funds for refugee programs diminish, the center receives financial support through income-generating projects and private sources. It also welcomes outsiders to sit on the twenty-three member board alongside Vietnamese, Cambodian, and Laotian members. Drawing on its long experience, the Indochinese Community Center now aids other refugee and immigrant groups—Ethiopians, Caribbeans, and Central Americans—and offers English and civics classes, translation services, immigration counseling, cultural preservation programs, emergency food and clothing, job counseling and placement, and a model multilingual AIDS prevention education and counseling program.

Signs of the Vietnamese, Cambodian, and Laotian communities' success are reflected in the institutions they have established: the temples, shopping centers, restaurants, and festivals. The Eden Center on Wilson Boulevard in suburban Fairfax County, Virginia, for example, is a large and growing shopping center of mostly Vietnamese-owned food markets, restaurants, and gift, fabric, appliance, and video-rental stores. Nearby, on Wilson and Arlington Boulevards, a refugee can find a Vietnamese lawyer, an insurance or real estate agent, or a Khmer-speaking dentist. Southeast Asian faces and dialects are also found when one gets a car repaired. While waiting for service, a patron can meet a friend or pick up a copy of *Capital Voices*, the local Vietnamese-language newspaper, to read about national or local events. The Cambodian and Laotian communities lack an equivalent of the Eden Center, though individual Cambodians and Laotians own food markets and restaurants throughout the Virginia and Maryland suburbs.

Southeast Asian businesses and institutions reflect a need to maintain and to share cherished traditions in a new environment. Foodways remain especially important. Refugees say that because traditional cooking takes more time, and because their children like American food, they generally cook both types at home. Ingredients for traditional cuisines are available in the Chinese and Pan-Asian food markets throughout the metropolitan area.

Restaurants are equally important in perpetuating food traditions among Southeast Asians and sharing them with the general community. Vietnamese, Sino-Vietnamese, and spicier Lao and Cambodian foods have become readily available to and popular among many of the region's residents. In addition to a few Cambodian restaurants in the Washington metropolitan area, Vietnamese restaurants abound along Wilson and Arlington Boulevards, spilling around corners onto the side streets as well. In Washington, Vietnamese and Sino-Vietnamese restaurants run by family groups flourish in the Georgetown and Adams Morgan neighborhoods.

Other visible signs of these new communities are their Buddhist temples, which they built with their own funds. Almost all Cambodians and Laotians, and some Vietnamese, are Buddhists. The large Khmer Buddhist temple, Wat Khmer, is in Silver Spring, Maryland; the Laotian temple, Wat Lao Buddhavongsa, is in rural Virginia near Manassas. These are vibrant spiritual and social centers, as well as refuges from what is new and often confusing. The Laotian temple draws devout worshippers from the entire eastern seaboard for spiritual celebrations. However, it is the local Laotians who regularly offer food and support to the monks in order to gain merit and to find peace and strength through the ancient rituals. The Laotian Buddhist monks are noted healers and herbalists; recently, eighteen young men were ordained and will remain with the monks at the temple for various periods before they return to the secular world.

The Vietnamese Buddhists follow a different tradition, one that blends Confucianism and Taoism with Buddhist teachings and is less centered on the temple itself. Several area Vietnamese Buddhist temples celebrate ancient rit-

Laotian Buddhist monks at the 1987 Festival of American Folklife. (Courtesy Smithsonian Institution)

uals and are crowded on special holidays. The Vietnamese Buddhist temple in Washington is on upper Sixteenth Street, NW.

Vietnam has long had a Catholic population, and Vietnamese Catholics attend Washington metropolitain-area Catholic churches where Mass is said in their native tongue by Vietnamese priests. Some Vietnamese, who converted to other Christian denominations in the refugee camps, attend churches of their choice in the larger community.

Vietnamese, Cambodians, and Laotians are also connected to the larger non-Asian community. As one Cambodian refugee said, they must "become part of the larger American family." They offer their cultural traditions to the general community and take from it American traditions, transforming them into Vietnamese American, Cambodian American, or Laotian American traditions. Thanksgiving, for example, is a popular holiday among these new residents—in part because they see few religious connotations connected to it, but mostly because it is a family holiday. They may roast the traditional turkey, but serve it with rice, lemon grass, coriander, and hot sauce.

Chum Chan Chavvy as the golden deer in the Khmer Traditional Arts Ensemble's July 1992 performance of "Riemkev," a classical drama. (Photograph by and courtesy Rick Reinhard)

Southeast Asians also share their cultural traditions at area ethnic fairs and festivals; and Washington residents have come to expect Vietnamese, Cambodian, or Laotian food at most street fairs in town. Washington is unusual in that the federal government often supports such events. Each summer the Smithsonian Institution's Festival of American Folklife offers opportunities to experience many people's cultural traditions. The local Laotian, Vietnamese, and Cambodian communities have participated in the festival, presenting their dances, songs, music, foods, crafts, and religious celebrations. They have also participated in the Commerce Department's yearly craft show.

The Vietnamese, Cambodians, and Laotians, through their temples and cultural preservation groups, also sponsor their own cultural projects. The Washington area was home to the renowned Khmer Traditional Arts Ensemble. Several dancers of the Khmer Royal Ballet who had survived Pol Pot's regime began to train promising youngsters in refugee camps in Thailand, and

Laotian women offer prayers and food at the 1987 Festival of American Folklife. (Courtesy Smithsonian Institution)

the entire group was subsequently admitted to the United States under a special cultural program. The teachers, dancers, costumers, and mask makers performed around the nation to promote Cambodian classical dance. Although juggling jobs, family obligations, practice, and performances proved too great a task, and the group dissolved, the musicians continue to perform at community events and a new dance group is emerging in Virginia.

The larger Washington community transmits its values and traditions to Southeast Asians in more subtle ways than festivals and fairs—namely through television and advertising, laws and regulations, and through such institutions as schools, hospitals, social-service agencies, police departments, parent-teacher associations, and government bureaucracies. Sometimes the larger community's customs and institutions conflict with Southeast Asians' traditions and provoke concern within their families. Many worry, for example, about the changing roles of women. In Vietnam, Cambodia, and Laos, many women are partners in family businesses, making decisions with and working beside their husbands for the family's welfare. Those involved in family businesses in the United States continue to do so, but many women also work outside family businesses—an unusual situation in their homelands—which causes conflict and ultimately changes the traditional responsibilities of relationships between men and women. Some Southeast Asian women who are experiencing this kind of independence for the first time find that divorce—unthinkable in Vietnam, Cambodia, or Laos—becomes tenable. Husbands are often under great stress when deprived of their former status in employment or when their traditional roles as economic heads of families are usurped by wives with better-paying jobs. Sometimes their frustrations find expression in alcoholism, physical or verbal abuse, or illness.

Vietnamese, Cambodian, and Laotian parents worry about drugs and violence, racial misunderstandings and how to avoid them, marriage partners for their children, and their children wanting to date or to choose their own, perhaps inappropriate, marriage partners. They worry as well about those family members they have left behind, and about having enough monks available to perform the rituals in honor of the ancestors. They are concerned about the breakdown of the traditional support systems that took care of the old, the sick, and the weak. They worry about whether they can provide sufficiently for their families and whether they are seen by others as good providers. Young people, on the other hand, wonder about the relevance of the old ways and their parents' emphasis on filial piety as they encounter the conflicting pulls of two different cultures.

Vietnamese, Cambodian, and Laotian parents want their children to be "American" enough to conduct family businesses, to succeed in careers, and to be good citizens, but not to the extent that they forget or ignore the traditional family values of respect and duty, or lose their native languages, which embody so much of the traditional respect. The parents also fear that American education and fluency in English, which they perceive as absolutely necessary, may ultimately deprive them of their children, their culture and language, and their links with the past and the future. Such concerns are not uncommon to first-generation immigrant groups across cultures.

The Washington area's Southeast Asian community, a community not so much of locality as of common memories and goals, is in reality several distinct communities that unite at times, sharing a concern for economic security and for rebuilding and reacquiring what they had lost. The Vietnamese, Cambodians, and Laotians who make their homes in the Washington area have changed and enriched the community at large. Economically, they have not only contributed a competent, eager, hardworking work force, but they have also injected new life and vigor into formerly run-down sections. They have whole-heartedly endorsed American free enterprise and have entered the market economy with imagination, tenacity, and enthusiasm reflecting the strength of the family unit. Culturally, they have contributed their religions, art, food, music, and dance to Washington's ethnic mosaic. They have also impressed everyone with their ability to survive.

NOTES

1. This essay is based on field research, interviews, and analyses (including that for government contracts and my Ph.D. dissertation) that I conducted in the Washington area's Vietnamese, Cambodian, and Laotian communities since 1981. Many community members have told me their stories and continue to help me understand what it means to be a refugee, a Vietnamese, Cambodian, or Laotian, and an American. The growing anthropological literature comparing Indochinese refugee experiences in the United States has also been useful. I would like to thank Kate Bond, Vilay Chalenreuth, Kim Oanh Cook, Priscilla Coudoux, Sylvain Coudoux, Nawon Kousom, Ruth Krufeld, Sroi Lim, Ong Robinson, and Jihan Y. Wu, whose comments, insights, and criticisms were important for this essay.

2. For the history and culture of Indochina, see G. Coedes, *The Making of South East Asia* (Berkeley: University of California Press, 1966); Daniel G. Hall, *A History of South-East Asia* (New York: St. Martin's Press, 1981); Charles F. Keyes, *The Golden Peninsula: Culture and Adaptation in Mainland Southeast Asia* (New York: Macmillan, 1977); Milton Osborne, *Southeast Asia* (Sydney: Allen and Unwin, 1985); and Ronald Provencher, *Mainland Southeast Asia: An Anthropological Perspective* (Pacific Palisades, Calif.: Goodyear Publishing Co., 1975).

3. Vilay Chalenreuth, director of the Indochinese Community Center, has monitored the movements of Vietnamese, Cambodians, and Laotians in the area. The center has responded by establishing branch offices in suburban areas to better serve its communities.

ADDITIONAL READING

Becker, Elizabeth. *When the War Was Over.* New York: Simon and Schuster, 1986.

Criddle, Joan D., and Teeda Butt Mam. *To Destroy You Is No Loss.* Boston: Atlantic Monthly Press, 1986.

Etcheson, Craig. *The Rise and Demise of Democratic Kapuchea.* Boulder, Colo: Westview Press, 1984.

Haines, David W. *Refugees in the United States.* Westport, Conn.: Greenwood Press, 1985.

Higgins, James, and J. Ross. *Southeast Asians: A New Beginning in Lowell.* Lowell, Mass.: Milltown Graphics, 1986.

Ngor, Haing. *A Cambodian Odyssey.* New York: Macmillan, 1987.

17.

"We Came Here with Dreams"
Koreans in the Nation's Capital

Meeja Yu and Unyong Kim

European immigrant groups in Washington—Italians, Germans, and Greeks, for example—have historically turned to operating small businesses to support themselves and to ease the transition into American life. As these more established groups vacated their businesses, they left a niche that newcomers filled. This pattern has persisted up to the present. Today, Korean immigrants are among the most visible entrepreneurs on the urban scene. Each morning in communities across the city, more than 1,100 Korean merchants open their shops, repeating a ritual familiar to hundreds of their immigrant predecessors.

By 7 A.M. fifty-year-old Mr. Chae opens the doors of Goody Cleaners in northeast Washington, as he does six days a week before he starts his twelve-hour workday. He described the difficulties in establishing his small business:

> For the past six years I've never taken a day off—except for Sundays. Americans can't understand how we can live like this. But I'm sure their ancestors worked the same way. I'd like Americans to think of that instead of negative aspects. We came here with dreams, just like the pioneers.

Mr. Oah, owner of W and W Liquors on Seventh Street, NW, is only thirty-five years old but often feels older. Since buying his store two years ago, he has worked from 9 A.M. to 10 P.M. and, like Mr. Chae, has put in a six-day week. Still, his hours are a relief compared with those he kept in his first business, where he worked from 7:30 A.M. until midnight:

> I've worked hard, and I've accomplished much. But I haven't gone anywhere. I haven't even visited the Smithsonian or the Washington Monument, both only

Mr. Oah and a customer in front of W and W Liquor Store circa 1991. (Photograph by and courtesy Meeja Yu)

five minutes away. It shows how busy life in America is. One moment I see flowers blooming, next I see leaves falling. I get older faster here.[1]

Mr. Oah and Mr. Chae are new faces on the Washington urban landscape, and their highly visible presence over the past decade as owners of mom-and-pop businesses has changed the cultural fabric of the city and the region.[2]

Naturally, such change requires adjustment on all sides. Contact between Korean merchants and African American customers, for example, has sometimes been fraught with tension. In part, such conflict arises from the fact that although 70 percent of the area's 44,000 Koreans have businesses in Washington, the majority live in the Maryland and Virginia suburbs, and only about 1,000 make their homes in the city. Although Koreans as businesspeople have become a major part of the city's economic life, as nonresidents they have limited opportunities for social exchange with Washington residents. Koreans' stories and perspectives are thus seldom heard.

*Edward Namtu Kuhms and his wife, Gloria Myong Suk, in their Anacostia store in July 1992.
(Photograph by Dudley M. Brooks, © Washington Post)*

The nature of the Washington area's economy has also shaped Korean newcomers' struggle to become established. As a city whose major industries are the federal government and tourism, Washington offers those with limited English-language skills service jobs in hotels or restaurants, and jobs cleaning office buildings, driving taxis, and vending souvenirs. Many Koreans have seized these opportunities. In addition, some also find wage work as auto mechanics, janitors, or sewing factory workers. Although such employment makes it difficult to achieve financial security, Koreans who have been in the area longer and have become established still manage to sponsor and to assist newly arrived relatives and friends.

Korean-owned small businesses provide jobs for family members. It is typical for relatives to do all the work and for close relatives to rely on each other, pooling capital for joint ventures. Few businesses take on nonfamily employees, partly because of Korean immigrants' insecurity with strangers, language differences, and the businesses' inability to carry the overhead of wages.

Many Korean immigrants aspire to get an education and to build a supportive foundation for their children. Thus, as soon as they have accumulated enough capital, they start their own businesses. Although few were shopkeepers in Korea, about 75 percent of all first-generation Korean Americans are thus engaged. Mr. Oah, after serving in the Korean army, emigrated from Seoul in 1980 with the hope of pursuing his education—a hope that soon gave way to the economic necessity of working for survival. Before starting his first business, he went to night school, where he earned fourteen credits in two years. Sometimes he went straight to school from his construction job without changing clothes. He remembers,

> My teacher told me to quit school because there was no need for me to go, but I told him about my thirst for knowledge. He understood and became a good friend. [The decision to leave school to go into business] was a struggle, but I couldn't let my parents suffer in their old age. I sacrificed my dream, but I'll pursue it when I'm more established and have more time.

Once his decision was made, Oah, like many other Korean merchants, discovered that he could afford to open a business only in one of the city's poorer neighborhoods. He therefore commutes to the city from his home in Rockville, Maryland, where he lives with his wife, two children, and parents. His father, formerly a well-paid Korean government worker, helps his son in the store. Coming from a society in which status, class, and tradition are important, Koreans such as Oah find that shopkeeping and blue-collar work do not always accord the respect they seek; this compounds the difficulty of choosing to go into business rather than to continue one's education in hopes of eventually securing a professional position.

Mr. Chae, who lives in Columbia, Maryland, had attended college in Korea and had come to the United States for graduate study at the age of forty-one. After his studies, he had intended to return home, where he had had his own business. However, when his wife and three children joined him a year later, he, like Mr. Oah, found that supporting his family had to take precedence over pursuing an education. In 1983 he opened a small clothing alteration shop in Baltimore, where he worked for several years until he accumulated enough savings to buy Goody Cleaners in the District. In retrospect he wonders if the pressure to achieve economic security for the future sometimes has made him and other Koreans short-sighted. He and his compatriots in the United States often find their lives "out of balance," with their families and their physical and emotional health suffering as a result:

> In order to raise children to be successful, parents have to be role models. We are immigrants, but within that boundary we have to live to the fullest. If we have that attitude, our children learn it too. What can they learn from parents who are not able to live their own lives? I work twelve hours a day and commute for two. That's fourteen hours, leaving only ten hours to sleep, eat, clean, and talk to my children. My dream is to work only five days a week so I can have some time for myself, to read and think for my own growth. . . .

Koreans also turn to operating small businesses because they believe it is nearly impossible for them to be successful in a white-dominated labor market. Like many Asian American professionals, Koreans frequently turn to self-employment after encountering the "glass ceiling," whereby they receive token promotions or advancement through the ranks only to find that they are bypassed for managerial positions.

Korean immigrants' mom-and-pop stores have thus become their most common source of income, affording control over their own livelihoods and freedom from the capricious labor market. Recent studies indicate that in the Washington area Korean Americans now own more than 50 percent of the labor-intensive small businesses—convenience stores, gas stations, groceries, shoe-repair shops, wholesale businesses, carryout restaurants, dry cleaners, liquor stores, tailor shops, and janitorial services.

Self-employment also minimizes the liability of limited English-language skills. A 1975 study of Korean immigrants over the age of twenty-three indicated that only 10 percent spoke English without difficulty, and 40 percent spoke no English at all. Koreans find that the demands of their twelve- to sixteen-hour workdays allow little time to become proficient in a new and complex language; however, their self-operated stores can be run without special training or English fluency.[3]

Some Koreans secure capital through *kae*, a traditional credit-rotating system in which close friends and relatives pool capital and take turns using the funds, the first borrower paying the most interest on the loan and the last borrower the least. In addition, as required by U.S. immigration law, Koreans bring with them money obtained from savings and from selling their possessions before uprooting. Koreans do not receive the type of U.S. government assistance provided to refugees from war or political persecution.

Koreans have the shortest history in the United States of any Asian group excepting the Indochinese. Before 1965 fewer than 70,000 Koreans lived in the United States. Over a decade later, the 1980 census counted 354,529 Koreans, and by 1989 the prevailing estimate was 500,000. Almost two-thirds of

Korean immigrants live in southern California, the center of the Korean American ethnic population. Those in the Washington area have generally come as permanent settlers, applying for citizenship once they meet the five-year residency requirements.

A difficult lesson for many first-generation Korean merchants is that hard work is not enough if the larger community does not support their success. Fear and ignorance perpetuate misunderstandings as well as stereotypes on the part of both merchants and customers. Often Koreans' uncertainty in unfamiliar circumstances triggers behaviors that others may view as unfriendly, rude, or authoritarian when, in fact, they simply mask underlying insecurity.

Mr. Oah believes that the best way for Korean shopkeepers to have good relationships with and to return something to the community is to learn to be more open with customers. Mr. Chae, in his struggle to achieve good business relationships with customers, has learned to reach across barriers to foster genuine human contact. He believes it is important to treat customers as individuals:

> They are important to me. They give me hope and become my friends, for I spend more than half the day at the store. I have tried an experiment in which, instead of just saying 'good morning,' I shake hands with my customers and call them by name. They appreciate and feel good about my gesture, and so do I. Now when customers complain about certain things, instead of getting mad, I just say, 'I'm sorry, I'll try better next time.'

Establishing good relations with customers and the community, however, remains an ongoing challenge. A number of recent violent anti-Asian incidents have made a strong impression on Korean merchants, who have come to realize that such behavior emanates in part from a lack of knowledge about the diversity of Asian national cultures. A series of firebombings several years ago plagued Asian-operated businesses along Georgia Avenue, NW. Although the arsonists remain unknown, merchants fear that anti-Asian bigotry motivated the violent acts. Such persistent crimes, including several tragic theft-related murders of Korean merchants, have reinforced deep fears, prejudices, and misunderstanding.

Korean merchants often sense real or perceived resentments from their host communities and generally respond by becoming withdrawn, assuming that they are unwelcome. They may also become defensive, anticipating victimization. Most Asian Americans, whether fifth- or first-generation, struggle with an awareness that others often and perhaps always will perceive them as "foreigners," no matter how long they have lived in the United States.

Many Korean merchants have been accused of giving little back to the urban communities in which they do business. Their apparent disinterest reflects in part feelings of alienation and a lack of knowledge about the social and economic history and the culture, needs, and interests of the people in whose neighborhoods they do business. Nonetheless, they fear that if they begin to address the communities' concerns, they will bear the brunt of a flood of pent-up frustrations.

In their homeland, Korean immigrants had experienced little sustained contact with non-Koreans; Korea remains one of the most homogeneous societies in the world, with a single language spoken by everyone. Traditional Korean society, offering little opportunity to develop tolerance for diversity, has valued cultural integrity, nationalism, tradition, and history. In this geographically vulnerable country, for many centuries poised precariously between two powerful imperial cultures, there has resulted a deep fear of "foreign-ness" that is both culturally and historically ingrained.

Mr. Oah, however, emphasizes the need for openness among Korean Americans:

> There are a lot more different ethnicities here in America, and Koreans need to learn to understand this. If you have a superior attitude, you block yourself from a meaningful relationship. Koreans share many commonalities [with African Americans]. You get back what you do to others. We should give [donations] to local churches and retirement homes; it's not that hard to do. And what do our customers know about Korea? Nothing. It's only through us that our customers can learn about Koreans and Korea.

Koreans are beneficiaries of the civil rights struggles of the 1950s and 1960s. The Immigration and Naturalization Act of 1965 was a direct result of that period of social action, which addressed unresolved issues of human rights and equality under law. The 1965 act made possible the largest immigration of Koreans and other Asians to the United States in its history, with the additional benefits of such civil rights policies as equal-opportunity housing and affirmative action.[4]

Recent history has been difficult and painful for many Korean immigrants, and their experiences have shaped their outlook. Many lived through the Japanese Occupation during World War II and are proud that their nation survived. In addition, at the end of the war in 1945 Korea was divided into a communist North and a capitalist South. In 1950 the North invaded the South, beginning the Korean War and thus generating further devastation and hardship. Families were uprooted, and Koreans' strong ties to their land, history, and tradition were disrupted. Many who fled the communist regime of the North to seek refuge in the South are also among those who later immigrated from Korea in great numbers to seek a new life in the United States. In fact, the proportion of residents from North Korea is today ten times greater in the United States than in South Korea.

Korean merchants in the United States are mostly post-1965 immigrants who left their country after the Korean War ended. They came not as refugees but often as professionals and skilled workers trained under South Korea's burgeoning economy. Surveys of Korean homeowners indicate that approximately 70 percent of those in the United States have college degrees and 71 percent of those who immigrated between 1966 and 1968 previously held professional and technical jobs in Korea. Statistically, Koreans in the United States have achieved the highest levels of education, higher even than that of their compatriots in Korea, where only about 10 percent of adults between the ages of twenty-five and thirty-nine have completed four years of college. Korean immigrants, therefore, find disheartening the downward job mobility that they experience in their initial transition into American society. They thus focus much of their energy on moving upward.

The fifth century B.C. Chinese philosopher Confucius deeply influenced Korean culture and values. The Confucian ethos, emphasizing self-discipline, self-sacrifice, the family, filial piety, respect for elders, social hierarchy, the work ethic, and a reserved demeanor, guides social relations of all kinds, including those between generations, family members, friends, and even business partners. Mr. Oah cherishes these values, and they have served him well in America. "We are taught to be modest," he said. "My parents educated me to share and give. I was also taught to not regret, to work hard, and to live to the fullest within my ability."

Merchants such as Mr. Oah with the most successful community relationships are able to avoid cultural conflicts. Others cope with them by relying on their Americanized children, who work in their shops, to be cultural intermediaries. The prevailing culture of American urban life appears more gregarious and individualistic than the reserved Confucian values underlying the traditional style of communication often used by Korean merchants. For example, an averted gaze indicates respect or humility in a Confucian value system, but may sometimes be perceived in other value systems as hostility, distrust, or guilt. Lively banter may express friendliness to an American, but to a

Korean American it may seem forward or rude—even between acquaintances. "Yes" may mean "I agree" to most Americans, but in a Confucian context it may mean "I hear what you say (but may not agree)." In a confrontational situation, a merchant's desire to save face through internal resolution of a problem may clash with the customer's desire to assert individual rights and to achieve justice through an airing of differences.

Although many parents depend upon their children to help them adjust to their adopted country, immigrant parents often find that their relationships with their children magnify the tensions of their new life. One major source of conflict grows out of Korean parents' traditional, all-consuming commitment to work, which means they may have little time to raise their children as they would wish to. Without sustained guidance from their parents, children may fail to fulfill family expectations, causing intergenerational frustration, anger, and resentment.

The generation gap is also a cultural gap: parents attempt to maintain traditional Korean values, while their children feel pressured to assimilate rapidly into the American culture and value system in order to be accepted at school and among their new peers. Many Korean children speak English as their first language. Since most of them were raised in the United States, they often do not understand their parents' drive or fully accept the notion of filial piety that is one of their parents' core operating assumptions. They may thus become alienated from their families and feel only a heavy sense of debt to their parents—a debt that many wish they did not owe so that they could pursue their own goals rather than those their parents have for them. Parents are often unable to earn their children's respect, and problems of delinquency, runaways, and school dropouts have increased in Korean American families. Because of the cultural ethic of keeping problems private and solving them internally, few outsiders know of these struggles.

Traditional Korean families tend to be male-oriented, patriarchal, authoritarian, and conservative, while American families are relatively more liberal and egalitarian. Koreans' adjustment to their new environment can be stressful, especially for men. Their roles as fathers, husbands, and providers are increasingly questioned by their children (who may challenge their authority), their wives (who may contribute equally to the family's financial support), and the communities in which they operate businesses (whose communication methods and cultural norms are strange and sometimes threatening to Korean men). In the worst cases these stresses can fuel alcoholism, strained marital and familial relations, and even divorce. Various Korean-run community-service

Jin Kim and her son, Christopher, examine produce at Korean Korner in July 1991. (Photograph by Joel Richardson, © Washington Post)

centers in the Washington metropolitan area provide support for Koreans who experience difficulty in adjusting to life in the United States. These centers assist them, for example, in taking an honest look at the costs of "achievement" and "success." The media, on the other hand, tend to neglect these social problems among Koreans, while extolling their "model minority" image.

Support systems for Korean merchants tend to be—in the order of their importance—the immediate family, the extended family, and friends and associates. Rarely do merchants look for support in the communities in which they do business. For those who can find time away from their businesses, Korean American churches in Maryland and Virginia provide a key support network.

Between 60 and 70 percent of Koreans in the United States are affiliated with a Christian church, compared with only 15 percent in Korea. In addition, immigration policies that were permissive with respect to the clergy made possible the establishment of many new congregations. The number of Korean American churches nationwide has increased from fewer than seventy-five in

Karl Kim at his family-owned record store in southeast Washington with Ken Weaver, a regular customer who is a disc jockey at a local public radio station, in July 1992. (Photograph by Dudley M. Brooks, © Washington Post)

1970 to more than 1,600 in 1985. Church-based activities include information exchanges, Korean language and culture classes for the young, and assistance to newcomers in locating jobs, housing, and business opportunities.

Some Korean Americans believe that although the churches preserve a sense of traditional identity and community, they also perpetuate Koreans' isolation from mainstream society. In some cities, however, including Washington, congregations have taken the lead in helping both the Korean and African American communities learn about each other's cultures and in organizing coalition-building projects.

Over the past several years, organized attempts to improve African American–Korean American relations through education, mediation, and joint charity projects have met with modest success in the District. In 1989 area residents, in cooperation with the Mayor's Office of Asian and Pacific Islander Affairs, formed the Afro-Asian Relations Council, whose programs included a speakers' bureau and the promotion of a multicultural public-school curriculum.[5] Other efforts to improve relations and to increase understanding included the D.C. Mediation Service's project to address conflicts between Asian merchants and mostly African American customers following the boycott of the Good Hope Carryout in Anacostia, and Korean merchant associations' contributions to help the homeless and the elderly in their communities, particularly during holidays.

Although Korean participation in organized community activities in the District is still minimal, there are notable examples of individual fellowship: an elderly black woman became an adopted *halmoni* (grandmother) to a Korean merchant's daughter and sewed clothes for her; and a Korean merchant asked a local minister to introduce him to his church's congregation in a community where he had recently opened a store. Individual efforts such as these and those undertaken by Mr. Chae and Mr. Oah can help shift prejudicial attitudes and create new human bonds.

Mr. Chae reflected on his hopes for the future:

> We work hard to achieve our dreams. Second- and third-generation Koreans will assimilate [into] the mainstream and become like [other] Americans. We should walk hand-in-hand with better understanding and sensitivity.

NOTES

1. Many merchants approached for interviews for this essay were reticent. For those who did share their stories and perspectives, it took a great deal of trust and courage, and we gratefully acknowledge our debt to them. The interviews (in the collection of the authors) were conducted in Korean and translated into English by Meeja Yu. The authors, both born in Korea and raised in the United States, offer the perspective of Korean Americans standing with a foot in each culture. Although many stories go untold, and there is little available literature on the new Korean immigrants, this essay is presented in hope of revealing the human face of Koreans living and working in Washington and its metropolitan area.

2. For an overview of Koreans in the Washington area, see Joel Garreau's three-part series, "Capitalizing on the American Dream: Koreans and the Changing Face of Small Business," *Washington Post,* 5, 6, and 7 July 1992. See also Charles Babington, "Korean Entrepreneurs Are Cornering the Markets: Large Store in Montgomery Offers Varied Taste of Home," *Washington Post,* 21 July 1991, B1, B4; and Karlyn Barker, "Mom-and-Pop Stores Selling Half of D.C. Lottery Tickets," *Washington Post,* 21 July 1991, B1, B4.

3. Ibid.

4. Eui-Yon Yu, "Korean Communities in America: Past, Present, and Future," *Amerasian Journal* 10 (fall/winter 1983): 23–51.

5. See "The Long Search for Racial Harmony," *Howard University Community News*, 12 April 1990.

ADDITIONAL READING

Coleman, Craig S. "Inside Koreatown." *Korean Culture* (spring 1990): 5–13.
Hurh, Won M. "The 1.5 Generation: A Paragon of Korean-American Pluralism." *Korean Culture* (spring 1990): 21–31.
Takaki, Ronald. *Strangers from a Different Shore: A History of Asian Americans*. Boston: Little, Brown and Co., 1989.

Contributors

OLIVIA CADAVAL is a curator at the Smithsonian Institution's Center for Folklife Programs and Cultural Studies. For over a decade she has conducted research on and collaborated in public programming with Washington's Caribbean and Latino communities. She is a former board member and chair of the Humanities Council of Washington D.C. She received her doctorate in American studies from George Washington University.

FRANCINE CURRO CARY is executive director of the Humanities Council of Washington, D.C. She taught women's history at the University of Toledo, directed a family violence prevention council, and served as an associate editor of the Freedom History project at the University of Maryland. She received a master's degree and a doctorate in American history from the University of Wisconsin.

ESTHER NGAN LING CHOW is professor of sociology at American University. Born in Hong Kong, she studied economics and sociology at the Chinese University of Hong Kong. She later received her doctorate in sociology from the University of California. She is coeditor and coauthor of *Women, the Family, and Policy: A Global Perspective* (1994); and *Common Bonds, Different Voices: Race, Class, and Gender* (forthcoming).

ELIZABETH CLARK-LEWIS is an associate professor and the director of the Public History Program at Howard University. She received her bachelor's and master's degrees from Howard University, and her doctorate in American studies from the University of Maryland. She is the author of *Living In, Living Out: African American Domestics in Washington, D.C., 1910–1940* (Smithsonian Institution Press, 1994). She is also coproducer of the award-winning documentary *Freedom Bags*.

SPENCER R. CREW is director of the Smithsonian Institution's National Museum of American History. He previously chaired the museum's Department of Social and

Cultural History and was the curator for the exhibition "Field to Factory: Afro-American Migration, 1915–1940." He received his bachelor's degree from Brown University, and his master's and doctorate degrees from Rutgers University. His latest exhibition and research explore the history and the role of black land grant colleges.

HASIA R. DINER is professor of American studies at the University of Maryland and a specialist in the history of immigration, ethnicity and race in the United States and American women's history. Her publications include *In the Almost Promised Land: American Jews and Blacks, 1915–1935* (1977); *Erin's Daughters in America* (1984); and *A Time for Gathering: The Second Migration, 1820–1880* (1992).

STEVEN J. DINER is professor of history at George Mason University. A specialist in U.S. urban history, race and ethnicity, the Progressive Era, and education in the United States, his publications include *A City and Its Universities: Public Policy in Chicago, 1892–1919* (1980); *Housing Washington's People: Public Policy in Retrospect* (1983); and *Democracy, Federalism, and the Governance of the Nation's Capital* (1985).

MONA E. DINGLE received a doctorate in economics from the University of California. From 1949 to 1965 she served the Board of Governors of the Federal Reserve System and the Federal Reserve Bank of New York as economist, senior economist, and section chief. She was professor of economics at the University of Missouri from 1965 to 1978. She has served as secretary of the board of the Historical Society of Washington D.C. and is currently a board member of the Washington Print Club.

WILLIAM M. GARDNER is professor of anthropology at Catholic University of America, where he has taught since 1967. Gardner received his doctorate in anthropology from the University of Illinois. An archeologist since 1963, he has worked in the southeastern, middlewestern, and middle Atlantic states. His fieldwork in the middle Atlantic has taken him from the Appalachian plateau in West Virginia to the Maryland's Eastern Shore, and he has worked on all time periods from the Paleoindian period of 9200 B.C. to a late nineteenth-century grocery store on Capitol Hill.

HOWARD GILLETTE JR. is professor of American civilization and history at George Washington University, where he specializes in U.S. urban and Washington history and was founding director of the Center for Washington Area Studies. He coedited two books on urban history and authored *Between Beauty and Justice: Race, Planning, and the Failure of Urban Policy in Washington, D.C.* (1995). He is the coauthor of *Washington Seen: A Photographic History, 1875–1965* (1995). Gillette served from 1992 to 1994 as editor of *Washington History.*

BEATRICE NIED HACKETT received her master's and doctorate degrees in anthropology from American University. She was the Humanities Council of Washington, D.C.'s first executive director, and is currently Anthropologist-in-Residence at American University, researching and lecturing on refugee and migrant experiences. She is author of *Pray God and Keep Walking* (1995), a book on refugee women's experiences.

JAMES OLIVER HORTON is professor of history and American civilization at George Washington University and director of the Afro-American Communities Project at the National Museum of American History. He received his doctorate in history from Brandeis University. His major publications include *Black Bostonians: Family Life and Community Struggle in an Antebellum City* (1979), coauthored with Lois E. Horton, and *Free People of Color: Inside the African American Community* (Smithsonian Institution Press, 1993). He is also the pilot series coeditor of *City of Magnificent Intentions: A History of the District of Columbia* (1983); and coeditor of *A History of African American People* (1995).

LOIS E. HORTON is associate professor of sociology and American studies at George Mason University. She received her doctorate from Brandeis University, where she wrote her dissertation on federal policy for African Americans during Reconstruction in Washington, D.C. Her publications include *Black Bostonians: Family Life and Community Struggle in an Antebellum City* (1979), coauthored with James Oliver Horton; the sections on the Civil War and Reconstruction in *City of Magnificent Intentions: A History of the District of Columbia* (1983); and *A History of African American People* (1995), which she coedited.

KATHRYN ALLAMONG JACOB received a master's degree in American history from Georgetown University and a doctorate in American history from Johns Hopkins University. Jacob has lectured and published on a range of subjects from the Lizzie Borden axe murders to Washington during the Gilded Age. She compiled *Guide to Research Collections of Former United States Senators* (1983), edited *The Biographical Directory of the American Congress* (1989), and wrote *Capital Elites: High Society in Washington, D.C., after the Civil War* (Smithsonian Institution Press, 1995).

UNYONG KIM was born in Seoul, Korea, and raised in the Washington area, where her parents were merchants in northern Virginia. She has studied liberal arts, psychology, and peer counseling and has worked as a mediator in disputes between Korean merchants and Washington residents. She currently heads the Asian Heritage Caucus of the National Coalition Building Institute in Washington, a nonprofit leadership-training organization.

ALAN M. KRAUT is professor of history at American University, where he specializes in U.S. immigration and ethnic history. His most recent book is *Silent Travelers: Germs, Genes, and the "Immigrant Menace"* (1994). In addition to many articles, he is author of *The Huddled Masses: The Immigrant in American Society, 1880–1921* (1982) and coauthor of *American Refugee Policy and European Jewry, 1933–1945* (1987).

MARGARET H. McALEER is an archivist in the Manuscript Division of the Library of Congress. Currently a doctoral candidate in history at Georgetown University, she is writing a dissertation on Irish immigrants in Philadelphia from 1785 to 1805.

BEREKET H. SELASSIE, a practitioner and scholar of law and politics, is the William E. Leuchtenburg professor of African studies at the University of North Carolina and was previously professor of law and politics at Howard University. His major works include *The Executive in African Government* (1974), *Conflict and Intervention in the Horn of Africa* (1980), *Behind the War in Eritrea* (1981, editor and contributor), and *Riding the Whirlwind* (1993). He is currently chairman of the Constitutional Commission of Eritrea, established to draft the Constitution of Eritrea.

KEITH Q. WARNER was born in Port of Spain, Trinidad. He holds a *licence en lettres* and a doctorate in French literature from the University of Caen. He is currently chair of the Department of Foreign Languages and Literatures at George Mason University. His publications include *Kaiso! The Trinidad Calypso: A Study of the Calypso as Oral Literature* (1982); a novel, *. . . And I'll Tell You No Lies* (1993); and translations into English of two French Caribbean novels: *Black Shack Alley* by Joseph Zobel (1980); and *The Bastards* by Bertène Juminer (1989).

CHRISTINE M. WARNKE, a native Washingtonian, is a governmental affairs advisor at the law firm of Hogan and Hartson, and serves on the board of directors of the National Institute of Building Sciences. A recipient of numerous awards for community service in promoting the arts and culture, Warnke has served on the board of governors of the Shakespeare Theatre Guild at the Folger Shakespeare Library and other organizations. She received a doctorate in modern Greek American studies from the University of Maryland.

MEEJA YU, born in Seoul, Korea, migrated to the United States when she was fifteen years old. Bicultural and bilingual, she earned her bachelor of science degree from Columbia University, a certificate in East Asian studies at the Yonsei University in Seoul, and a master's degree in international development at American University. She is currently special assistant to the mayor for Asian and Pacific Island affairs in the District of Columbia.

Index

Page numbers in italics refer to illustrations.